From
Nuremberg to
My Lai

PROBLEMS IN
EUROPEAN CIVILIZATION

Under the editorial direction of
John Ratté
Amherst College

From Nuremberg to My Lai

Edited and with an introduction by

Jay W. Baird
Miami University

83-679

D. C. HEATH AND COMPANY
Lexington, Massachusetts Toronto

CONTENTS

IV THE MEANING OF NUREMBERG

V FROM YAMASHITA TO EICHMANN

VI THE LEGAL DEBATE OVER AGGRESSION IN VIETNAM

VII WAR CRIMES: NUREMBERG AND VIETNAM

INTRODUCTION

The significance of the Nuremberg trials in shaping a just world order has yet to be resolved despite the fact that over a quarter of a century has passed since those historic judicial proceedings. Some authorities have judged Nuremberg to be a milestone in the development of international law, while others have condemned the trials as a travesty of justice. The Nuremberg trials pitted the major victor nations of World War II, the United States, the Soviet Union, Great Britain, and France, sitting as the International Military Tribunal and the prosecution, against the leaders of Nazi Germany, sitting as the defense. The trials spanned the period from November 1945 to October 1946 and resulted in the sentence of death by hanging for most of the defendants. The complex legal issues involved have made Nuremberg the subject of one of the major controversies of the twentieth century.

Debate over those issues cannot be divorced from the historical milieu immediately following World War II, when the enormity of the Nazi crimes evoked an emotional response characterized by cries for revenge as well as justice. Statements by two prominent government officials at that time offer remarkable testimony to the climate of opinion. On the one hand, Justice Henry Jackson, who became Chief Counsel for the United States at Nuremberg, went on record with many temperate pleas for equity. But Attorney General Tom Clark declared that it was his hope that the Nuremberg court would "deal out what we in Texas call 'law west of the Pecos'—fast justice, particularly fast."

Yet another consideration must be made in assessing the problem of justice and the Nuremberg trials. Above all, Nuremberg represented a basic clash of two world views: that of the Nazis based on authoritarianism, racism, elitism, and the Führer principle of leadership, and that of the United States, Great Britain, and France, grounded in the liberal traditions of the West. The fact that the Soviet Union also sat on the Tribunal at Nuremberg further complicated the debate, because the Russians' record of crimes against humanity was equally as appalling as that of the Nazis. Thus radically opposed political traditions clashed at Nuremberg.

Had Germany waged a traditional aggressive war, Nuremberg might never have ensued. But the Nazi master plan coupled the drive for Continental power with genocide, an attempt to exterminate world Jewry referred to in Nazi jargon as "the final solution of the Jewish question." It was this "final solution" and the Nazi liquidations of their other racial enemies which set the stage for Nuremberg. One possible course of action would have been to hang the Nazis immediately, because according to international law the victor nations had the right to execute their enemies summarily. This clearly was out of the question; the crimes of the enemy were so unspeakable that the option of not holding a trial was never given very serious consideration. Justice demanded that a trial be held, despite the lack of precedent for such judicial proceedings and regardless of the fact that the Tribunal would be subject to attack for the innovations in international law which by force of circumstances it would institute.

The Allies hoped to carry out their task in the most just manner possible, but they realized that they must surmount immense difficulties. Furthermore, the speed with which it seemed most propitious to act precluded a more judicious handling of the hundreds of thousands of items included in files of the captured German documents, which comprised the most complete collection of government papers ever to fall into the hands of a victor nation. As Justice Robert H. Jackson wrote to President Truman in a report dated June 7, 1945, theirs was "a task so immense that it can never be done completely or perfectly, but which we hope to do acceptably."

The first major step on the road to Nuremberg was the Declaration of London of August 8, 1945, an agreement signed by the governments of the United States, Britain, Soviet Russia, and France. The importance of the Declaration of London was twofold. First, it called for the establishment of the International Military Tribunal to try the war criminals. Secondly, it published the Charter of the International Military Tribunal which outlined the avenues which the prosecution would take in making its case. The Nazis were to be tried on three counts: (1) crimes against peace, (2) war crimes, and (3) crimes against humanity. Furthermore, the Charter made it clear that individuals would be charged with crimes they perpetrated as Hitler's agents. As a result, no Nazi could hope to escape prosecution with the plea that individuals were not liable for actions carried out in their governmental capacity. Nor would "orders from superiors" be considered an acceptable plea. Even more far-reaching as an innovation in international law was the statement in the Charter that certain organizations might be branded as criminal. To buttress their claim that fairness would characterize the proceedings, the Allies included all the protections for the defense to be found in Continental, British, and American law.

The trial opened in Nuremberg on November 20, 1945. Robert Jackson had his finest hour when he delivered an eloquent opening statement for the United States, outlining the prosecution's case. Jackson's most effective ploy was to equate the Allies' standard with the defense of civilization itself. The noted international legal authority Quincy Wright concludes the first section by offering an analysis of the problems presented by Nuremberg.

Any consideration of the trials would be incomplete without a description of those days in Nuremberg—once a symbol of a grand medieval past and the scene of Hitler's annual Reich Party rallies— but in ruins in 1945 and inhabited by a shattered and hungry population. The world waited with great anticipation for the reports from the courtroom describing the behavior of the party luminaries as the crimes of the Third Reich were laid before the International Tribunal. The dispatches of John Dos Passos in *Life* and Genet in the *New Yorker* were remarkable descriptions of the drama at Nuremberg. A selection from the prosecution's cross-examination of the unrepentant Hermann Göring follows, offering noteworthy testimony to his flamboyant career.

Section III offers the case for the defense and raises many controversial points of law which have never been resolved satisfactorily. Ironically, the leading critics in the West based their misgivings about the trials on many of these identical arguments. Those contending that Nuremberg did not serve the cause of justice have laid particular emphasis on the following issues:

1. The International Tribunal operated on no legal precedent, and was thus in effect an innovation in international law.
2. The Tribunal was not in fact international in composition, and could not judge in a case involving international law. Instead the Tribunal was a front for the military services of the Allies, which dispensed drumhead justice, indeed justice of the victors.
3. The Tribunal served at once as the source of new law, as prosecution, as judge, and as jury.
4. The Tribunal violated the ancient legal tenet against dispensing ex post facto justice (*nullum crimen, sine lege*).
5. By charging that the Reich had illegally waged war, the Tribunal deprived the German government of the timeless right of national sovereignty.
6. International stability had broken down in the 1930s and, as a result, Germany was not guilty of waging aggressive war.
7. According to international law, individuals cannot be tried for crimes of state.
8. The individuals charged with crimes acted only according to their sacred oath to follow the commands of the Führer who alone was responsible for crimes perpetrated during the war.
9. The Soviet Union was not fit to sit on the Tribunal. What guilt Germany bore, the Russians bore also.

Taken together, the thrust of these objections to the Nuremberg proceedings seriously challenged the case for the prosecution. Two selections for the defense firmly grounded the German case in international law. The "Motion Adopted by All Defense Counsel," signed by Dr. Stahmer, offers the initial articulation of the defense's position. Counsel for defendant Jodl, Dr. Hermann Jahrreiss, attempted to absolve Germany of the guilt of waging aggressive war by tracing the breakdown of the international security system in the 1930s. Jahrreiss opened a running sore when he broached the subject of Soviet Russia's cooperation with Germany in shoring up the unstable situation in Central Europe by dividing Poland among the two of them, as well as by his pointed references to the Russo-Finnish War which proved embarrassing to the Soviet members of the Tribunal. His attempt to absolve the Nazis of guilt by the "superior orders" argument was less telling.

Perhaps the most controversial of the charges against the Nazis was that their "conspiracy" to plan and wage aggressive war violated international law. Professor Sheldon Glueck of Harvard has written the most convincing defense of the prosecution's case, arguing that the illegality of aggressive war was implicit in international law despite the fact that there was no international agreement forbidding it. In so doing, he dispenses with the Nazi defense based on claims of the illegality of retroactive justice (*nullum crimen, sine lege*). Glueck also argues points upholding the legality of prosecuting individuals for acts of state, and attacks the Nazis' defense regarding "superior orders."

Although the proceedings of the International Tribunal were widely applauded, some world leaders vehemently denounced Nuremberg as a travesty of justice. Criticism came from the most unexpected quarters. Perhaps the most outstanding case of this was the address delivered by Senator Robert A. Taft of Ohio at Kenyon College in October 1946, in which he denounced the trials as a miscarriage of justice. Basing his accusations on the Tribunal's "trials for ex post facto crimes" which he termed a "denial of justice," Senator Taft offered a critique based entirely on tenets of international law. The Senator's address became a trumpet call for a torrent of abuse against him more often based on emotion than law.

On the other hand former Secretary of State and Secretary of Defense Henry L. Stimson, as well as the distinguished Columbia professor of law Herbert Wechsler, both argued that Nuremberg served the cause of justice and the development of world order. They clearly demonstrated that under the circumstances there was no alternative to the International Tribunal. The Allies made the best of a situation which offered no easy solutions, and as a result significantly shaped the body of international law. They do not accept the contention that the Nazis were subjected to ex post facto justice. According to Stimson and Wechsler international law is a changing entity; genocide and other crimes against humanity did not need to be made the subject of an explicit international statute prior to 1945 to be considered illegal at Nuremberg.

The Nuremberg precedent on war crimes and genocide was reinforced and given a broader legal basis in the years immediately subsequent to the trials. Soon after the judgment of the court was announced, the United Nations underwrote the Charter law in General Assembly Resolution 1 (95) dated December 11, 1946. Further, the United Nations passed the Genocide Convention in 1948, and the Geneva Convention on Prisoners of War of 1949. Yet aggressive war has remained undefined in international law; teams of distinguished international lawyers have wrestled with this problem under the United Nations' auspices without success since the end of World War II.

The Nuremberg trials so captured the world's imagination that the very important proceedings in the Far East—the Japanese War Crimes Tribunal—paled in comparison. The *Yamashita* case was the single notable exception to this rule and the controversy surrounding the proceedings against Yamashita became a cause célèbre during the Truman years. General Yamashita was the commander of the Japanese Army in the Philippines Theater. As his forces retreated they commited unspeakable atrocities against combatants and civilians alike. Following V-J Day, General MacArthur appointed a military commission to try Yamashita. Acting with undue haste and proceeding in a manner which denied the defendant the benefits of a fair trial, the military commission held Yamashita responsible for the conduct of his troops despite convincing evidence to the contrary. He was found guilty and was executed. The Supreme Court refused to hear the case, although justices Murphy and Rutledge wrote scathing minority opinions. The Yamashita case was significant not only in the context of World War II—it did raise serious questions about Army justice and justice of the victors—but it also placed military commanders of future wars in a most precarious position. Further, it enabled the opponents of the United States involvement in Vietnam to cite the Yamashita precedent in their relentless search for scapegoats on whom to blame the tragedy.

A. Frank Reel, an Army attorney named to the Yamashita defense counsel in 1945, raised a storm of controversy with the publication of his book, *The Case of General Yamashita,* which detailed in a highly readable account what he considered to be a regrettable miscarriage of justice. The work stirred the waters from the White House to General MacArthur's occupation headquarters in Tokyo, and the Army felt pressed to prepare a brief which at once reviewed the prosecution's case against Yamashita and questioned A. Frank Reel's loyalty to the United States. But Reel was not one to confuse loyalty with universal standards of justice, as Charles S. Lyon's review of *The Case of General Yamashita* for the *Columbia Law Review* reveals. A memorandum written by Brigadier General Courtney Whitney from General Headquarters, Supreme Commander for the Allied Powers, Tokyo, is appended. It scores Reel for his "inflammatory material designed to arouse irresponsible Japanese elements into active opposition," for his questioning of "the righteousness of American justice," and because he allegedly endangered "American prestige, American dignity, and American security."

During the years between the death of Yamashita and the American involvement in Vietnam the *Eichmann* case overshadowed all others in both its legal implications and dramatic intensity. During the Third Reich Adolf Eichmann served his Führer as Chief of the Jewish Affairs Section of the Reich Security Head Office in Himmler's SS organization. As such, this banal figure assumed a role in the "final solution of the Jewish question" of far less significance than either Israel or the world press ascribed to him during his trial in Jerusalem in 1961 following his abduction from Argentina. There is more agreement on the symbolic nature of the trial than there is regarding the legality of the proceedings and the substantive legal issues which led to the hanging of Eichmann. Robert Woetzel analyzes these disputed issues in an article entitled "The Eichmann Case in International Law" which appeared in the *Criminal Law Review,* London.

American involvement in the war in Vietnam led to a bitter controversy which has been waged in part over the legal and moral implications of our intervention. Much of this debate has focused on the relevance of Nuremberg to Vietnam, and a great deal of confusing and unlearned parallels have been drawn between the two. It is the purpose of section VI of this book to bring the legal issues involved into clear focus.

Any discussion of Nuremberg and Vietnam is most clearly understandable when debated within the framework of the three central Nuremberg counts: (1) the conspiracy and the waging of aggressive war, (2) war crimes and atrocities, and (3) genocide. Each charge shall be dealt with in turn.

That aggression is difficult to define is attested by the fact that the United Nations' Special Committee on the Question of Defining Aggression has been unable to present the General Assembly with a workable code which a majority of the members will accept. The implication of this is twofold: first, it raises serious reservations about the Nuremberg precedent on aggression, and second it adds yet another counter-argument to the arsenal of those rejecting the designation of the United States as the aggressor in Vietnam where guerilla warfare has rendered the legal fog nearly impenetrable.

Nevertheless, the United States has been scored as the aggressor in many quarters. In response to this criticism, the Office of the Legal Adviser of the Department of State released in 1966 a defense of American intervention entitled "The Legality of United States Participation in the Defense of Viet-Nam." Acting as spokesman for the Johnson Administration, the Legal Adviser argued that our involvement was not only legal but consonant with both our SEATO commitments and international law. The document alleged that North Vietnam launched a war of aggression against the sovereign state of South Vietnam and that according to Article 51 of the United Nations Charter both the United States and South Vietnam have the right to participate in the collective defense of that nation.

This State Department memorandum elicited considerable reaction. Richard A. Falk of the Woodrow Wilson School of International Affairs at Princeton emerged as one of the more capable and articulate spokesmen among the dissidents. In an article entitled "International Law and the United States' Role in the Vietnam War" published in the *Yale Law Journal,* Falk questioned many of the Administration's assumptions. He raised the following disputed points of law: (1) that the sovereignty of South Vietnam is open to question, (2) that the United States did not follow the letter of the Geneva Accords of 1954, (3) that the war might well be termed a civil war, which further complicates the legality of American participation, (4) that guerilla insurgency by the National Liberation Front does not constitute aggression according to international law; at the very least this "indirect aggression" must be judged as aggression by an international body before Washington can act on this assumption, (5) that the United States had not exhausted all peaceful avenues of settlement before becoming heavily engaged in Vietnam (a violation of Article 33 of the U.N. Charter), and (6) that the United States did not approach the problem in Vietnam according to the Nuremberg spirit of operating through the international community; instead, the Administration sought negotiations only when it became clear that victory on the field of battle was not forthcoming.

General Telford Taylor, professor of law at Columbia University, undertook in his work *Nuremberg and Vietnam* to bring the rather confused public dialogue about these matters into clearer perspective. He was admirably suited for the task, because he served at Nuremberg as chief prosecutor for the United States with the rank of Brigadier General; he thus represented a link with Nuremberg law, and his opinions were not lightly regarded. General Taylor probes the nuances of both sides of the question of assessing guilt for aggression in Vietnam, and demonstrates that whereas at Nuremberg the aggressor was easily identifiable, the opposite was the case in Vietnam. Further, he reflects on the complications arising from the American governmental system in which there are various foci of power, and shows that locating "the aggressor" is a most difficult task, considering the conflict for power waged between the President and the Congress. Finally, Taylor rejects Falk's contention that the courts of the United States, even the Supreme Court, should pass judgment on the actions of the President. Such responsibility, Taylor argues, clearly resides with the Congress, not the courts.

The next question to be treated is the relevance of Nuremberg to My Lai. No one will deny that the massacre of My Lai cast a pall over the world's conscience; the tragedy was morally reprehensible by any standard. This fact is not mooted here. More important, however, is the relationship between My Lai and international law. It should be noted from the outset that the executions carried out by the Nazis were the result of a calculated state policy, whereas those perpetrated by the Americans in Vietnam were not. There are few precedents for a nation at war undertaking to court-martial its own soldiers for atrocities committed against the enemy while hostilities were still in progress.

The cases of Lieutenant William Calley and the twelve other army men court-martialed for the murder of civilians at My Lai were remarkable both for the relentless attempt by the prosecution to reveal every detail of the event, and for the dissimulation of the army elite as it attempted to protect its own. In the first document devoted to My Lai, Lieutenant Calley speaks for himself in a most revealing manner.

In Calley's mind, every Vietnamese was the enemy, and their death was at once a service to Jesus Christ, the American way of life, and Western culture. His description of the murders of the women and children—which he attributed to the chaos of war—is both shocking and understandable in the guerilla context. The irony of the affair is that according to the Yamashita precedent, General West-moreland himself would have stood in the dock.

The horrors of the Vietnam war were not lost on the American people, and their response was reflected in the Congress. Early in 1970 a group of concerned legislators sponsored the Congressional Conference on War and National Responsibility which featured a distinguished group of participants ranging from Hannah Arendt to Hans Morgenthau, who pondered the moral implications of the United States' intervention in Vietnam. The transcript of the conference leaves one with the impression that massacres on the scale of My Lai were by no means the exception, but instead flow naturally from the conditions imposed on those forced to fight a war with no stable battle front against an enemy wearing neither recognizable insignia nor uniforms.

The Russell International War Crimes Tribunal, on the other hand, took a radical view of the American presence in Vietnam. Sponsored by Lord Bertrand Russell and Jean Paul Sartre, the Tribunal met on the neutral soil of Denmark and Sweden in 1967 where they staged a "trial" with remarkable fanfare and propagandistic expertise. There were no witnesses for the defense or even defendants in the dock. Instead an overwhelming mass of detail was presented to designate the United States as a technological giant gone mad, waging a war of suppression against a peace-loving Asiatic people. The United States stood guilty, according to the Russell Tribunal, of all three Nuremburg counts: aggression, atrocities, and genocide.

The article by Telford Taylor entitled "War Crimes: Son My" should be read as an antidote to the Russell Tribunal. General Taylor, while admitting the tragic nature of My Lai, nevertheless subjects the event to the merciless scrutiny of international law and finds the case for the Vietcong wanting. Not only has the enemy failed to comply with the 1949 Geneva Conventions on "Prisoners of War" and the "Protection of Civilian Persons in Time of War," but they have also refused to wear insignia making them recognizable as the foe, a clear violation of international law. Further, My Lai lay deep in enemy territory and the American units involved had every reason to believe that they would face hostile fire there. Finally, the Vietcong have sworn off the Geneva Conventions because they were not signatories to the treaties. The implication from the enemy's point of view is clear: the United States is expected to comply with the Geneva Conventions and international law but the guerilla insurgents are not. Taylor does not mean to exonerate the American forces for murdering men, women, and children at My Lai; instead, his goal is to demonstrate that the Vietcong themselves were responsible for the My Lai massacre, because of their consistent refusal to wage war according to the principles of international law.

Richard Falk brings the discussion of Nuremberg and My Lai full circle in the final selection, and his review symposium of Taylor's work serves as a vehicle for an article of much wider dimensions. In it he analyzes the state of international law as we enter the last quarter of the twentieth century. It is Falk's contention that the United States made a significant contribution to the orderly progression of justice and international law at Nuremberg, where we opted for a multinational approach to the formulation of international legal principles. Nevertheless, he notes regrettably, within a matter of two decades after Nuremberg the United States turned its back on the principle of internationalism—the ideal which served to inspire the Charter of the United Nations—and reverted to the traditional politics of unilateral power and national interest. Professor Falk warns that the future of the international community hangs in the balance.

Acknowledgments

I would like to thank Professor Richard R. Baxter of the Harvard Law School, Editor-in-Chief of the *American Journal of International Law* and presently director of the Office of the Legal Adviser, Department of State, for a most informative conversation in the fall of 1971 on the legal problems of Nuremberg and My Lai. I acknowledge also the loyal support of my graduate assistant, Mr. Steven Hurst, for his assistance in preparing the manuscript.

Conflict of Opinion

This Tribunal, while it is novel and experimental, is not the product of abstract speculations nor is it created to vindicate legalistic theories. This inquest represents the practical effort of four of the most mighty of nations, with the support of seventeen more, to utilize International Law to meet the greatest menace of our times—aggressive war.

JUSTICE ROBERT H. JACKSON

The opinion of the Nuremberg Tribunal marks an important step in the development of international criminal law. . . . The world shattered by two world wars needs to have its confidence in law restored. Such confidence can only develop if people believe that formal law embodies justice and that it will be enforced. The Nuremberg trial is likely to contribute to both of these ends.

QUINCY WRIGHT

The present trial . . . cannot invoke existing international law, it is rather a proceeding pursuant to a new penal law, a penal law enacted only after the crime. This is repugnant to a principle of jurisprudence sacred to the civilized world. . . .

GERMAN ALL DEFENSE COUNSEL

By 1 September 1939 the various experiments which had been tried since the First World War with a view to replace the "anarchic world order" of classical international law by a better, a genuine, order of peace . . . had failed in the opinion of the major powers of the time.

HERMANN JAHRREISS

The claim that in the absence of a specific, detailed, pre-existing code of international penal law to which all states have previously subscribed, prosecution for the international crime of aggressive war is necessarily ex post facto because no world legislature has previously spoken is specious. . . . In the international field . . . part of the system of prohibitions implemented by penal sanctions consists of customary or common law. . . . In assuming that an act of aggressive war is not merely lawless but also criminal, the Nuremberg court would merely be following the age-old precedent of courts which enforce not only the specific published provisions of a systematic code enacted by a legislature, but also "unwritten" law.

SHELDON GLUECK

I believe that most Americans view with discomfort the war trials which have just been concluded in Germany and are proceeding in Japan. They violate that fundamental principle of American law that a man cannot be tried under an ex post facto statute. The trial of the vanquished by the victors cannot be impartial no matter how it is hedged about with the forms of justice. . . . About this whole judgment there is the spirit of vengeance, and vengeance is seldom justice. The hanging of the eleven men convicted will be a blot on the American record which we shall long regret.

SENATOR ROBERT A. TAFT

The charge of aggressive war is unsound . . . only if the community of nations did not believe in 1939 that aggressive war was an offense. Merely to make such a suggestion, however, is to discard it. Aggression is an offense, and we all know it; we have known it for a generation. It is an offense so deep and heinous that we cannot endure its repetition. The law made effective by the trial at Nuremberg is righteous law long overdue.

HENRY L. STIMSON

. . . Nuremberg . . . was the assumption of an irrevocable obligation— to build a world of just law that shall apply to all, with institutions strong enough to carry it into effect. . . . If we succeed in that great venture . . . Nuremberg will stand as a cornerstone in the house of peace. If we fail, we shall hear from the German ruins an attack on the Nuremberg judgment as the second "diktat" of Versailles.

HERBERT WECHSLER

General Yamashita . . . did not have a fair trial. . . . He was held accountable for crimes committed by persons other than himself, crimes committed without his knowledge and, in fact, against his orders. [He] was held so accountable on the basis of a "principle" of command responsibility, a principle that in this perverted form has no basis in either law or logic. . . . We have been unjust, hypocritical, and vindictive. We have defeated our enemies on the battlefield, but we have let their spirit triumph in our hearts.

A. FRANK REEL

It must be concluded . . . that the court in the *Eichmann* case was not justified in claiming a basis in customary international law for the extension of the universal principle of jurisdiction to crimes against humanity involving genocide. . . . The argument that Israel has a moral right to try crimes against Jews regardless of where or when they were committed does not have much basis in law. . . . The competence of the Israeli court in trying crimes against the Jewish people, therefore, clearly derived from national law and not from international law or practice.

ROBERT K. WOETZEL

The United States and South Vietnam have the right under international law to participate in the collective defense of South Vietnam against armed attack.

DEPARTMENT OF STATE

A Tribunal such as ours will be necessary until the last starving man is fed and a way of life is created which ends exploitation of the many by the few. Vietnam struggles so others may survive.

RUSSELL INTERNATIONAL WAR CRIMES TRIBUNAL

"God," people say. "But these were old men, women, and children." I tell you: I didn't see it. I had this mission, and I was intent upon it: I only saw, *They're enemy.*

Lt. WILLIAM CALLEY

As of 1971, the United States has clearly not carried forward the Nuremberg tradition. . . . Our indebtedness to Telford Taylor, Daniel Ellsberg, and the Berrigans is essentially the same: they remind us of our ideals in a period of national and international danger.

RICHARD A. FALK

And so it has come to this; that the anti-aggression spirit of Nuremberg and the United Nations Charter is invoked to justify our venture in Vietnam. . . . Somehow we failed ourselves to learn the lessons we undertook to teach at Nuremberg, and that failure is today's American tragedy.

TELFORD TAYLOR

I THE CASE FOR THE PROSECUTION

Quincy Wright

THE LAW OF THE NUREMBERG TRIAL, PART I

Professor Quincy Wright (1890–1970) was one of the outstanding figures in the field of international law in the twentieth century. He achieved renown as president of the American Society of International Law, as a professor at both Chicago and Virginia, and as a member of the board of editors of The American Journal of International Law. *Among his significant works were* The Causes of War and the Conditions of Peace *and* The Role of International Law in the Elimination of War, *and he had the added distinction of being nominated for a Nobel Peace Prize. He saw service at Nuremberg as a technical adviser for the American members of the International Military Tribunal. In the following selection Professor Wright offers a concise statement regarding the origins, proceedings, and judgment of the Tribunal.*

On the afternoon of October 1, 1946, the International Military Tribunal at Nuremberg sentenced twelve of the twenty-two Nazi defendants to death by hanging and seven to imprisonment for terms ranging from ten years to life. Three were acquitted. Three of the six accused organizations were found to be criminal. The reading of these sentences was preceded by the reading, through the whole of September 30, of the general opinion of the Tribunal on the four counts of the indictment and, on the morning of October 1, of the opinion on the charges against each defendant. The Control Council for Germany considered applications for clemency for most of those convicted but did not grant them and carried out the executions of those sentenced to death on October 16 with the exception of Martin Bormann who had not been found and Hermann Goering who had succeeded in committing suicide a few hours earlier. Thus came to an end what President Truman described as "the first international criminal assize in history." "I have no hesitancy in declaring," continued the President, "that the historic precedent set at Nuremberg abundantly justifies the expenditure of effort, prodigious though it was. This precedent becomes basic in the international law of the

"The Law of the Nuremberg Trials" by Quincy Wright, originally published in the *American Journal of International Law* 41 (January 1947). From *International Law in the Twentieth Century,* copyright © 1969. By permission of Appleton-Century-Crofts, Educational Division, Meredith Corporation. (Footnotes omitted.)

future. The principles established and the results achieved place International Law on the side of peace as against aggressive warfare."

A similar thought was expressed by Warren R. Austin, Chief Delegate of the United States, in his opening address to the General Assembly of the United Nations on October 30:

> Besides being bound by the law of the United Nations Charter, twenty-three nations, members of this Assembly, including the United States, Soviet Russia, the United Kingdom and France, are also bound by the law of the Charter of the Nuremberg Tribunal. That makes planning or waging a war of aggression a crime against humanity for which individuals as well as nations can be brought before the bar of international justice, tried and punished.

Origin of the Trial

The trial originated in the declaration of German atrocities by Roosevelt, Churchill, and Stalin "speaking in the interest of the thirty-two United Nations" and released at the Moscow Conference on November 1, 1943. This declaration provided that:

> Those German officers and men and members of the Nazi party who have been responsible for, or have taken a consenting part in the above atrocities, massacres and executions, will be sent back to the countries in which their abominable deeds were done in order that they may be judged and punished according to the laws of these liberated countries and of the free governments which will be created therein . . . without prejudice to the case of the major criminals, whose offenses have no particular geographical localization and who will be punished by the joint decision of the Governments of the Allies.

Trials in accord with the first part of this declaration have been carried on in Allied military commissions and criminal courts and hundreds of war criminals have been dealt with. A plan for carrying out the second part concerning major criminals was proposed in his report to the President on June 7, 1945, by Justice Robert H. Jackson who had been appointed Chief of Counsel for the United States in prosecuting the principal Axis war criminals. In accordance with this plan Justice Jackson negotiated for the United States with representatives of Great Britain, France, and the Soviet Union with the result that an agreement for the establishment of an International Military Tribunal was signed in London on August 8, 1945.

The Charter and the Trial

Attached to this agreement was "The Charter of the International Military Tribunal." This document provided for a tribunal composed of one judge and one alternate from each of the four powers; for a procedure designed to assure the defendants a fair trial; and for jurisdiction "to try and punish persons who, acting in the interests of the European Axis countries, whether as individuals or as members of organizations," committed any of the crimes defined in the Charter. The Charter authorized a committee consisting of the chief prosecutors of each country to prepare the indictment and present the evidence on the basis of the law set forth in the Charter.

The Tribunal was promptly established, consisting of Lord Justice Geoffrey Lawrence of the British Court of Appeals as President; Francis Biddle, former Attorney General of the United States; Major General I. T. Nikitchenko, Vice-Chairman of the Soviet Supreme Court; and Donnedieu de Vabres, professor of law at the University of Paris. The alternates were Sir Norman Birkett, Judge of the High Court of England; John J. Parker, Judge of the United States Circuit Court of Appeals; Lt.-Col. A. F. Volchkov, Judge of the Moscow District Court; and Robert Falco, Judge of the Court of Cassation of France. The Tribunal held its first public meeting in Berlin on October 18, 1945, and received the indictment from the Committee of the Chief Prosecutors consisting of Justice Robert H. Jackson for the United States, Sir Hartley Shawcross for Great Britain, Francois de Menthon for France, and General R. A. Rudenko for the Soviet Union. Twenty-four Nazi leaders were indicted, each on two or more counts.

The Tribunal then established itself in the Palace of Justice at Nuremberg where it decided upon its rules and assisted the defendants, who had been brought there, to find the counsel of their choice and to obtain the witnesses necessary for the defense. It also decided that Gustav Krupp von Bohlen, who had been indicted, was too sick to be tried; that Martin Bormann, who had not been found, should be tried *in absentia;* that Rudolph Hess, who was alleged to be suffering from loss of memory, was not in such a condition as to prevent his trial and that Julius Streicher was not in such a mental condition as to prevent his trial. One defendant, Robert Ley, committed suicide while in custody. Thus only twenty-one defendants were present in person during the trial.

The trial was begun on November 20, 1945, and continued until October 1, 1946. It was conducted in four languages facilitated by a simultaneous interpretation device. The case of the prosecution was opened by the Americans who dealt with the first count, conspiracy to commit war crimes, on which all defendants had been indicted. The British prosecution followed with the second count, planning, preparing, initiating or waging aggressive war on which sixteen defendants had been indicted. The French prosecution then dealt with counts 3 and 4, as applied to the West, and the Soviet prosecution followed with the same counts in the East. Count 3 charged violation of the laws and customs of war, and count 4, crimes against humanity. Nineteen defendants were indicted under each of these counts. The prosecution consumed three months. The defense, represented by able German lawyers, then presented its case with many witnesses during five months, concluding with legal arguments in behalf of each defendant. The prosecution made its final arguments during the last days of July 1946. The case of the accused organizations was then heard. On the last day of August the defendants each made final statements. After a few weeks' adjournment the Court read its opinion and sentenced the defendants on the first of October. Three of the defendants (Schacht, von Papen, and Fritzsche) were found not guilty on any counts. Seven (Hess, Funk, Doenitz, Raeder, von Schirach, Speer, and von Neurath) were sentenced to prison terms varying from ten years to life. The remaining twelve (Goering, von Ribbentrop, Keitel, Kaltenbrunner, Rosenberg, Frank, Frick, Streicher, Saukel, Jodl, Bormann and Seyss-Inquart) were sentenced to hang. The Soviet judge dissented from the acquittals and thought Hess should have been sentenced to death.

Of the seventy-six counts on the indictment against the twenty-two defendants the Court sustained fifty-two. All those sentenced to hang were found guilty of crimes against humanity and in most cases of other crimes also. Four defendants—Funk, Neurath, Schirach, and Speer—though found guilty of crimes against humanity, were given

The courtroom at Nuremberg; the defendants' dock. (*Photo no. 238-NT-574 in the National Archives*)

prison sentences because of mitigating circumstances. Defendants found guilty of aggressive war or conspiracy to commit that crime were given life sentences (Hess, Raeder, and Funk) unless there were mitigating circumstances as in the case of Neurath and Doenitz.

The Tribunal also declared that the SS (Black Shirts) and its subsidiary the SD, the Gestapo, and the Leadership Corps of the Nazi Party were criminal. The SA (Brown Shirts), the Reich Cabinet and the General Staff and High Command were acquitted without prejudice to the individual liability of members. The Soviet judge dissented from the acquittal of the two latter organizations.

THE LONDON AGREEMENT AND THE CHARTER OF THE INTERNATIONAL MILITARY TRIBUNAL, AUGUST 8, 1945

The London Agreement, the essential document which prepared the way for the trials, announced to the world that the Allies were in accord regarding the decision to try the war criminals despite their mutual suspicions and differing social and governmental systems. The Charter of the International Military Tribunal which was appended to the London Agreement provided for procedural matters during the trials and declared that the jurisdiction of the court embraced crimes against peace, war crimes, and crimes against humanity; it stated further that leaders of state would be prosecuted for acts of government, that individuals could not plead superior orders, and that selected Nazi organizations might be held criminal. As a result, the bitter controversy over the trials began with the Charter itself.

From International Military Tribunal, *Trial of the Major War Criminals before the International Military Tribunal*, 42 vols. [Blue Series] (Nuremberg, 1949), 1:8–16.

*AGREEMENT BY THE GOVERNMENT OF THE
UNITED STATES OF AMERICA, THE PROVISIONAL
GOVERNMENT OF THE FRENCH REPUBLIC, THE
GOVERNMENT OF THE UNITED KINGDOM OF
GREAT BRITAIN AND NORTHERN IRELAND AND
THE GOVERNMENT OF THE UNION OF SOVIET
SOCIALIST REPUBLICS FOR THE PROSECUTION AND
PUNISHMENT OF THE MAJOR WAR CRIMINALS OF
THE EUROPEAN AXIS.*

Whereas the United Nations have from time to time made declarations of their intention that War Criminals shall be brought to justice;

And Whereas this Declaration was stated to be without prejudice on German atrocities in Occupied Europe stated that those German Officers and men and members of the Nazi Party who have been responsible for or have taken a consenting part in atrocities and crimes will be sent back to the countries in which their abominable deeds were done in order that they may be judged and punished according to the laws of these liberated countries and of the free Governments that will be created therein;

And Whereas this Declaration was stated to be without prejudice to the case of major criminals whose offenses have particular geographic location and who will be punished by the joint decision of the Governments of the Allies;

Now Therefore the Government of the United States of America, the Provisional Government of the French Republic, the Government of the United Kingdom of Great Britain and Northern Ireland and the Government of the Union of Soviet Socialist Republics (hereinafter called "the Signatories") acting in the interests of all the United Nations and by their representatives duly authorized thereto have concluded this Agreement.

Article 1. There shall be established after consultation with the Control Council for Germany an International Military Tribunal for the trial of war criminals whose offenses have no particular geographical location whether they be accused individually or in their capacity as members of organizations or groups or in both capacities.

Article 2. The constitution, jurisdiction and functions of the International Military Tribunal shall be those set out in the Charter annexed to this Agreement, which Charter shall form an integral part of this Agreement.

Article 3. Each of the Signatories shall take the necessary steps to make available for the investigation of the charges and trial the major war criminals detained by them who are to be tried by the International Military Tribunal. The Signatories shall also use their best endeavors to make available for investigation of the charges against and the trial before the International Military Tribunal such of the major war criminals as are not in the territories of any of the Signatories.

Article 4. Nothing in this Agreement shall prejudice the provisions established by the Moscow Declaration concerning the return of war criminals to the countries where they committed their crimes.

Article 5. Any Government of the United Nations may adhere to this Agreement by notice given through the diplomatic channel to the Government of the United Kingdom, who shall inform the other Signatory and adhering Governments of each such adherence.

Article 6. Nothing in this Agreement shall prejudice the jurisdiction or the powers of any national or occupation court established or to be established in any allied territory or in Germany for the trial of war criminals.

Article 7. This Agreement shall come into force on the day of signature and shall remain in force for the period of one year and shall continue thereafter, subject to the right of any Signatory to give, through the diplomatic channel, one month's notice of intention to terminate it. Such termination shall not prejudice any proceedings already taken or any findings already made in pursuance of this Agreement.

In Witness Whereof the Undersigned have signed the present Agreement.

Done in quadruplicate in London this 8th day of August 1945 each in English, French and Russian, and each text to have equal authenticity.

For the Government of the United States of America
                                                  Robert H. Jackson

For the Provisional Government of the French Republic
                                                  Robert Falco

For the Government of the United Kingdom of Great Britain and Northern Ireland

Jowitt

For the Government of the Union of Soviet Socialist Republics
I. T. Nikitchenko (and) A. N. Trainin

CHARTER OF THE INTERNATIONAL MILITARY TRIBUNAL

I. Constitution of the Tribunal

Article 1. In pursuance of the Agreement signed on the 8th day of August 1945 by the Government of the United States of America, the Provisional Government of the French Republic, the Government of the United Kingdom of Great Britain and Northern Ireland and the Government of the Union of Soviet Socialist Republics, there shall be established an International Military Tribunal (hereinafter called "the Tribunal") for the just and prompt trial and punishment of the major war criminals of the European Axis.

Article 2. The Tribunal shall consist of four members, each with an alternate. One member and one alternate shall be appointed by each of the Signatories. The alternates shall so far as they are able, be present at all sessions of the Tribunal. In case of illness of any member of the Tribunal or his incapacity for some other reason to fulfill his functions, his alternate shall take his place.

Article 3. Neither the Tribunal, its members nor their alternates can be challenged by the prosecution, or by the Defendants or their Counsel. Each Signatory may replace its member of the Tribunal or his alternate for reasons of health or for other good reasons, except that no replacement may take place during a Trial, other than by an alternate.

Article 4.

(a) The presence of all four members of the Tribunal or the alternate for any absent member shall be necessary to constitute the quorum.

(b) The members of the Tribunal shall, before any trial begins, agree among themselves upon the selection from their number of a President, and the President shall hold office during that trial, or as may otherwise be agreed by a vote of not less than three members.

The principle of rotation of presidency for successive trials is agreed. If, however, a session of the Tribunal takes place on the territory of one of the four Signatories, the representative of that Signatory on the Tribunal shall preside.

(c) Save as aforesaid the Tribunal shall take decisions by a majority vote and in case the votes are evenly divided, the vote of the President shall be decisive: provided always that convictions and sentences shall only be imposed by the affirmative votes of at least three members of the Tribunal.

Article 5. In case of need and depending on the number of the matters to be tried, other Tribunals may be set up; and the establishment, functions, and procedure of each Tribunal shall be identical, and shall be governed by this Charter.

II. Jurisdiction and General Principles

Article 6. The Tribunal established by the Agreement referred to in Article 1 hereof for the trial and punishment of the major war criminals of the European Axis countries shall have the power to try and punish persons who, acting in the interests of the European Axis countries, whether as individuals or as members of organizations, committed any of the following crimes.

The following acts, or any of them, are crimes coming within the jurisdiction of the Tribunal for which there shall be individual responsibility:

(a) *Crimes Against Peace:* namely, planning, preparation, initiation or waging of a war of aggression, or a war in violation of international treaties, agreements or assurances, or participation in a common plan or conspiracy for the accomplishment of any of the foregoing;

(b) *War Crimes:* namely, violations of the laws or customs of war. Such violations shall include, but not be limited to, murder, ill-treatment or deportation to slave labor or for any other purpose of civilian population of or in occupied territory, murder or ill-treatment of prisoners of war or persons on the seas, killing of hostages, plunder of public or private property, wanton destruction of cities, towns or villages, or devastation not justified by military necessity;

(c) *Crimes Against Humanity:* namely, murder, extermination, enslavement, deportation, and other inhumane acts committed against any civilian population, before or during the war; or persecutions on political, racial or religious grounds in execution of or in connection with any crime within the jurisdiction of the Tribunal, whether or not in violation of domestic law of the country where perpetrated.

Leaders, organizers, instigators and accomplices participating in the formulation or execution of a common plan or conspiracy to commit any of the foregoing crimes are responsible for all acts performed by any persons in execution of such plan.

Article 7. The official position of defendants, whether as Heads of State or responsible officials in Government Departments, shall not be considered as freeing them from responsibility or mitigating punishment.

Article 8. The fact that the Defendant acted pursuant to order of his Government or of a superior shall not free him from responsibility, but may be considered in mitigation of punishment if the Tribunal determine that justice so requires.

Article 9. At the trial of any individual member of any group or organization the Tribunal may declare (in connection with any act of which the individual may be convicted) that the group or organization of which the individual was a member was a criminal organization.

After receipt of the Indictment the Tribunal shall give such notice as it thinks fit that the prosecution intends to ask the Tribunal to make such declaration and any member of the organization will be entitled to apply to the Tribunal for leave to be heard by the Tribunal upon the question of the criminal character of the organization. The Tribunal shall have power to allow or reject the application. If the application is allowed, the Tribunal may direct in what manner the applicants shall be represented and heard.

Article 10. In cases where a group or organization is declared criminal by the Tribunal, the competent national authority of any Signatory shall have the right to bring individuals to trial for membership therein before national, military or occupation courts. In any such case the criminal nature of the group or organization is considered proved and shall not be questioned.

Article 11. Any person convicted by the Tribunal may be charged before a national, military or occupation court, referred to in Article

10 of this Charter, with a crime other than of membership in a criminal group or organization and such court may, after convicting him, impose upon him punishment independent of and additional to the punishment imposed by the Tribunal for participation in the criminal activities of such group or organization.

Article 12. The Tribunal shall have the right to take proceedings against a person charged with crimes set out in Article 6 of this Charter in his absence, if he has not been found or if the Tribunal, for any reason, finds it necessary, in the interests of justice, to conduct the hearing in his absence.

Article 13. The Tribunal shall draw up rules for its procedure. These rules shall not be inconsistent with the provisions of this Charter.

III. Committee for the Investigation and Prosecution of Major War Criminals

Article 14. Each Signatory shall appoint a Chief Prosecutor for the investigation of the charges against and the prosecution of major war criminals.

The Chief Prosecutors shall act as a committee for the following purposes:

(a) to agree upon a plan of the individual work of each of the Chief Prosecutors and his staff,

(b) to settle the final designation of major war criminals to be tried by the Tribunal,

(c) to approve the Indictment and the documents to be submitted therewith,

(d) to lodge the Indictment and the accompanying documents with the Tribunal,

(e) to draw up and recommend to the Tribunal for its approval draft rules of procedure, contemplated by Article 13 of this Charter. The Tribunal shall have power to accept, with or without amendments, or to reject, the rules so recommended.

The Committee shall act in all the above matters by a majority vote and shall appoint a Chairman as may be convenient and in accordance with the principle of rotation: provided that if there is an equal division of vote concerning the designation of a Defendant to be tried by the Tribunal, or the crimes with which he shall be charged, that proposal will be adopted which was made by the party which proposed that the particular Defendant be tried, or the particular charges be preferred against him.

Article 15. The Chief Prosecutors shall individually, and acting in collaboration with one another, also undertake the following duties:

(a) investigation, collection and production before or at the Trial of all necessary evidence,

(b) the preparation of the Indictment for approval by the Committee in accordance with paragraph (c) of Article 14 hereof,

(c) the preliminary examination of all necessary witnesses and of the Defendants,

(d) to act as prosecutor at the Trial,

(e) to appoint representatives to carry out such duties as may be assigned to them,

(f) to undertake such other matters as may appear necessary to them for the purposes of the preparation for and conduct of the Trial.

It is understood that no witness or Defendant detained by any Signatory shall be taken out of the possession of that Signatory without its assent.

IV. Fair Trial for Defendants

Article 16. In order to ensure fair trial for the Defendants, the following procedure shall be followed:

(a) The Indictment shall include full particulars specifying in detail the charges against the Defendants. A copy of the Indictment and of all the documents lodged with the Indictment, translated into a language which he understands, shall be furnished to the Defendant at a reasonable time before the Trial.

(b) During any preliminary examination or trial of a Defendant he shall have the right to give any explanation relevant to the charges made against him.

(c) A preliminary examination of a Defendant and his Trial shall be conducted in, or translated into, a language which the Defendant understands.

(d) A defendant shall have the right to conduct his own defense before the Tribunal or to have the assistance of Counsel.

(e) A defendant shall have the right through himself or through his Counsel to present evidence at the Trial in support of his defense, and to cross-examine any witness called by the Prosecution.

V. Powers of the Tribunal and Conduct of the Trial

Article 17. The Tribunal shall have the power

(a) to summon witnesses to the Trial and to require their attendance and testimony and to put questions to them,

(b) to interrogate any Defendant,

(c) to require the production of documents and other evidentiary material,

(d) to administer oaths to witnesses,

(e) to appoint officers for the carrying out of any task designated by the Tribunal including the power to have evidence taken on commission.

Article 18. The Tribunal shall

(a) confine the Trial strictly to an expeditious hearing of the issues raised by the charges,

(b) take strict measures to prevent any action which will cause unreasonable delay, and rule out irrelevant issues and statements of any kind whatsoever,

(c) deal summarily with any contumacy, imposing appropriate punishment, including exclusion of any Defendant or his Counsel from some or all further proceedings, but without prejudice to the determination of the charges.

Article 19. The Tribunal shall not be bound by technical rules of evidence. It shall adopt and apply to the greatest possible extent expeditious and nontechnical procedure, and shall admit any evidence which it deems to have probative value.

Article 20. The Tribunal may require to be informed of the nature of any evidence before it is offered so that it may rule upon the relevance thereof.

Article 21. The Tribunal shall not require proof of facts of common knowledge but shall take judicial notice thereof. It shall also take judicial notice of official governmental documents and reports of the United Nations, including the acts and documents of the committees set up in the various allied countries for the investigation of war crimes, and the records and findings of military or other Tribunals of any of the United Nations.

Article 22. The permanent seat of the Tribunal shall be in Berlin. The first meetings of the members of the Tribunal and of the Chief Prosecutors shall be held at Berlin in a place to be designated by the Control Council for Germany. The first trial shall be held at Nürnberg, and any subsequent trials shall be held at such places as the Tribunal may decide.

Article 23. One or more of the Chief Prosecutors may take part in the prosecution at each Trial. The function of any Chief Prosecutor may be discharged by him personally, or by any person or persons authorized by him.

The function of Counsel for a Defendant may be discharged at the Defendant's request by any Counsel professionally qualified to conduct cases before the courts of his own country, or by any other person who may be specially authorized thereto by the Tribunal.

Article 24. The proceedings at the Trial shall take the following course:

(a) The Indictment shall be read in court.

(b) The Tribunal shall ask each Defendant whether he pleads "guilty" or "not guilty."

(c) The prosecution shall make an opening statement.

(d) The Tribunal shall ask the prosecution and the defense what evidence (if any) they wish to submit to the Tribunal, and the Tribunal shall rule upon the admissibility of any such evidence.

(e) The witnesses for the Prosecution shall be examined and after that the witnesses for the Defense. Thereafter such rebutting evidence as may be held by the Tribunal to be admissible shall be called by either the Prosecution or the Defense.

(f) The Tribunal may put any question to any witness and to any Defendant, at any time.

(g) The Prosecution and the Defense shall interrogate and may cross-examine any witnesses and any Defendant who gives testimony.

(h) The Defense shall address the court.

(i) The Prosecution shall address the court.

(j) Each Defendant may make a statement to the Tribunal.

(k) The Tribunal shall deliver judgment and pronounce sentence.

Article 25. All official documents shall be produced, and all court proceedings conducted, in English, French, and Russian, and in the language of the Defendant. So much of the record and of the proceedings may also be translated into the language of any country in which the Tribunal is sitting, as the Tribunal considers desirable in the interests of justice and public opinion.

VI. Judgment and Sentence

Article 26. The judgment of the Tribunal as to the guilt or the innocence of any Defendant shall give the reasons on which it is based, and shall be final and not subject to review.

Article 27. The Tribunal shall have the right to impose upon a Defendant on conviction, death or such other punishment as shall be determined by it to be just.

Article 28. In addition to any punishment imposed by it, the Tribunal shall have the right to deprive the convicted person of any stolen property and order its delivery to the Control Council for Germany.

Article 29. In case of guilt, sentences shall be carried out in accordance with the orders of the Control Council for Germany, which may at any time reduce or otherwise alter the sentences, but may not increase the severity thereof. If the Control Council for Germany, after any Defendant has been convicted and sentenced, discovers fresh evidence which, in its opinion, would found a fresh charge against him, the Council shall report accordingly to the Committee established under Article 14 hereof, for such action as they may consider proper, having regard to the interests of justice.

VII. Expenses

Article 30. The expenses of the Tribunal and of the Trials, shall be charged by the Signatories against the funds allotted for maintenance of the Control Council for Germany.

Robert H. Jackson

OPENING STATEMENT FOR THE UNITED STATES BEFORE THE INTERNATIONAL MILITARY TRIBUNAL, NOVEMBER 21, 1945

The Honorable Robert H. Jackson (1892–1954) was Attorney General of the United States when President Roosevelt named him Associate Justice of the Supreme Court in 1941, a position he held until his death in 1954. But he will be remembered chiefly for the role he played as Chief of Counsel for the United States at Nuremberg from 1945 to 1946. Although Justice Jackson's familiarity with the Nazi state has been questioned, his strength of character, determination, and quest for justice have remained above reproach. The following selection is taken from his eloquent opening statement for the United States, which reflects the idealism that characterized the country at mid-century, when friend and enemy, justice and injustice, right and wrong were absolutely clear and unquestioned.

INTERNATIONAL MILITARY TRIBUNAL NO. I

The United States of America, the French Republic, the United Kingdom of Great Britain and Northern Ireland, and the Union of Soviet Socialist Republics

AGAINST   83-679

Hermann Wilhelm Göring, Rudolf Hess, Joachim von Ribbentrop, Robert Ley, Wilhelm Keitel, Ernst Kaltenbrunner, Alfred Rosenberg, Hans Frank, Wilhelm Frick, Julius Streicher, Walter Funk, Hjalmar Schacht, Gustav Krupp von Bohlen und Halbach, Karl Dönitz, Erich Raeder, Baldur von Schirach, Fritz Sauckel, Alfred Jodl, Martin Bormann, Franz von Papen, Artur Seyss-Inquart, Albert Speer, Constantin von Neurath, and Hans Fritzsche,

Individually and as Members of Any of the Following Groups or Organizations to which They Respectively Belonged Namely: Die Reichsregierung (Reich Cabinet); Das Korps der Politischen Leiter der Nationalsozialistischen Deutschen Arbeiterpartei (Leadership Corps of the Nazi Party); Die Schutzstaffeln der Nationalsozialistischen Deutschen Arbeiterpartei (commonly known as the "SS") and including Die Sicherheitsdienst (commonly known as the "SD"); Die Geheime Staatspolizei (Secret State Police, commonly known as the "Gestapo"); Die Sturmabteilungen der

From International Military Tribunal, *Trial of the Major War Criminals before the International Military Tribunal*, 42 vols. [Blue Series] (Nuremberg, 1949), 2:98–155.

*N.S.D.A.P. (commonly known as the "SA") and the General Staff and High
Command of the German Armed Forces.*

DEFENDANTS

MAY IT PLEASE YOUR HONORS:

The privilege of opening the first trial in history for crimes against
the peace of the world imposes a grave responsibility. The wrongs
which we seek to condemn and punish have been so calculated, so
malignant and so devastating, that civilization cannot tolerate their
being ignored because it cannot survive their being repeated. That
four great nations, flushed with victory and stung with injury stay
the hand of vengeance and voluntarily submit their captive enemies
to the judgment of the law is one of the most significant tributes that
Power ever has paid to Reason.

This Tribunal, while it is novel and experimental, is not the product
of abstract speculations nor is it created to vindicate legalistic
theories. This inquest represents the practical effort of four of the
most mighty nations, with the support of seventeen more, to utilize
International Law to meet the greatest menace of our times—aggressive war. The common sense of mankind demands that law shall
not stop with the punishment of petty crimes by little people. It must
also reach men who possess themselves of great power and make
deliberate and concerted use of it to set in motion evils which leave
no home in the world untouched. It is a cause of this magnitude that
the United Nations will lay before Your Honors.

In the prisoners' dock sit twenty-odd broken men. Reproached by
the humiliation of those they have led almost as bitterly as by the
desolation of those they have attacked, their personal capacity for
evil is forever past. It is hard now to perceive in these miserable
men as captives the power by which as Nazi leaders they once
dominated much of the world and terrified most of it. Merely as
individuals, their fate is of little consequence to the world.

What makes this inquest significant is that these prisoners represent sinister influences that will lurk in the world long after their
bodies have returned to dust. They are living symbols of racial
hatreds, of terrorism and violence, and of the arrogance and cruelty
of power. They are symbols of fierce nationalisms and of militarism,
of intrigue and war-making which have embroiled Europe generation

after generation, crushing its manhood, destroying its homes, and impoverishing its life. They have so identified themselves with the philosophies they conceived and with the forces they directed that any tenderness to them is a victory and an encouragement to all the evils which are attached to their names. Civilization can afford no compromise with the social forces which would gain renewed strength if we deal ambiguously or indecisively with the men in whom those forces now precariously survive.

What these men stand for we will patiently and temperately disclose. We will give you undeniable proofs of incredible events. The catalogue of crimes will omit nothing that could be conceived by a pathological pride, cruelty, and lust for power. These men created in Germany, under the *Führerprinzip,* a National Socialist despotism equaled only by the dynasties of the ancient East. They took from the German people all those dignities and freedoms that we hold natural and inalienable rights in every human being. The people were compensated by inflaming and gratifying hatreds toward those who were marked as "scapegoats." Against their opponents, including Jews, Catholics, and free labor, the Nazis directed such a campaign of arrogance, brutality, and annihilation as the world has not witnessed since the pre-Christian ages. They excited the German ambition to be a "master race," which of course implies serfdom for others. They led their people on a mad gamble for domination. They diverted social energies and resources to the creation of what they thought to be an invincible war machine. They overran their neighbors. To sustain the "master race" in its war-making, they enslaved millions of human beings and brought them into Germany, where these hapless creatures now wander as "displaced persons." At length bestiality and bad faith reached such excess that they aroused the sleeping strength of imperiled Civilization. Its united efforts have ground the German war machine to fragments. But the struggle has left Europe a liberated yet prostrate land where a demoralized society struggles to survive. These are the fruits of the sinister forces that sit with these defendants in the prisoners' dock.

In justice to the nations and the men associated in this prosecution, I must remind you of certain difficulties which may leave their mark on this case. Never before in legal history has an effort been made to bring within the scope of a single litigation the developments of a decade, covering a whole Continent, and involving a score of nations, countless individuals, and innumerable events. Despite the magnitude of the task, the world has demanded immediate action. This demand has had to be met, though perhaps at the cost of finished craftsmanship. In my country, established courts, following familiar procedures, applying well-thumbed precedents, and dealing with the legal consequences of local and limited events seldom commence a trial within a year of the event in litigation. Yet less than eight months ago today the courtroom in which you sit was an enemy fortress in the hands of German SS troops. Less than eight months ago nearly all our witnesses and documents were in enemy hands. The law had not been codified, no procedures had been established, no Tribunal was in existence, no usable courthouse stood here, none of the hundreds of tons of official German documents had been examined, no prosecuting staff had been assembled, nearly all the present defendants were at large, and the four prosecuting powers had not yet joined in common cause to try them. I should be the last to deny that the case may well suffer from incomplete researches and quite likely will not be the example of professional work which any of the prosecuting nations would normally wish to sponsor. It is, however, a completely adequate case to the judgment we shall ask you to render, and its full development we shall be obliged to leave to historians.

Before I discuss particulars of evidence, some general considerations which may affect the credit of this trial in the eyes of the world should be candidly faced. There is a dramatic disparity between the circumstances of the accusers and of the accused that might discredit our work if we should falter, in even minor matters, in being fair and temperate.

Unfortunately, the nature of these crimes is such that both prosecution and judgment must be by victor nations over vanquished foes. The world-wide scope of the aggressions carried out by these men has left but few real neutrals. Either the victors must judge the vanquished or we must leave the defeated to judge themselves. After the First World War, we learned the futility of the latter course. The former high station of these defendants, the notoriety of their acts, and the adaptability of their conduct to provoke retaliation make it hard to distinguish between the demand for a just and measured retribution, and the unthinking cry for vengeance which arises from the anguish of war. It is our task, so far as humanly possible, to draw the line between the two. We must never forget that the record on which we judge these defendants today is the record on which history will judge us tomorrow. To pass these defendants a poisoned chalice is to put it to our own lips as well. We must summon such detachment and intellectual integrity to our task that this trial will commend itself to posterity as fulfilling humanity's aspirations to do justice.

At the very outset, let us dispose of the contention that to put these men to trial is to do them an injustice entitling them to some special consideration. These defendants may be hard pressed but they are not ill-used. Let us see what alternative they would have to being tried.

More than a majority of these prisoners surrendered to or were tracked down by forces of the United States. Could they expect us to make American custody a shelter for our enemies against the just wrath of our Allies? Did we spend American lives to capture them only to save them from punishment? Under the principles of the Moscow Declaration, those suspected war criminals who are not to be tried internationally must be turned over to individual governments for trial at the scene of their outrages. Many less responsible and less culpable American-held prisoners have been and will be turned over to other United Nations for local trial. If these defendants should succeed, for any reason, in escaping the condemnation of this Tribunal, or if they obstruct or abort this trial, those who are American-held prisoners will be delivered up to our Continental Allies. For these defendants, however, we have set up an International Tribunal and have undertaken the burden of participating in a complicated effort to give them fair and dispassionate hearings. That is the best-known protection to any man with a defense worthy of being heard.

If these men are the first war leaders of a defeated nation to be prosecuted in the name of the law, they are also the first to be given a chance to plead for their lives in the name of the law. Realistically, the Charter of this Tribunal, which gives them a hearing, is also the source of their only hope. It may be that these men of troubled conscience, whose only wish is that the world forget them, do not regard a trial as a favor. But they do have a fair opportunity to defend themselves—a favor which these men, when in power, rarely extended to their fellow countrymen. Despite the fact that public opinion already condemns their acts, we agree that here they must be given a presumption of innocence, and we accept the burden of proving criminal acts and the responsibility of these defendants for their commission.

When I say that we do not ask for convictions unless we prove crime, I do not mean mere technical or incidental transgression of international conventions. We charge guilt on planned and intended conduct that involves moral as well as legal wrong. And we do not mean conduct that is a natural and human, even if illegal, cutting of corners, such as many of us might well have committed had we been in the defendants' positions. It is not because they yielded to the normal frailties of human beings that we accuse them. It is their abnormal and inhuman conduct which brings them to this bar.

We will not ask you to convict these men on the testimony of their foes. There is no count of the Indictment that cannot be proved by books and records. The Germans were always meticulous record-keepers, and these defendants had their share of the Teutonic passion for thoroughness in putting things on paper. Nor were they without vanity. They arranged frequently to be photographed in action. We will show you their own films. You will see their own conduct and hear their own voices as these defendants re-enact for you, from the screen, some of the events in the course of the conspiracy.

We would also make clear that we have no purpose to incriminate the whole German people. We know that the Nazi Party was not put in power by a majority of the German vote. We know it came to power by an evil-alliance between the most extreme of the Nazi revolutionists, the most unrestrained of the German reactionaries, and the most aggressive of the German militarists. If the German populace had willingly accepted the Nazi program, no Stormtroopers would have been needed in the early days of the Party and there would have been no need for concentration camps or the Gestapo, both of which institutions were inaugurated as soon as the Nazis gained control of the German state. Only after these lawless innovations proved successful at home were they taken abroad.

The German people should know by now that the people of the United States hold them in no fear, and in no hate. It is true that the

Germans have taught us the horrors of modern warfare, but the ruin that lies from the Rhine to the Danube shows that we, like our Allies, have not been dull pupils. If we are not awed by German fortitude and proficiency in war, and if we are not persuaded of their political maturity, we do respect their skill in the arts of peace, their technical competence, and the sober, industrious and self-disciplined character of the masses of the German people. In 1933, we saw the German people recovering prestige in the commercial, industrial and artistic world after the setback of the last war. We beheld their progress neither with envy nor malice. The Nazi regime interrupted this advance. The recoil of the Nazi aggression has left Germany in ruins. The Nazi readiness to pledge the German word without hesitation and to break it without shame has fastened upon German diplomacy a reputation for duplicity that will handicap it for years. Nazi arrogance has made the boast of the "master race" a taunt that will be thrown at Germans the world over for generations. The Nazi nightmare has given the German name a new and sinister significance throughout the world which will retard Germany a century. The German, no less than the non-German world, has accounts to settle with these defendants.

The fact of the war and the course of the war, which is the central theme of our case, is history. From September 1, 1939, when the German armies crossed the Polish frontiers, until September 1942, when they met epic resistance at Stalingrad, German arms seemed invincible. Denmark and Norway, The Netherlands and France, Belgium and Luxembourg, the Balkans and Africa, Poland and the Baltic States, and parts of Russia, all had been overrun and conquered by swift, powerful, well-aimed blows. That attack upon the peace of the world is the crime against international society which brings into international cognizance crimes in its aid and preparation which otherwise might only be internal concerns. It was aggressive war, which the nations of the world had renounced. It was war in violation of treaties, by which the peace of the world was sought to be safeguarded.

This war did not just happen—it was planned and prepared for over a long period of time and with no small skill and cunning. The world has perhaps never seen such a concentration and stimulation of the energies of any people as that which enabled Germany twenty years after it was defeated, disarmed, and dismembered to come so near carrying out its plan to dominate Europe. Whatever else we may say of those who were the authors of this war, they did achieve a stupendous work in organization, and our first task is to examine the means by which these defendants and their fellow conspirators prepared and incited Germany to go to war.

In general, our case will disclose these defendants all uniting at some time with the Nazi Party in a plan which they well knew could be accomplished only by an outbreak of war in Europe. Their seizure of the German state, their subjugation of the German people, their terrorism and extermination of dissident elements, their planning and waging of war, their calculated and planned ruthlessness in the conduct of warfare, their deliberate and planned criminality toward conquered peoples—all these are ends for which they acted in concert; and all these are phases of the conspiracy, a conspiracy which reached one goal only to set out for another and more ambitious one. We shall also trace for you the intricate web of organizations which these men formed and utilized to accomplish these ends. We will show how the entire structure of offices and officials was dedicated to the criminal purposes and committed to use of the criminal methods planned by these defendants and their co-conspirators, many of whom war and suicide have put beyond reach.

It is my purpose to open the case, particularly under Count One of the Indictment, and to deal with the common plan or conspiracy to achieve ends possible only by resort to crimes against peace, war crimes, and crimes against humanity. My emphasis will not be on individual barbarities and perversions which may have occurred independently of any central plan. One of the dangers ever-present is that this trial may be protracted by details of particular wrongs and that we will become lost in a "wilderness of single instances." Nor will I now dwell on the activity of individual defendants except as it may contribute to exposition of the common plan.

The case as presented by the United States will be concerned with the brains and authority back of all the crimes. These defendants were men of a station and rank which does not soil its own hands with blood. They were men who knew how to use lesser folks as tools. We want to reach the planners and designers, the inciters and leaders without whose evil architecture the world would not have been for so long scourged with the violence and lawlessness, and wracked with the agonies and convulsions of this terrible war. . . .

*   *   *

The Responsibility of this Tribunal

To apply the sanctions of the law to those whose conduct is found criminal by the standards I have outlined, is the responsibility committed to this Tribunal. It is the first court ever to undertake the difficult task of overcoming the confusion of many tongues and the conflicting concepts of just procedure among diverse systems of law, so as to reach a common judgment. The tasks of all of us are such as to make heavy demands on patience and good will. Although the need for prompt action has admittedly resulted in imperfect work on the part of the prosecution, four great nations bring you their hurriedly assembled contributions of evidence. What remains undiscovered we can only guess. We could, with witnesses' testimony, prolong the recitals of crime for years—but to what avail? We shall rest the case when we have offered what seems convincing and adequate proof of the crimes charged without unnecessary cumulation of evidence. We doubt very much whether it will be seriously denied that the crimes I have outlined took place. The effort will undoubtedly be to mitigate or escape personal responsibility.

Among the nations which unite in accusing these defendants the United States is perhaps in a position to be the most dispassionate, for, having sustained the least injury, it is perhaps the least animated by vengeance. Our American cities have not been bombed by day and by night, by humans and by robots. It is not our temples that have been laid in ruins. Our countrymen have not had their homes destroyed over their heads. The menace of Nazi aggression, except to those in actual service, has seemed less personal and immediate to us than to European peoples. But while the United States is not first in rancor, it is not second in determination that the forces of law and order be made equal to the task of dealing with such international lawlessness as I have recited here.

Twice in my lifetime, the United States has sent its young manhood across the Atlantic, drained its resources, and burdened itself with debt to help defeat Germany. But the real hope and faith that has sustained the Amercan people in these great efforts was that victory for ourselves and our Allies would lay the basis for an ordered international relationship in Europe and would end the centuries of strife on this embattled continent.

Twice we have held back in the early stages of European conflict in the belief that it might be confined to a purely European affair. In the United States, we have tried to build an economy without armament, a system of government without militarism, and a society where men are not regimented for war. This purpose, we know now, can never be realized if the world periodically is to be embroiled in war. The United States cannot, generation after generation, throw its youth or its resources onto the battlefields of Europe to redress the lack of balance between Germany's strength and that of her enemies, and to keep the battles from our shores.

The American dream of a peace-and-plenty economy, as well as the hopes of other nations, can never be fulfilled if those nations are involved in a war every generation so vast and devastating as to crush the generation that fights and burden the generation that follows. But experience has shown that wars are no longer local. All modern wars become world wars eventually. And none of the big nations at least can stay out. If we cannot stay out of wars, our only hope is to prevent wars.

I am too well aware of the weaknesses of juridical action alone to contend that in itself your decision under this Charter can prevent future wars. Judicial action always comes after the event. Wars are started only on the theory and in the confidence that they can be won. Personal punishment, to be suffered only in the event the war is lost, will probably not be a sufficient deterrent to prevent a war where the war-makers feel the chances of defeat to be negligible.

But the ultimate step in avoiding periodic wars, which are inevitable in a system of international lawlessness, is to make statesmen responsible to law. And let me make clear that while this law is first applied against German aggressors, the law includes, and if it is to serve a useful purpose it must condemn aggression by any other nations, including those which sit here now in judgment. We are able to do away with domestic tyranny and violence and aggression by those in power against the rights of their own people only when we make all men answerable to the law. This trial represents mankind's desperate effort to apply the discipline of the law to statesmen who have used their powers of state to attack the foundations of the world's peace and to commit aggressions against the rights of their neighbors.

The usefulness of this effort to do justice is not to be measured by considering the law or your judgment in isolation. This trial is part of the great effort to make the peace more secure. One step in this direction is the United Nations organization, which may take joint political action to prevent war if possible, and joint military action to insure that any nation which starts a war will lose it. This Charter and this trial, implementing the Kellogg-Briand Pact, constitute another step in the same direction—juridical action of a kind to insure that those who start a war will pay for it personally.

While the defendants and the prosecutors stand before you as individuals, it is not the triumph of either group alone that is committed to your judgment. Above all personalities there are anonymous and impersonal forces whose conflict makes up much of human history. It is yours to throw the strength of the law back of either the one or the other of these forces for at least another generation. What are the real forces that are contending before you?

No charity can disguise the fact that the forces which these defendants represent, the forces that would advantage and delight in their acquittal, are the darkest and most sinister forces in society—dictatorship and oppression, malevolence and passion, militarism and lawlessness. By their fruits we best know them. Their acts have bathed the world in blood and set civilization back a century. They have subjected their European neighbors to every outrage and torture, every spoliation and deprivation that insolence, cruelty, and greed could inflict. They have brought the German people to the lowest pitch of wretchedness, from which they can entertain no hope of early deliverance. They have stirred hatreds and incited domestic violence on every continent. These are the things that stand in the dock shoulder to shoulder with these prisoners.

The real complaining party at your bar is Civilization. In all our countries it is still a struggling and imperfect thing. It does not plead that the United States, or any other country, has been blameless of the conditions which made the German people easy victims to the blandishments and intimidations of the Nazi conspirators.

But it points to the dreadful sequence of aggressions and crimes I have recited, it points to the weariness of flesh, the exhaustion of resources, and the destruction of all that was beautiful or useful in so much of the world, and to greater potentialities for destruction in the days to come. It is not necessary among the ruins of this ancient and beautiful city, with untold members of its civilian inhabitants still buried in its rubble, to argue the proposition that to start or wage an aggressive war has the moral qualities of the worst of crimes. The refuge of the defendants can be only their hope that International Law will lag so far behind the moral sense of mankind that conduct which is crime in the moral sense must be regarded as innocent in law.

Civilization asks whether law is so laggard as to be utterly helpless to deal with crimes of this magnitude by criminals of this order of importance. It does not expect that your juridical action will put the forces of International Law, its precepts, its prohibitions and, most of all, its sanctions, on the side of peace, so that men and women of good will in all countries may have "leave to live by no man's leave, underneath the law."

Quincy Wright
THE LAW OF THE NUREMBERG TRIAL, PART II

There has been much confusion about Nuremberg in the past because many people have refused to separate the moral and political issues from the legal principles involved in the debate. In the following selection, Quincy Wright makes this distinction and proceeds to bring the controversy into focus by commenting on several disputed points of law. Among other questions he discusses the jurisdiction of the International Military Tribunal, the fairness of the trial proceedings, ex post facto justice, the legality of prosecuting individuals for acts of state, and genocide as an international crime.

"The Law of the Nuremberg Trial," *American Journal of International Law* 41 (January 1947). From *International Law in the Twentieth Century,* copyright © 1969. By permission of Appleton-Century-Crofts, Educational Division, Meredith Corporation. (Footnotes omitted.)

Critics from a legal point of view have contended that the Tribunal had no jurisdiction in international law and that it applied ex post facto law. Related to these criticisms have been the contention that morally the trial was unfair because constituted by one side in a war or because some of the prosecuting states had been guilty of the same offenses for which they were trying their enemies, and that politically the trial was inexpedient because it may make conciliation between victor and vanquished more difficult, because it may make heroes and martyrs of the defendants, or because its principles if generally accepted may reduce the unity of the state, increase the difficulties of maintaining domestic order, and deter statesmen from pursuing vigorous foreign policies when necessary in the national interests. These moral and political arguments depend upon ethical, psychological, and sociological assumptions which are controversial. They should be distinguished from the legal arguments which alone are under consideration here. . . .

Sovereign states, it is true, cannot be subjected to a foreign jurisdiction without their consent but no such principle applies to individuals. The Nuremberg Tribunal did not exercise jurisdiction over Germany but over certain German individuals accused of crimes.

Furthermore, the equitable principle of "clean hands" is not recognized as a defense in criminal trials. Whether or not statesmen or individuals of the United Nations have been guilty of any of the offenses for which the defendants were tried was not a question legally relevant to this trial, nor is it legally relevant to consider whether other persons who have not been indicted or who were not within the jurisdiction of the Tribunal may have been guilty of the same offenses. . . .

The Charter of the Tribunal recognized principles generally believed to be essential for a law-governed world under present conditions, and naturally those who are afraid of the restriction of a law-governed world upon the nation or who think world opinion has not developed to a point that would make such a world possible, view these principles with apprehension. The United Nations in the Charter of the International Military Tribunal, as in the Charter of the United Nations, performed an act of faith in, and commitment to, a law-governed world and the principles which must be accepted and applied if there is to be such a world. The Tribunal did not hesitate to accept these principles as established in developing international law at the time the acts for which the defendants were being tried were committed. . . .

The Tribunal's Jurisdiction

The making of the Charter (said the Tribunal) was the exercise of the sovereign legislative power by the countries to which the German Reich unconditionally surrendered; and the undoubted right of these countries to legislate for the occupied territories had been recognized by the civilized world. The Charter is not an arbitrary exercise of power on the part of the victorious nations, but in the view of the Tribunal, as will be shown, it is the expression of international law existing at the time of its creation; and to that extent is itself a contribution to international law.

The signatory powers created this Tribunal, defined the law it was to administer, and made regulations for the proper conduct of the Trial. In doing so, they have done together what any one of them might have done singly; for it is not to be doubted that any nation has the right thus to set up special courts to administer laws. With regard to the constitution of the court, all that the defendants are entitled to ask is to receive a fair trial on the facts and law.

This statement suggests two distinct grounds of jurisdiction—that enjoyed by the four powers as the government of Germany and that enjoyed by any state to administer law. The latter statement is far from complete. International law does not permit states to administer criminal law over any defendant for any act. There are limits to the criminal jurisdiction of a state. Every state does, however, have authority to set up special courts to try any person within its custody who commits war crimes, at least if such offenses threaten its security. It is believed that this jurisdiction is broad enough to cover the jurisdiction given by the Charter. If each party to the Charter could exercise such jurisdiction individually, they can agree to set up an international tribunal to exercise the jurisdiction jointly. The context of the court's statement suggests that the Tribunal intended this limitation. . . .

The derivation of the Tribunal's jurisdiction from the sovereignty of Germany also appears to be well grounded. The Nazi government of Germany disappeared with the unconditional surrender of Germany in May 1945, and on June 5, 1945, the four Allied powers, then in complete control of Germany by public declaration at Berlin, assumed "supreme authority with respect to Germany, including all the powers possessed by the German government, the High Command, and any state, municipal, or local government or authority" in order "to make provision for the cessation of any further hostilities on the part of the German armed forces, for the maintenance of order in Germany, and for the administration of the country," but without intention to "effect the annexation of Germany." Under international law a state may acquire sovereignty of territory by declaration of annexation after subjugation of the territory if that declaration is generally recognized by the other states of the world. The Declaration of Berlin was generally recognized, not only by the United Nations but also by neutral states. This Declaration, however, differed from the usual declaration of annexation in that it was by several states, its purposes were stated, and it was declared not to effect the annexation of Germany. . . .

The four Allied powers assumed the sovereignty of Germany in order, among other purposes, to administer the country until such time as they thought fit to recognize an independent German government. Their exercise of powers of legislation, adjudication, and administration in Germany during this period is permissible under international law, limited only by the rules of international law applicable to sovereign states in territory they have subjugated. Their powers go beyond those of a military occupant. It would appear, therefore, that the four states who proclaimed the Charter of August 8, 1945, had the power to enact that Charter as a legislative act for Germany provided they did not transgress fundamental principles of justice which even a conqueror ought to observe toward the inhabitants of annexed territory.

The idea that the four powers acting in the interest of the United Nations had the right to legislate for the entire community of nations, though given some support by Article 5 of the Moscow Declaration of November 1, 1943, and by Article 2 (6) of the Charter of the United Nations was not referred to by the Tribunal. The preamble of the agreement of August 8, 1945, however, declares that the four powers in making the agreement "act in the interests of all the United Nations" and invited any government of the United Nations to adhere, and nineteen of them did so. Since the Charter of the United Nations assumed that that organization could declare principles binding on nonmembers, it may be that the United Nations in making the agreement for the Nuremberg Tribunal intended to act for the community of nations as a whole, thus making universal international law. While such an assumption of competence would theoretically be a novelty in international law, it would accord with the practice established during the nineteenth century under which leading powers exercised a predominant influence in initiating new rules of international law. It is not, however, necessary to make any such assumption in order to support the right of the parties to the Charter to give the Tribunal the jurisdiction it asserted. That right can be amply supported by the position of these powers as the government of Germany or from the sovereign right of each to exercise universal jurisdiction over the offenses stated.

Procedure of the Trial

"With regard to the constitution of the court," said the Tribunal, "all that the defendants are entitled to ask is to receive a fair trial on the facts and law." International law requires that any state or group of states in exercising criminal jurisdiction over aliens shall not "deny justice." The Charter provided suitable procedure with this in view.

The rules adopted by the Tribunal in pursuance of Article 13 of the Charter elaborated these provisions by assuring each individual defendant a period at least thirty days before his trial began to study the indictment and prepare his case, and ample opportunity to obtain the counsel of his choice, to obtain witnesses and documents, to examine all documents submitted by the prosecution, and to address motions, applications, and other requests to the Tribunal, and by assuring members of accused organizations opportunity to apply to be heard. At the first public session of the Tribunal, held in Berlin on October 18, 1945, the Presiding Judge, General Nikitchenko, called attention to these rules and said a "special clerk of the Tribunal has been appointed to advise the defendants of their rights and to take instructions from them personally as to their choice of counsel, and generally to see that their rights of defense are made known to them."

In addition to requiring that the trial be "fair," the Charter required that it be "expeditious" and that the Tribunal "take strict measures" to prevent "unreasonable delay" and rule out "irrelevant issues and statements." Some critics have deplored the length of the trial but few have suggested any unfairness in the procedure. The counsel of the defendants mildly objected to some rulings on the relevance of evidence or argument, to some limitation on the length of speeches, and to some admissions of affidavit evidence presented by the prosecution. The Tribunal, if anything, leaned over backwards to assure the defendants an opportunity to find and present all relevant evidence, to argue all legal problems related to the case and to present motions concerning the mental and physical competence of defendants which might bear upon their triability.

The Supreme Court of the United States held that General Yamashita was given due process of law in his trial by a United States Military Commission in the Philippines, but two dissenting Justices thought the admission of hearsay and opinion evidence and the haste of the proceedings giving the defense insufficient opportunity to present its case denied "due process of law." The latter charge has not been made against the Nuremberg Tribunal. Like other international tribunals, like military commissions, and like continental European criminal courts, it did not apply common law rules of evidence, but it has never been contended that those rules of evidence are required by international law.

It seems to be generally recognized that the application of ex post facto laws in criminal cases constitutes a denial of justice under international law. Constitutional guarantees and proposed bills of human rights have usually forbidden the application of ex post facto criminal law. Though few international claims have turned on this issue, that may be because modern states have rarely applied such laws. The Supreme Court of the United States in the Yamashita case and the Nuremberg Tribunal seem to have assumed that the application of ex post facto laws would be a denial of justice because both took pains to show that the rules of international law which they applied were not ex post facto. They treated the issue as one of substantive law and not of procedure or jursdiction.

The Law Applied

The law, defining the crimes and the conditions of liability to be applied in the trial, was set forth in the Charter and the Tribunal recognized that the law "is decisive and binding upon the Tribunal." Was this law declaratory of preexisting international law binding the defendants at the time they committed the acts charged? The issue has been discussed particularly in regard to the crime of "aggressive war."

The Tribunal listened to argument on the question and concluded that a rule of international law, resting upon "general principles of justice," affirmed in this respect by several international declarations that aggressive war is an international crime, had been formally accepted by all the states concerned when they ratified the Pact of Paris which condemned recourse to war for the solution of international controversies and renounced it as an instrument of national policy. This rule had made "resort to a war of aggression not merely illegal but criminal."

The Tribunal therefore considered that the well-known legal maxim *nullum crimen sine lege* had been duly observed in the case.

It quoted the text of the Pact of Paris of August 27, 1928, binding sixty-three nations, including Germany, Italy, and Japan at the outbreak of the war in 1939, referred to the analogous situation of the Hague Convention, violation of which created individual criminal liability, and held that the result was to make the waging of aggressive war illegal and those committing the act criminally liable. The Tribunal then cited various draft treaties, and resolutions of the League of Nations and the Pan American Organization declaring aggressive war a crime and added:

> *All these expressions of opinion, and others that could be cited, so solemnly made, reinforce the construction which the Tribunal places upon the Pact of Paris, that resort to a war of aggression is not merely illegal, but is criminal. The prohibition of aggressive war demanded by the conscience of the world, finds its expression in the series of Pacts and Treaties to which the Tribunal has just referred.*

Turning to the status of the individual in international law the Tribunal said:

It was submitted that international law is concerned with the actions of sovereign states, and provides for no punishment for individuals; and further, that where the action in question is an act of state, those who carry it out are not personally responsible, but are protected by the doctrine of the sovereignty of the State. In the opinion of the Tribunal both these submissions must be rejected. That international law imposes duties and liabilities upon individuals as well as upon states has long been recognized. . . .

The Tribunal said that individuals could be held responsible for criminal acts even if committed on behalf of their states "if the state in authorizing action moves outside its competence under international law." Furthermore they could not shelter themselves behind a plea of superior orders if "moral choice was in fact possible."

These statements of the Tribunal will be commented on by examining the concept of offenses against the law of nations as it has developed in international practice and custom, the applicability of the ex post facto rule in a legal system which develops by practice, the extent to which the specific offenses laid down in the charter had been recognized in customary international law with especial reference to aggressive war and criminal conspiracy and organization, and the extent to which international law recognized "act of state" as a defense against criminal charges.

Offenses against the Law of Nations

The concept of offenses against the law of nations (*delicti juris gentium*) was recognized by the classical text-writers on international law and has been employed in national constitutions and statutes. It was regarded as sufficiently tangible in the eighteenth century so that United States Federal Courts sustained indictments charging acts as an offense against the law of nations, even if there were no statutes defining the offense. Early in the nineteenth century it was held that the criminal jurisdiction of federal courts rested only on statutes though the definition of crimes denounced by statutes might be left largely to international law. Thus "piracy as defined by the law of nations" is an indictable offense in federal courts and all offenses against the law of nations are indictable at common law in state courts.

In the nineteenth century the development of the positivist doctrine that only states are subject to international law and that individuals are bound only by the municipal law of states with jurisdiction over them led to a decline in the application of the concept of offenses against the law of nations. This idea, however, has acquired renewed vigor in the twentieth century and has been discussed by numerous text writers and in many international conferences. There is, however, still disagreement as to the scope of the concept. An analysis of general principles of international law and of criminal law suggests the following definition: A crime against international law is an act committed with intent to violate a fundamental interest protected by international law or with knowledge that the act will probably violate such an interest, and which may not be adequately punished by the exercise of the normal criminal jurisdiction of any state.

States ordinarily punish crime in the interest of their own peace and security and those interests are often parallel to the general interests of the community of nations, defined by international law. Consequently the latter interests are in considerable measure protected by the normal exercise of criminal jurisdiction by states. There are, however, circumstances when this exercise of normal criminal jurisdiction is not adequate. To protect itself in such circumstances international law has recognized four methods of supplementing the normal criminal jurisdiction of states.

International law has imposed obligations on states to punish certain acts committed in their territory, punishment of which is primarily an interest of other states or of the community of nations and which therefore might be neglected in the absence of such a rule. Offenses against foreign diplomatic officers, against foreign currencies, or against the security of foreign states fall in this category.

International law has permitted a state to exercise jurisdiction over acts committed by aliens abroad either on the ground that such acts endanger the prosecuting state's security or on the ground that they endanger all states or their nationals. The jurisdiction of military commissions over offenses against the laws of war, of prize courts against contraband carriers and blockade runners, of admiralty courts against pirates, and of criminal courts against offenses defined in general international conventions or customary international law are of this character.

International law has recognized the competence of states to establish international tribunals for the trial of grave offenses not dealt with by national tribunals such as terrorism and aggression.

International law has favored or, in the opinion of some writers, required, the cooperation of states in the apprehension and punishment of fugitive criminals through extradition or other treaties. This cooperation concerns particularly persons accused of universally recognized crimes such as murder, rape, mayhem, arson, piracy, robbery, burglary, forgery, counterfeiting, embezzlement, and theft. Political and military offenses are normally excluded. Consequently many of the offenses dealt with in the preceding categories have escaped this procedure.

From a consideration of the obligation arising from these principles of international law, of the fundamental interests of states and of the community of nations protected by international law, of the acts which violate these obligations and threaten these interests, and of the circumstances which are likely to prevent punishment of such acts by the exercise of the normal jurisdiction of states, it is possible to determine whether a given act is a crime against the law of nations.

The Ex Post Facto Principle

The sources of general international law are general conventions, general customs, general principles, judicial precedents and juristic analysis. International law, therefore, resembles the common law in its developing character. According to Sir James Stephen the common law is less like a series of commands than "like an art or a science, the principles of which are first enunciated vaguely, and are gradually reduced to precision by their application to particular circumstances."

That such a conception of the ex post facto principle must apply in international law was recognized by the Tribunal when it said: "This law is not static, but by continual adaptation follows the needs of a changing world." Baron Wright, Lord of Appeal in Ordinary and Chairman of the United Nations War Crimes Commission, has recently developed this thought:

> *The common lawyer is familiar with the idea of customs which developed into law and may eventually receive recognition from competent*

Courts and authorities. But the Court does not make the law, it merely declares it or decides that it exists, after hearing the rival contentions of those who assert and those who deny the law. . . .

International Law is progressive. The period of growth generally coincides with the period of world upheavals. The pressure of necessity stimulates the impact of natural law and of moral ideas and converts them into rules of law deliberately and overtly recognized by the consensus of civilized mankind. The experience of two great world wars within a quarter of a century cannot fail to have deep repercussions on the senses of the peoples and their demand for an International Law which reflects international justice. I am convinced that International Law has progressed, as it is bound to progress if it is to be a living and operative force in these days of widening sense of humanity. An International Court, faced with the duty of deciding if the bringing of aggressive war is an international crime, is, I think, entitled and bound to hold that it is.

Considering international law as a progressive system, the rules and principles of which are to be determined at any moment by examining all its sources, "general principles of law," "international custom," and the "teachings of the most highly qualified publicists" no less than "international conventions" and "judicial decisions," there can be little doubt that international law had designated as crimes the acts so specified in the Charter long before the acts charged against the defendants were committed.

War Crimes and Crimes against Humanity

No one has questioned this conclusion as regards the "war crimes" in the narrow sense. Military commissions in wars of the past have habitually tried and punished enemy persons captured and found to have been guilty of acts in violation of the customary and conventional law of war. The Tribunal considered that the Hague Convention on land warfare was declaratory of customary international law binding all the belligerents, and that it bound Germany in all the territories it had occupied, but that the defendants were entitled to the benefit of the principle of reprisals recognized in the customary law of war. . . .

The Tribunal had no doubt that the acts in pursuance of policies of "genocide" and clearing land by extermination of its population, if carried on in occupied territories or against enemy persons, constituted "war crimes.". . .

The idea that the individual is entitled to respect for fundamental rights, accepted by the earlier writers on international law, has come under extensive consideration recently and has been accepted in the United Nations Charter, one of whose purposes is "to achieve international cooperation in promoting and encouraging respect for human rights and for fundamental freedoms for all without distinction as to race, sex, language or religion. . . ."

The Tribunal had no difficulty in assuming that war crimes and crimes against humanity in the narrow sense of the Charter were crimes under customary international law at the time the acts were committed and felt it unnecessary to give to this question the elaborate discussion which it devoted to the "crimes against peace." It merely said:

> In so far as the inhuman acts charged in the Indictment, and committed after the beginning of the war, did not constitute war crimes, they were all committed in execution of, or in connection with, the aggressive war, and therefore constituted crimes against humanity. . . .

Criminal Conspiracy and Criminal Organization

The evidence showed that concrete plans to make aggressive war were made as early as November 5, 1937. Consequently persons aware of and aiding in these plans after that date were guilty of the conspiracy charge. The prosecution's theory that "any significant participation in the affairs of the Nazi party or government is evidence of a participation in a conspiracy that is in itself criminal" was rejected:

> In the opinion of the Tribunal the conspiracy must be clearly outlined in its criminal purpose. It must not be too far removed from the time of decision and of action. The planning, to be criminal, must not rest merely on the declarations of a party program, such as are found in the twenty-five points of the Nazi party, announced in 1920, or the political affirmations expressed in Mein Kampf in later years. The Tribunal must examine whether a concrete plan to wage war existed, and determine the participants in that concrete plan.

In this sense the Tribunal found that the evidence "establishes the permanent planning to prepare and wage war by certain of the defendants" and considered it immaterial whether there were several plans or a single conspiracy. Furthermore, they were not impressed by the idea of the defense that a dictatorship was incompatible with "common planning.". . .

With this interpretation, the court found only twelve of the twenty-two defendants indicted on the conspiracy charge guilty, that is, those whom the evidence showed were significantly engaged in the inner Nazi circle after November 1937 and who participated in the planning of aggressive war. The Austrian and Czech occupations, though aggressive acts, were not aggressive wars. Consequently, activities intended to bring about these occupations such as those of von Papen who was German ambassador to Austria, did not in themselves prove guilt on this charge unless there was specific evidence that the defendant was aware of the plan to resort to aggressive war in these cases if it had proved necessary. In its treatment of the conspiracy charge the Tribunal applied the rule of strict construction of criminal statutes and gave the defendants the benefit of the doubt when the evidence of criminal intent was not clear. . . .

While the Tribunal would not hesitate to declare an organization or group criminal because "the theory of group criminality is new" or "because it might be unjustly applied by some subsequent tribunals," the Tribunal "should make such declaration of criminality so far as possible in a manner to insure that innocent persons will not be punished." It therefore applied the following definition:

> *A criminal organization is analogous to a criminal conspiracy in that the essence of both is cooperation for criminal purposes. There must be a group bound together and organized for a common purpose. The group must be formed or used in connection with the commission of crimes denounced by the Charter. Since the declaration with respect to the organizations and groups will, as has been pointed out, fix the criminality of its members, that definition should exclude persons who had no knowledge of the criminal purposes or acts of the organization and those who were drafted by the State for membership, unless they were personally implicated in the commission of acts declared criminal by Article 6 of the Charter as members of the organization. Membership alone is not enough to come within the scope of these declarations. . . .*

It is clear that in dealing with the problem of conspiracy and criminal organization the Tribunal took great care to observe the principles of criminal justice which interpret criminal statutes restrictively, which consider criminal responsibility an individual matter, and which give the benefit of the doubt to the accused. Under its rules no person could be convicted unless as an individual he had conspired in criminal activities or purposes. . . .

The opinion of the Nuremberg Tribunal marks an important step in the development of international criminal law. . . . Especially significant is the clear pronouncement that aggressive war is an individual crime, and the development of the conception of that crime. . . . The world shattered by two world wars needs to have its confidence in law restored. Such confidence can only develop if people believe that formal law embodies justice and that it will be enforced. The Nuremberg trial is likely to contribute to both of these ends.

II DRAMA AT NUREMBERG

John Dos Passos
REPORT FROM NÜRNBERG

John Dos Passos (1896–1970), the author of 42nd Parallel, The Big Money, *and* Midcentury, *was seldom thought of as a reporter. Yet he had a passionate desire to witness historical events from close range. He covered both the European and Pacific fronts during World War II, and his articles were collected in a volume entitled* Tour of Duty, *a series of vignettes which poignantly captured the mood of the war. Thereafter he appeared at Nuremberg, and his description of the city and the courtroom during the early days of the trial was both accurate and colorful.*

November 19

A sharp sun searches out every detail of the heaped ruins of the old city of toymakers. Around the statue of Albrecht Dürer stocky German women, surrounded by a pack of towheaded children, are putting potatoes to boil on a stove made out of a torn sheet of galvanized roofing. Their hands are red with cold. Their swollen knuckles are blue. On a post down the street a freshly chalked swastika stares us in the face.

At the great battered building of the Bavarian Palace of Justice there is a bustle of jeeps, command cars and converted German buses. MPs scrutinize your pass. Thronging the corridors are Americans with a familiar Washington look about their faces. The vaults resound with the cheerful clack of the heels of American girl secretaries. There are all the uniforms of the four nations.

November 20

The freshly redecorated courtroom with its sage-green curtains and crimson chairs seems warm and luxurious and radiant with silky white light. Interpreters sit behind their glass screen, tinkering with the five-way earphones. Great clusters of floodlights hang from the ceiling. A GI is smoothing out the folds of the four flags that stand behind the judges' dais.

The prisoners are already there, sitting in two rows under a rank of young American guards. The guards stand still against the wall with the serious faces of a high-school basketball team waiting to be photographed. Under them, crumpled and torn by defeat, are the faces that glared for years from the front pages of the world. There is Göring in a pearl-gray double-breasted uniform with brass buttons and that wizened look of a leaky balloon of a fat man who has lost a great deal of weight. Hess's face has fallen away till it is nothing but a pinched nose and hollow eyes and chinless mouth. Ribbentrop in dark glasses has the uneasy trapped look of a defaulting bank cashier. Streicher is a horrible cartoon of a Foxy Grandpa. Funk is a little, round, sallow man with hanging bloodhound jowls. Schacht stares out like an angry walrus. The military men with wooden chins sit up straight and quiet and separate. Except for Hess, who slumps on the bench almost in a coma, the prisoners have an easy, expectant look, as if they had come to see the play rather than to act in it. Göring is very much the master of ceremonies. Sometimes he has the naughty-boy expression of a repentant drunkard. He bows to a lady he knows in the press seats. All the while a big American sailor with a shock of red hair moves cheerfully and carefully among them checking on their earphones.

"Attenshun," calls a tall man in a frock coat. The black-robed judges are filing in. First come two Frenchmen with little wedge-shaped white bibs, one with a bushy Clemenceau mustache. Then come the two Americans. The light gleams on Biddle's tall forehead above his long face with its long thin nose. Then the two Britishers in wing collars and, last, the two Russians in uniform. There is not a sound in the courtroom. The two British judges bow slightly for the defense, who sit in front of the prisoners, some in purple robes, some in black robes and pork-pie hats, some in civilian clothes. Justice Lawrence starts talking in a low, precise, casual voice. The earphones resound hollowly. At first the voices seem to come from far away, down some echoing prison corridor. Sidney Alderman of the American prosecution staff has started to read the indictment. An Englishman takes his place, then a Frenchman, then a Russian. All day the reading goes on. Out of the voices of the prosecutors, out of the tense, out-of-breath voices of the interpreters a refrain is built up in your ears, *"Shooting, starvation* and *torture. Tortured* and *killed. Shooting, beating* and *hanging."*

Göring shakes his head with an air of martyrdom. Streicher develops a tick in the corners of his mouth. Keitel, looking more a buck sergeant than ever, is woodenly munching on a piece of bread. Rosenberg, when his name is mentioned, sits up, suddenly pulls at the neck of his blue shirt and straightens his tie.

"And *crimes against humanity* and *on the high seas.*"

November 21

Justice Lawrence has overruled a defense motion that called into question the jurisdiction of the court and has granted a recess for the defendants to consult with their lawyers before pleading. In varying tones, defiant, outraged, deprecatory, the defendants have pleaded *"nicht schuldig."*

Robert Jackson steps quietly to the microphone to open the case for the prosecution. He has a broad forehead and an expression of good humor about his mouth. He wears round spectacles. The brown hair clipped close to his round head has a look of youth. He talks slowly in an even, explanatory tone without betraying a trace of self-importance in his voice: "The privilege of opening the first trial in history for crimes against the peace of the world imposes a grave responsibility. . . ." Deceived perhaps by his mild unassuming manner, the prisoners at the bar listen at first quite cheerfully. Being able to hear their own voices in court when they plead has made them feel important again. Even Göring's broad countenance has lost the peevish spoiled-child look it took on when Justice Lawrence refused to allow him to make a statement. ". . . In the prisoners' dock sit 20-odd broken men. Reproached by the humiliation of those they have led almost as bitterly as by the desolation of those they have attacked, their personal capacity for evil is forever past. . . ."

As the day wears on and Jackson, reasonably, dispassionately, with magnificent clarity, unfolds the case against them, taking the evidence out of their own mouths, out of their own written orders, a change comes over the prisoners' box. They stir uneasily in their seats. They give strange starts and shudders when they hear their own words, their own secret diaries quoted against them. When the prosecutor reaches the crimes against the Jews they freeze into an agony of attention. The voice of the German translator follows the prosecutor's voice like a shrill echo of vengeance. Through the glass partition beside the prisoners' box you can see the taut face between gleaming earphones of the dark-haired woman who is making the translation. There is a look of horror on her face. Sometimes her throat seems to stiffen so that she can hardly speak the terrible words. They are cringing now. Frank's dark eyes seem bulging out of his head. Rosenberg draws the stiff fingers of one hand down his face. Schact's red face is drawn into deep creases of nightmare. Streicher's head leans far over on his shoulder as if it were about to fall off his body. Jackson's voice goes on, quietly and rationally describing in common-sense American phrases the actions of madmen. Sometimes there is a touch of puzzlement in his tone as if he could hardly believe the authentic documents from which he is reading. His voice is that of a reasonable man appalled by the crimes he has discovered, but echoing it is the choked, sterile German of the woman interpreter that hovers over the prisoners' box like a gadfly. The Nazi leaders stare with twisted mouths out into the white light of the courtroom. For the first time they have seen themselves as the world sees them.

"... You will say I have robbed you of your sleep. But these are things which have turned the stomach of the world. ..."

Jackson turns a page on his manuscript. The paper rustles in the silent courtroom. As the tension relaxes, people stir a little in their seats. Behind the glass windows you can see the intent, screwed-up faces of photographers. From somewhere comes the gentle whir of a moving-picture camera. A pale young GI with the harassed manner of the property boy in a high-school play is rolling up the white screen on the side wall to uncover a map that shows with colored bands the progressive stages of Nazi aggression. With the calm, explanatory voice of a man delivering a lecture in a history course, Jackson begins his exposition of the assault on Europe. Occasionally he points to the map.

The defendants are sitting up attentively, except for Hess, who sags with his thin blue jowl dropped on his chest, paying no attention to anything. They listen as if all this were news to them. They have managed to pull their faces together; their lips are tight. Ribbentrop has taken off his glasses and is stroking his heavy eyes with the tips of his fingers. The military men sit with squared shoulders. Göring goes out to the latrine between two guards. When he comes back, walking with the jaunty, self-important stride of a small boy who is

Top: Deputy Führer Rudolf Hess and Foreign Minister Joachim von Ribbentrop fidget in the dock *(Photo no. 238-NT–627 in the National Archives). Bottom:* Ernst Kaltenbrunner, the trusted lieutenant of Reichsführer Heinrich Himmler, in the witness stand testifying in his own behalf *(Photo no. 238-NT–680 in the National Archives).*

late to school, there's almost a smile on his great fatty countenance. He settles into his seat to listen in an attitude of genuine interest. Austria, Czechoslovakia, Poland, the history of the early years of the war unfolds. Gradually, as the afternoon slips by, we forget to look in the ranked faces of the prisoners.

His voice firmer and louder, Jackson has launched into the theory, which he is laying down in behalf of the U.S., that aggressive war is in itself a crime under the law of nations. "To apply the sanctions of the law to those whose conduct is found criminal by the standards I have outlined is the responsibility committed to this tribunal. It is the first court ever to undertake the difficult task of overcoming the confusion of many tongues and the conflicting concepts of just procedure among diverse systems of law so as to reach a common judgment. . . . The real complaining party at your bar is civilization. . . . It points to the weariness of flesh, the exhaustion of resources, and the destruction of what was beautiful or useful in so much of the world. . . . Civilization asks whether law is so laggard as to be utterly helpless to deal with crimes of this magnitude by criminals of this order of importance. . . ." Robert Jackson has finished speaking. The court rises. People move slowly and thoughfully from their seats. I doubt if there is a man or woman in the courtroom who does not feel that great and courageous words have been spoken. We Americans rise to our feet with a feeling of pride because it was a countryman of ours who spoke them.

Genet

LETTERS FROM NUREMBERG

Janet Flanner has been the Paris correspondent for the New Yorker *since the magazine was founded in 1925. Writing under the pseudonym "Genet," her "Letters" have revealed an intimate knowledge of the political, social, and cultural life of twentieth-century France. In 1945, the* New Yorker *sent*

her to cover the proceedings at Nuremberg; today her reports remain a de-
light at once to the student and the social historian.

December 17, 1945

There are two sights in Germany which seem equally to give dramatic
proof that the Allies won the war. One is the vast spectacle of any
ruined German city, open to the skies, and the other is the small
tableau of the Nazi-filled prisoners' box, beneath the floodlights, in
the war-crimes courtroom in Nuremberg. Almost everything else in
Germany—in the American zone, at least—seems to be some sort of
sign that we Allies are at a loss in the peace. But the mere sight of
Hermann Göring—for once sitting down, silent and almost slender, as
a civilian and a prisoner in the same town where, during the second
great *Parteitag,* ten years ago, he was baying *"Heil"* as he strutted the
swastika-hung streets, fat, decorated, in uniform, and loose on society—is a stimulating, satisfying proof that at least we Allies won
the war the Nazis started. When you look at the startling ruins of
Nuremberg, you are looking at a result of the war. When you look at
the prisoners on view in the courthouse, you are looking at twenty-
one of the causes. It is an astonishing view of humanity.

Ex-Reichsmarschall Göring's twenty colleagues seem dominated
by him in the prisoners' dock, just as they were when they were all free.
By his superior supply of theatrical energy, fancy clothes, and interest
in the proceedings, and by his air of participation, Göring maintains
his position of Prisoner No. 1, sitting in the dock's most prominent
and only comfortable seat—first row on the aisle. Behind him he has
one level of the dock balustrade to rest his back against, and at his
side a lower level to rest his right elbow and write upon. At this ad-
vantageous corner post, he scribbles like a busybody diarist with a
perfect view of the terrible goings on. Of all the Nazis' hierarchy
whose faces were already famous when they appeared at the big
Parteitag, his has since changed the least. Then it looked like the face
of an aging, fat tenor; now it looks like the face of a middle-aged,
fleshy contralto (but in either case a star). Hess seems the most
altered. Once the lower part of his dark countenance was heavy, not
only with confidence but with a disciple's swollen sentimentality.
Now his face is blanched, sharp, disillusioned, and irascible, and if he

finds himself being stared at by a foreigner, he stares back with humorous hostility.

Some of the journalists have equipped themselves with mother-of-pearl opera glasses or with black Army binoculars to squint at the prisoners, fifty feet away, in an attempt to discover enlarged signs of shame, alarm, or guilt on their features. Now, in the fourth week of the trial, the twenty-one Nazi faces show nothing—at any rate to the naked eye—but occasional reflexes of strained attentiveness, as when a Nazi soldier's private movie of highlights in a Warsaw pogrom were being shown to the courtroom. Maybe the prisoners are by now so accustomed to the faint lights which illuminate their faces when the room is darkened for a film that they have learned to hide their feelings. Or maybe they have recently seen and heard so many horrible proofs of what they and theirs did that their faces, like their memories, are used to it all.

To the rest of us, this pogrom picture seemed rather special. Part of the negative had been burned, perhaps in one of the ghetto fires which, as some Nazi snapshots showed, were getting out of hand. (The snapshots also showed Jews jumping from fourth-story windows. Smoking them out had been the fun and the goal of the day's job, according to the Nazi military report read aloud at the trial.) However, enough was left of the burned movie, which was shown twice in succession and at half speed, to give a clear view of naked Jews, male and female, moving with a floating, unearthly slowness and a nightmare-like dignity among the clubs and kicks of the laughing German soldiers. One nude Jew still had his hat, which he modestly held before him. One thin young Jewess, lying on a sidewalk was helped to her feet by an officer so that she could be knocked down again. The movies and snapshots were presented by the American prosecution as illustrations to texts read aloud from the diary of Nazi Governor General Frank of Poland. After seeing these pogrom pictures and hearing excerpts from Frank's Polish memoirs ("My attitude toward the Jews will therefore be based only on the expectation that they will disappear. They must be done away with. We must annihilate the Jews"), one might have thought that Christian prisoner Frank kept his eyes cast down because he was ashamed to look the court in the face. However, as it later turned out, his eyes were really cast down upon a note of protest he was hastily scribbling to his lawyer.

The one good result of the interruption by the lawyer when he got the note was that momentarily, anyway, it cut the reading aloud of documents by the American prosecution. Thrice in one sitting of the fourth week, Tribunal President Sir Geoffrey Lawrence was driven to protest that the trial would never end if our lawyers continued to read aloud documents they had already read aloud twice before. Even Hess showed that he was not mad when he offered to get his memory back if it would only speed up the trial. It would seem that we Americans, prosecuting the most nebulous possible charge—crimes against humanity—have, ever since our own Chief Prosecutor Jackson's precise, idealistic, impressive opening, weakened our case, already difficult because the charge lacks precedence, by our irrelevancies and redundancies. In three and a half days the British presented their case against the Nazis for waging a war of aggression on Poland, Norway, Denmark, Belgium, Holland, Greece, and Yugoslavia—a lot of ground. We Americans took five days merely for the case of Austria and Czechoslovakia, and broke up the resultant boredom in court only with the irrelevant diversion of horror movies of Belsen, Dachau, and Buchenwald, which are not in either country. On the whole, our lawyers have succeeded in making the world's most completely planned and horribly melodramatic war dull and incoherent. And, though it may be less important, several of our legal men have evidenced an ignorance of Europe, politically and historically, which might have seemed patriotic back home but seems something else at what has been earnestly described as the greatest trial in history. . . .

Whatever else the German population is thinking, it is not thinking much about the Nuremberg trial. The *Nürnberger Nachrichten,* which is the local newspaper licensed by our Military Government, had to be prodded by us to give the trial a bit more space and lately has been allotting it three-quarters of the second of its four pages. Its account lays typically Teutonic emphasis on the trial's occasional allusions to the Nazi war plans, such as the Barbarossa Plan, which was the full-fledged plan of attack on Russia, or the still-born Felix Plan, which was to have been the attack on Gibraltar. The same

German ex-professor says that the reasons the Germans are what he calls utterly uninterested in the trial are: First, everyone has too many private troubles, such as the loss of a husband or son, no coal, no window panes, or not enough good food, and no longer cares about political characters like Göring but wants news of where his son died or about his neighbors' disasters. Second, after twelve years of propaganda, the Germans do not believe anything they read, so they don't bother to read it, but look in their papers only to see what trains are running or to study, say, the American Military Government's order that in divorce proceedings and for the reading of wedding banns, both interested parties must be present. Third, the humbler classes, which, he says, lived on their emotions and did not care for ideas, are now too dazed to learn to put their minds on an editorial. Fourth, the educated classes refuse to listen to talk of the trials. They have heard too much of those twenty-one men and now do not wish to hear even about their guilt. In any case, they think the trial is an effort at propaganda rather than at justice, a myth they have forgotten about and so no longer believe in. Fifth, the Germans of all classes are now abnormal, like people who have come out of a boiler factory and cannot hear small noises any more. They are deaf. They are apathetic. No one, not even the upper classes, has any impulse toward responsibility now. All use our Military Government as an excuse for deciding nothing and consider Germans who work with our Military Government collaborators.

In summing up, the ex-professor says that the four elements in Hitler's ideology which most affected the German mind was militarism, anti-Semitism, nationalism (or pan-Germanism), and totalitarianism, of which ideas only the first has been weakened by defeat. As for democracy, the Bavarians, at least, think it might be wonderful if anybody seemed to know exactly what it was or is. Because we Americans have authorized six Bavarian political parties to function, the Germans deduce that this must be democracy. But since five of the parties have the same program, they say it is silly. Above all, the German people, amid their rubble and their muddy memory of an orderly and cruel belief in empire, are shocked at our laissez-faire, at our uncertainty and untidiness in the face of what are to them accumulating and anguishing complications. They have only ideas to divert them from their daily dilemma. Seven out of every ten Germans, according to the ex-professor, seem to believe that the next war will come within six months, that it will obviously be the Americans and British against the barbarous Russians, and that what is left of us Anglo-Saxons will one day declare that the German fear of having Russia in Europe was indeed justified. Not one German in ten, or in ten thousand, seems to have enough grasp of recent history to recall that it was Germany which pulled Russia into the center of Europe in the first place. . . .

February 27 (by Wireless)

The trial of the twenty-two criminal characters here has reached its midpoint. The Allied prosecution has rested its case. The defense of the Nazis has begun. There must be millions of people, especially the Europeans that suffered under them for years, who have wondered with bitter curiosity what in God's name the Germans could say for themselves on the reckoning day. Now they have started to say it. Since last November, when the trials began, the American, British, French, and Russian prosecutions' principal task has been to prove to the court that the Nazis did wrong. In the few hours the Germans have just taken to outline their defense, it has become clear that they are not going to try to disprove that they did wrong. They are actually and characteristically going to try to prove that they did right. Reichsmarschall Göring's defense lawyer has gone even further. One of the novelties he has offered is that it was really the Allies who had committed the original wrongs.

While the war was going on, the Allies had a threefold declared aim: to defeat the German Army, to bring the Nazi leaders to trial, and to re-educate the German mind. What the opening Nuremberg defense counsel have just offered is more than a mere display of Grade-B legal talent; it is an absolute first-rate demonstration of the still unreconstructed prewar German mind. The mental qualities the German defense has shown so far sound comical but are no laughing matter—egomania, mythomania, paranoia, superiority complex, and a general falling flat in those areas in which, in civilized men's minds, logic and morality have always been supreme.

It is significant that of the two German lawyers chosen to carry the principal presentation of the defense, one is old enough to have matured under the Kaiser, the other is young enough to have grown up under the Weimar Republic, and, in defending their Nazis, they see eye to eye. The one who opened the case was Göring's lawyer, Dr. Otto Stahmer, who is in his sixties, cropheaded, and truculent, and who has none of the long-white-haired elegance which several of the other senior German bar members at the trial affect. The second major figure is von Ribbentrop's representative, young Dr. Martin Horn, who had not previously appeared because, German rumor candidly said, he wanted as little contact as possible with a courtroom so full of Jews. Horn's hair is long but black. He is remarkable for his superior air, for his ignorance of English politics, and finally, when he gets into deep water, for repeatedly having to leave the lectern to beg some quick advice from Admiral Raeder's counsel, one of the picturesque, older, long-haired set. Another, though less important and less impressive, personage is Hess's lawyer, little Dr. Alfred Seidel, whose chin barely comes up to the pulpit and splendid Sir David Maxwell Fyfe, acting Allied chief prosecutor, cluster around their glasses of water, their fine legal points, and their microphone.

The first important point about the German lawyers' buildup for their clients was their inability to comprehend the difference between the relevant and the irrelevant. In their national lack of logic, anything was relevant to them if it suited their book. The oddest incident during their presentation of their fantastic list of Allied witnesses and writings whom and which they wanted to question and to cite was the long, patient, pedagogic effort, led by Court President Sir Geoffrey Lawrence (and in which the American, British, French, and Russian prosecutors all finally joined in), to din into the Göring, Ribbentrop, and Hess lawyers' heads what the word "relevant" has meant for centuries in law. As Sir Geoffrey dryly announced to the third of these, "I have amply explained it three times. I shall now make a fourth and final endeavor." The irrelevancy of some of the witnesses the Germans named was as obvious as the air of persecution with which German lawyers fought for their inclusion. Göring's lawyer asked to have called, as a character witness who could testify to Göring's having disapproved of terror bombing, a certain Luftwaffe doctor whose relevancy consisted of his having been Göring's physician but having nevertheless refused to take part in some grisly experiments at Dachau with five hundred living Poles' brains. To prove that Ribbentrop had not desired war with France, His ex-Excellency's lawyer

wanted as witnesses the French accused-collaborationist Count de
Castellane and the ditto Marquis and Marquise de Polignac; to prove
he had not wanted war with England, he wanted as witness a member
of the Bath Club whom Ribbentrop had asked in London, in 1936, to
introduce him to Premier Baldwin. The payoff was Ribbentrop's call
for an English party named Professor Cornwall Evans, whom Sir
David, whose job it was to check over the witness list, frankly declared he'd never heard of and who is not in *Who's Who*. . . .

It was odd to sit in the Nuremberg court and hear young Dr. Horn
. . . state that it might well have been the international London Naval
Conference of 1935 that drove Hitler's hypersensitive Third Reich
into rearmament, obviously making the war John Bull's and not
Adolf's fault. In the summer of 1936, in this then-picturesque and
intact city of Nuremberg, the Nazis were staging (in the great Zeppe-
lin Stadium, now used as a football bowl by Allied soldiers) their
grandiose fourth Party Day military displays. These consisted of an
eight-day parading of military strength and of equipment of a blitz-
krieg type then unknown in England or western Europe—the public
premiere of Panzer divisions, of a brand-new Luftwaffe roaring over-
head, of demonstrations by the ace Udet of dive-bombing, of flame-
throwers in rows, of motorcycle corps in formation, of solid city
blocks of whippet and giant tanks, of miles of marching, goose-step-
ping, uniformed men, and, above all, of hundreds of thousands of
civilian German faces lifted to bay to the blue Bavarian skies, "Today
Germany, tomorrow the world."

It was . . odd to hear Horn demand the anti-"Nahsi" Winston
Churchill as a witness, claiming that Churchill's sentiments had more
than anything else to do with Germany's preparing for war because
at that time he had been "somewhat of an official as the leader of
His Majesty's loyal Opposition." When Sir David politely explained
that the loyal opposer of that time had been Clement Attlee and that
Churchill had then been merely an uninfluential back-bencher, it was
the Allies' turn to smile in court. The Germans' turn had come shortly
before, when their side had demanded as a witness the Nazi military
attaché in Moscow at the time of the signing of the Russo-German
non-aggression pact. It was a tense moment in the courtroom, except
for the levity in the prisoners' box, whose occupants presumably had
been tipped off to what was coming and were leaning forward eagerly,

with wide smiles; Göring, who had been sitting with a G.I. blanket wrapped around him like a smart steamer rug, wriggled with delight. This inevitable, potentially troublesome, first allusion to the pact, which everyone on the Allied side had been waiting for, some with trepidation, others with blatant complacency, nevertheless left the British president and the Allied prosecution chief floundering, until Russian Prosecutor Rudenko strode the lectern and swiftly declared that it was not the signing of the pact but its violation by the Germans that came within the scope of those criminal charges which are the exclusive concern of the Nuremberg court. It was a brilliant recovery. It even dimmed Göring's smile, temporarily.

Last on the Allied alphabetical list, the Russians dominated the trials with their brief, dramatic peroration and with their special nationalistic vocabulary, no matter in which of the four courtroom languages it was heard. Theretofore the Germans had been referred to by the Allies simply as "the Germans" or "the Nazis," without adjectives. The Russians are more literary, elaborate, and inventive. In reporting on what the war meant to them back home, they referred with angry, often hyphenated flourishes to pogrom-maker Hitler, Fascist-German conspirators, Hitlerian hordes, Hitlerite pirates, Fascist barbarians, and German-Fascist intruders, the last being their favorite. The Russians have taken under their wing the Czechs, Yugoslavs, Latvians, Lithuanians, and Estonians, and when the Soviet's Assistant Prosecutor Raginsky cried, "Your Honor, the whole world knows about the Hitlerite misdeeds at Lidice!," he produced a thrilling effect, even in translation and through earphones.

Among the few Russian witnesses brought from the Soviet Republics was the curator of the Hermitage Museum, in Leningrad, notable not only for his vast, dignified gray beard, which is practically the size of a broom, but also for having produced the one burst of unchecked laughter in court the Bench has yet permitted. Under German cross-examination (after he had told how the Germans had willfully shelled his precious museum and after he had given citations from a ninety-page document on the German destruction of Russian art in general), a German counsel imprudently asked how he knew that the destruction of the Hermitage was intentional; was he, as well as an art expert, also an authority on artillery fire? The fine furious old man answered, with the greatest simplicity, that the Nazis had hit the neighboring bridge only once but had hit his beloved museum thirty times and that even he knew enough about artillery to figure out that the Germans weren't such bad shots as that.

Most of the Russian information was not funny, especially for the prisoners. As the other Allied prosecutors had done before them, the Russians pinned down each prisoner with copies of his own damning signed, personal, and often secret documents, since each prisoner, whatever his pompous, ministerial title, had, during and before the war, actually worked knowingly, busily, and competently at his terrible tasks of cruelty, torture, devastation, injustice, arrogance, and death. The Russians spiked Prisoner No. 7, Governor General of Poland Frank, with a quotation from what they quaintly described as his "calico-bound diary." In it he commented on his beloved Führer's new, especially important orders to him about "my task of pacifying Warsaw—that is, razing Warsaw to the ground." And then the Russians introduced his self-congratulatory telegram to Hitler, which began, "The city of Warsaw is wreathed in flames. The burning of the houses is the most reliable method of preventing the escape of the insurgents," meaning the citizenry. Prisoner No. 4, Keitel, Chief of the High Command was accused by the Russians of having complained, in writing, of the lack of ruthlessness toward the Russians. Even No. 14, Baldur von Schirach, though officially only the Leader of the Hitler Youth, was praised by Göring in a 1941 conference report to his Gauleiters for having had the brilliant idea of helping starve the Ukrainians by carting off their butter and eggs to a local German noodle factory for the benefit of the fat Volk of Berlin. Of unimportant Prisoner No. 15, Gauleiter Sauckel, Göring declared, in the same conference report, "I don't want to praise Sauckel. He doesn't need it. But what he achieved in obtaining workers from all over Europe and putting them into our industries is unique"—which it was. Of Sauckel's eight and a half million slave laborers, whom he himself wittily declared in writing "he had not removed for pleasure or for fun," at least a million died of overwork. . . .

March 15

Shortly before Göring himself stepped to the witness stand, he had been described by his sinister four-year-plan economic expert, a one-star S.S. general, as "the last great figure from the Renaissance."

When Göring stood up to take his oath, he undeniably looked the bravura personality in his vast, sagging, dove-colored jacket and his matching voluminous breeches, with his fine, high, maroon boots and his maroon neckerchief, and above it his hard, blue eyes and what is left of the familiar fleshiness of his mobile, theatrical face. Then, in an agreeable, reedy baritone voice that never halted but merely swerved to follow the movement of his memories, he began the story of his political life. "I was against the Republic," he said. "In November of the year 1922, on a Sunday in Munich, I attended a protest meeting. Toward the end, Adolf Hitler appeared. I had heard his name mentioned briefly and wanted to hear what he had to say. He refused to speak. But he spoke the next day on the Peace of Versailles. He said that until Germany was strong it was useless to protest. This was my thought in the depth of my soul. We spoke together of things dear to our hearts. I told him he could dispose of me and of my person as he saw fit. Later, I joined his Party." That was the way it all started.

During the next three days, as Göring narrated his and his Führer's extraordinary past together, building it up again from his powerful memory and with the agile intelligence that had aided in its construction in the first place, into the courtroom came the repeated muffled boom of dynamite clearing the wreckage of Nuremberg. Göring's recital was an astonishing performance. It was the greatest success story of a failure in modern times. A narrative delivered ad lib but with the vocabulary and coherence of a high-class serial, it developed into a dramatic study of two men's minds and their planned effect on the body of Europe. Göring's stream of words swept away all the Germans' legal efforts and false pleas to save him, and themselves, which had preceded him in court. What he offered his judges was no *mea culpa* but a dissertation on the technique of power. On the witness stand, he didn't wait to be asked questions by the Allied prosecution; he told them the German answers first. The Reichsmarschall made Machiavelli's Prince look like a dull apologist; Göring was decidedly more amoral, and funnier. The horrifying weakness in everything he said was that it took no account of the destruction it had caused in other men's or nations' lives. What he offered, essentially, was the Teutonic fallacy that the divine right of kings, which used to be limited to one individual, had been bestowed upon the German nation, which was therefore free to do anything to anybody.

Everybody in court had suffered, one way or another, from Göring's mind, but few had ever before sat and listened to it work. There was considerable surprise, though there should not have been, that behind his fancy tailoring, his fat, and his medals he had one of the best brains of a period in history when good brains were rare. On the stand, he was malicious and disturbing. He pointed out that only rich nations could afford the luxury of democracy, with its wasteful political squabbles and parliamentary inefficiencies, so he and his Führer, as he constantly called him, had aimed at the economy of single power for poor Germany. He said he probably didn't understand freedom, but he nevertheless had freed German workers from both the strikes and the lockouts that bother the democracies in their liberty. He cited the Communist Party and the Catholic Church as two flourishing institutions that operate on his theory of one-man, totalitarian power. He spoke candidly of having sent his young fliers in rotation to Franco's war so that they could try their wings in a sort of rehearsal. To pique the British, he said that the American Air Forces had assured the Allied victory, and to annoy America, he said he had hoped to develop a bomber strong enough to go to the States and back. He recounted that he had once apologized to the German Communist Ernst Thaelmann for his having been hit on the head by the Gestapo and had added that if the Communists and not the Nazis had won, he, Göring, wouldn't have been hit on the head but would have had it cut off by the G.P.U. To which the Communist "agreed in the friendliest fashion."

Then Göring began on the sellout of Europe, country by country. The Anschluss had been a walkover; earlier, France and England had been prepared to offer him a free hand in Austria if Germany had been willing to swap it for sanctions in Spain. Czechoslovakia was more dangerous; he had hobnobbed with some English at San Remo and afterward was able to tell the Führer that the British had swallowed the Anschluss but might be upset by Czechoslovakia, and that he didn't want to "have to bomb beautiful Prague," and that, anyway, those Britishers might toss out useful Chamberlain and bring in anti-Nazi Churchill. The night of the Anschluss, at a ball in Berlin, Göring had given his word of honor to the frightened Czech ambassador that Germany was only marching into Austria, not into Czechoslovakia. "But I did not give my word of honor that we *never* would march in,"

Göring said stiffly. Yes, the Nazis had subsidized Quisling. They knew that the Russians and British had been pouring bribes into Norway. Unfortunately, Göring left the bribing of Quisling to the Nazi foreign office and he frankly thought they had been niggardly. "I always remember the trouble we had in the first war," he reminisced genially, "because we didn't give Rumania enough." He was sorry about Poland; he had formerly had pleasant times there. He did not say if he was sorry about ruined Germany. Göring insisted throughout on taking his share of the responsibilities: the Anschluss and Munich were his doing; Danzig was the Führer's. Apparently, like partners in power, they divided the jobs up, as in any office. Göring had been furious about the march into Norway, but only because somebody forgot to tell him about it in advance. When asked by his counsel if the High Command had been consulted about starting the war, he said, "German generals are never asked to vote on war. One way to prevent war might be to ask the generals if they want to fight or go home." There was strained laughter in the court at this want-to-go-home jibe at the Americans.

Aside from its pungent flashes of humor, which were like footnotes, Göring's twenty-one hours on the witness stand amounted to an alarmingly serious lecture given by an active, if captive, historian on the most cynical military period in Europe's history. What his lecture featured was economic warfare, in the modern manner, which marks the difference between military murder in the nineteenth century and the twentieth. The court transcript of Göring's speech is a bibliographic item for future historians to collect. It was the complicated narrative of a brain without a conscience. Except for the constant reference to airplanes, it did indeed sound like something read from a family parchment in the Renaissance. Within its own framework, the story had veracity. None of the diplomatic observers in court thought he told any lies. They agreed that he had been, in fact, illuminating.

There were not more than a few hundred people in the courtroom. They had the awful privilege of listening to the personal recital of a man who helped tear apart millions of lives, as if with those large, white hands that gestured as he sat on the Nuremberg witness stand.

March 22 (by wireless)

On a recent visit to Nuremberg, a noted British lawyer optimisti-
cally wrote to a colleague, "I expect you feel, as I do, that the first
really great and dramatic moment of this trial will come when Göring
is cross-examined by the American prosecutor, Jackson. It will be a
duel to the death between the representative of all that is worth while
in civilization and the last important surviving protagonist of all that
was evil. In a sense, the whole result of the trial depends upon the
outcome of that duel, and whilst the world could see the importance
of the great and decisive battles fought out between the armed forces
arrayed against each other, I hope that they may see the immense
importance of the decisive battle of ideas to be fought out that day
in the courtroom. It will color this trial from now on and it may very
well color the thoughts of men for generations to come."

The future thoughts of democratic men will have to take their hue
from other, rosier episodes in the trial, for in that extremely important
Göring-Jackson duel it was, unhappily, Prosecutor Jackson who lost.
When the former Reichsmarschall strode from the witness stand to
the prisoners' box after his last session with Mr. Jackson, he was
congratulated and smiled upon by his fellow-Nazis there, like a
gladiator who has just won his fight. He had even won it noisily,
which added to the blaring, triumphal note. He had successfully
shouted at Prosecutor Jackson, who back home is a Justice of the
Supreme Court. There had been no "battle of ideas," because Jackson seemed not to be able to think of any. There had been nothing
more—and that much was bad enough—than an important struggle
between two opposing men's brains and personalities, and Göring
showed more of both. He displayed, besides, a phenomenal memory
and a remarkable gift for casuistic maneuver, and he was naturally
more knowledgeable about Nazi and other European history. Also, he
showed a diabolical skill in drawing on American and English history
for familiar paradoxes and damaging precedents. As a fantastic and
formidable personality, he temporarily produced an even greater confusion in the sensible legal minds at Nuremberg than Laval did in
Paris at the trial of Petain.

As the trial moved out of its preparatory period of massive, static
documentation and entered its period of skirmishing and battle in the
open, where the brains and personalities of the opponents were what

counted, Jackson began to show inadequacies as the leading Allied man. Up to then his main contribution to this very special legal scene had been the high humanitarianism which marked his fine opening address in November. Beneath that humanitarianism there lies his burning private conviction that the Nazi prisoners are mere common criminals. This, too, logically led to his treating them in a blustering policecourt manner, which was successful with the craven small fry but disastrous for him in cross-examining that uncommon criminal, Göring, himself accustomed to blustering in a grander way. Even physically, Jackson cut a poor figure. He unbuttoned his coat, whisked it back over his hips, and, with his hands in his back pockets, spraddled and teetered like a country lawyer. Not only did he seem to lack the background and wisdom of our Justice Holmes tradition, but his prepared European foreground was full of holes, which he fell into en route to setting traps for Göring.

In view of the fact that the Russian Chief Prosecutor, Roman Andreyevich Rudenko, and the British Chief Prosecutor, Sir David Maxwell Fyfe, had to be sent in as cross-examiners to master Göring and to obtain what amounted to the first confession from him, perhaps the American domination of the court will from now on decline. As the Court sees it, the Nuremberg trial is a Yalta Conference idea of President Roosevelt's, and though the Russians, British, and French gravely and fully have joined in, they have modestly regarded what goes on in the courthouse as mostly an American show. For this reason, the opening cross-examination of Göring was left, as a compliment, to what it was hoped would be typical Yankee shrewdness. The French know nothing of cross-examining, the Russians supposedly knew nothing, and the British know so much that, even belatedly, they were able to save the day. Of the four charges brought against the Nazis—conspiracy (which includes breaking treaties), crimes against peace, war crimes, and crimes against humanity—the British have concentrated on the charge of breaking treaties. And while the Russians and French addressed themselves to the charges of war of aggression (crimes against peace) and war crimes, the Americans took on the overall charge of crimes against humanity. We seem to have overlooked the importance of choosing men who could carry the heavy burden we volunteered for. For instance, among the early minor figures on the American legal team there was an unfor-

tunately memorable young captain who opened his court speech to
and about a troubled world with the peculiarly personal confidence
that if the microphone recorded any special disturbances, they would
be the quaking of his knees, shaking as they had not shaken since his
wedding day. Then Sidney S. Alderman, a member of the American
prosecuting staff, may be a noted expert on American railroads, but
he certainly was lost in Nuremberg among the terrible documents
whose relative values in the timetable of Europe's ruin he couldn't be
expected to make head or tail of. On the whole, the American team
has consisted of simple Davids sent in against the Nazi Goliaths on
faith rather than with equipment—Davids entitled, symbolically, to
their small stature because their cause was great. . . . In the end, it is
probably the British who will dominate this Allied gathering. . . . It
is not only the British worldiness and sense of history that give them
a special place in the trial; it is their legal prestige, exemplified in
the person of the Court President, Sir Geoffrey Lawrence. The mere
sight of his bald, wise, Dickensian head sets the tone of the bench.
His courtesy to the German lawyers has been cutting; a sample,
shown to Göring's Dr. Stahmer: "What you have just said seems to
me the acme of irrelevance." One of the sights outside the courthouse
is the glorious daily arrival of Sir Geoffrey in a magnificent black
limousine, glistening against the dusty ruin of the bombed walls. At-
tired in a long, blue broadcloth coat and a bowler, he passes through
the courthouse door while the Allied guards of the day—the Russians
with medals or the French with berets or the Tommies with battle
ribbons or the Americans in snow-white helmets—stiffly present
arms. In the courthouse itself, the same physical dignity and sartorial
elegance of Prosecutor Sir David Maxwell Fyfe, impeccable in his
Foreign Office attire, have unquestionably affected the Nazis, hypersensitive to formality and chic in the male.

As the cross-examiner who forced a weary Göring to admit that, by
deduction, at least, Hitler had been a murderer, Sir David was
polished, courteous, and artful. His strength lay in conducting the
cross-examination in a manner that clearly kept Göring guessing
about what was coming next, and each question made his line of
thought more baffling. During this vital cross-examination, Sir David's
professional affability disappeared. The pitying patience with which
he had politely referred to "our young friend," when von Ribbentrop's

Hermann Göring in a pensive mood during a court recess. *(Photo no. 238-NT–625 in the National Archives)*

youthful Dr. Horn made a bloomer, and his handsome way of referring to our Justice Biddle, on the bench, as "the learned American judge"—these easy verbal gestures were gone. With his excellent mind, his vast legal knowledge, and the added passion of a just inquisition, he stood behind his lectern and prosecuted the seated Göring into at least a partial state of destruction. He succeeded in doing what had not yet been done: he forced Göring to separate himself intellectually from the Nazi myth, he forced him to admit the difference between the glorified Nazi plan and the ghastly human results.

THE CROSS-EXAMINATION OF HERMANN GÖRING

Reichsmarschall Hermann Göring (1893–1946) was the leading figure in the dock at Nuremberg, a role he assumed with not a little sense of the dramatic moment. Unlike many of the accused who were remorseful and severely depressed, Göring's behavior and rhetoric were reminiscent of Caesar Borgia. Göring had been close to Hitler from the early days of the Nazi Party; the Führer named him to command functions in the Gestapo, the economy, and the Luftwaffe, and finally as his successor as well. The cross-examination of Göring was remarkable for the light it shed not only on the career of a leading figure in the Nazi hierarchy, but on the entire Fascist era.

Hermann Göring, defendant, appearing as a witness in his own behalf was cross-examined for the United States by Mr. Justice Jackson:

Q. You are perhaps aware that you are the only living man who can expound to us the true principles of the Nazi Party and the inner workings of its leadership?

A. I am perfectly clear on that subject.

Q. You, from the very beginning, together with those who were associated with you, intended to overthrow, and later did overthrow, the Weimar Republic?

A. That was my firm intention.

Q. And upon coming into power, you immediately abolished parliamentary government in Germany?

A. It was no longer necessary. . . .

Q. You established the leadership principle which you have described as a system under which authority exists only at the top and is passed downward and is imposed on the people below; is that correct?

A. In order to avoid any misunderstanding, I should like to explain it once more as I understand it. In previous German parliaments, the responsibility resided in the highest offices and it represented the anonymous power of the whole. In the Führer principle we arranged for the opposite of that, and the authority went from above to below and the permission was given from the lowest to the above.

From International Military Tribunal, *Trial of the Major War Criminals before the International Military Tribunal,* 42 vols. [Blue Series] (Nuremberg, 1949), 9:417–456, 499–571.

Q. In other words, you did not believe in and did not permit government as we do, in which the people, through their representatives, are the possessors of power and authority.

A. That is not entirely correct. We repeatedly called on the population from time to time to express their opinion of our system, only by a different way than was previously used, and in a different way than is used in other countries. We also were of the point of view that, of course, the Government could maintain itself through the Führer principle that had some sort of confidence in its population. If it no longer has such confidence, then it had to rule with bayonets, and the Führer was always of the opinion that that was impossible in the long run.

Q. You did not permit the election by the people of those who should act with authority, but they were designated from the top, were they not?

A. The conduct of the government was entirely up to the Führer. The individual representatives were not chosen by the people, but their leaders were. . . .

Q. The principles of the government which you set up required, as I understand you, that there should be no opposition by political parties which might oppose the policy of the Nazi Party?

A. Let us understand this correctly. We lived long enough through that period of opposition. It was now time not to have a party of opposition, but to build up.

Q. After you came to power, you believed it necessary in order to maintain power to suppress all opposition parties?

A. We found it necessary that we permit no opposition to us.

Q. And you also held the theory that you should suppress all individual opposition lest it should develop a party of opposition?

A. So far as opposition is concerned in any form, the opposition of each individual person was not tolerated unless it was a matter of unimportance.

Q. Now, in order to make sure that you suppressed the parties and individuals also, you found it necessary to have a secret political police to detect opposition?

A. I have already stated that I knew that to be necessary just as previously the political police existed. Only, we did this to a stronger and larger degree.

Q. And upon coming into power, you also considered it immediately necessary to establish concentration camps to take care of all incorrigible opponents?

A. I have already stated that the idea of the concentration camps did not arise in such a way. One might say that there were a number of people in opposition to us who should be taken into custody. The idea arose as an immediate measure against the Communists who were attacking us in thousands, and we could not accommodate them in prisons, so it was necessary to erect camps. . . .

Q. And protective custody meant you were taking people into custody who had not committed any crime but who you thought might possibly commit a crime?

A. Yes. People were arrested and taken into protective custody who had committed no crime, but of whom one could expect that if they remained in freedom they would do all sorts of things to damage the German state.

Q. Now, it is also a necessity in that kind of state that you have some kind of organization to carry propaganda down to the people and to get their reactions and inform the leadership of it, is it not?

A. Of course we carried on propaganda, and for that reason organized a propaganda department.

Q. You carried that on through the Leadership Corps of the Nazi Party?

A. The Leadership Corps was there to inform the people of the propaganda and our attitude.

Q. Through your system of Gauleiters and Kreisleiters, down to Blockleiters, commands and information went down from the higher authority, and information as to the people's reactions came back to the leadership, didn't it?

A. That is correct. The orders that were given for propaganda or other purposes were passed down the line as far as necessary. On the other hand, it was a matter of course that the reactions on the part of the people were again transmitted up through the various offices, in order to keep us informed of the mood of the people.

Q. And you also had to have certain organizations to carry out orders—executive organizations, organizations to fight for you, if necessary, did you not?

A. Administrative organizations were, of course, necessary. I don't understand exactly what organizations you mean. For what fights?

Q. Well, if you wanted certain people killed you have to have some organization that would kill them, didn't you? Röhm and the rest of them were not killed by Hitler's own hands nor by yours, were they?

A. Röhm—I explained that that was a matter of state necessity.

Q. But whether it was state necessity to kill somebody, you had to have somebody to do it, didn't you?

A. I also know other states where it is called secret service or something else. . . .

Q. At what time did the SS perform this function of acting as an executor of the Nazi policy?

A. After the seizure of power the police came to be more and more in the hands of Himmler, and it can no longer be understandable to somebody outside this picture where the SS was active and where the Gestapo was active. They worked very closely, hand in hand. It is known that the SS guarded concentration camps later.

Q. And carried out other functions in the camps?

A. What functions do you refer to?

Q. All of the functions of the camps, didn't they?

A. If an SS unit was guarding a camp and an SS leader was in charge of it, then it could only be that unit that carried out all the functions necessary in the camp. . . .

Q. Part of the effectiveness of a secret police and a part of the effectiveness of concentration camp penalties is that the people do know that there are such agencies, isn't it?

A. It is true that if everyone knows that if he acts against the state he will end up in a concentration camp or will be accused before a court of high treason—that is to our advantage. But the original reason why concentration camps were created was to handle enemies of the state. . . .

Q. You have related to us the manner in which you and others cooperated in concentrating all authority in the German state in the hands of the Führer, is that right?

A. I was speaking about myself and how far I was connected in this direction.

Q. Now, I want to call your attention to the fruits of this system. You, as I understand it, were informed in 1940 of an impending attack by the German Army on Soviet Russia?

A. I have already mentioned just how far I was informed of these matters.

Q. You believed the attack not only to be unnecessary but also to be unwise from the point of view of Germany itself?

A. At that time I was of the opinion that this attack should be postponed in order to take care of more important tasks.

Q. You didn't see any military necessity for an attack at that time even from the point of view of Germany?

A. I saw the effort of Russia in the direction of a mobilization, but hoped to put through measures which would be useful, and thought that time would prevent a danger toward Germany. Later on I was of the opinion that perhaps at any time this period of danger for Germany would arrive and might arrive at any later moment.

Q. I will repeat my question, which I think you have not answered: Did you at that time see any military necessity for an attack by Germany on Soviet Russia?

A. I personally believed that at that period of time, the danger had not reached its zenith; therefore, at that time, the attack might not be necessary, but I emphasize that that was my personal view.

Q. And you were the number two man at that time in all Germany?

A. It has nothing to do with my position of second importance. Two points of view were contradictory. The Führer saw one danger, and the Führer was the number one man, and if you wish to put it that way, had I wished to put another strategic measure through and if my plans had gone through, then I would have become the number one man, but since the number one man was of a different opinion and I was only the second man, his opinion naturally prevailed.

Q. I have understood from your testimony—and I think you can answer this yes or no, and I would greatly appreciate it if you would —I have understood from your testimony that you were opposed, and told the Führer that you were opposed, to an attack upon Russia at that time. Am I right or wrong?

A. That is correct.

Q. Now, you were opposed to it because you thought that it was a dangerous move for Germany to make; is that correct?

A. Yes, I was of the opinion that the moment—and I emphasize again that at that time the decisive moment—had not come and that more expedient measures should have been taken for Germany. . . .

Q. At what time did you know that the war, so far as achieving the objectives that you had in mind, was a lost war?

A. It is extraordinarily difficult to say that. According to my con-

viction, relatively late—and by that I mean at a late period of time—
the conviction grew within me that the war had been lost. Previous to
that time, I thought we would have a chance, and I was hoping for a
chance.

Q. Well, in November 1941 the offensive in Russia broke down,
did it not?

A. That is not right at all. We had reverses because of adverse
weather, and the aims that we had set out for were not won. The
push-through of 1943 proved that a military collapse is not even to be
thought of. Some corps which had advanced were thrown back, or
were taken back, and the frost that set in before we expected it was
the cause of all of this. . . . When the push-through of the Russian
offensive of January 12, 1945, advanced as far as the Oder, and
simultaneously the Ardennes offensive was not successful, at that
period of time I thought—and I could not think otherwise—that
slowly, in all possibility, a defeat would result. Before that period of
time, I had always hoped that perhaps either at Weichsel—the position would change toward the East or perhaps towards the West
Wall and could be held until new weapons would be put in production
and used in such strength so that the American air war could be
weakened.

Q. Now, will you fix that by date? You told us when it was by
events.

A. I just said January 1945—middle or end of January 1945. At
that point I saw no hope any longer. . . .

Q. By the time of January 1945 you also knew that you were unable to defend the German cities against the air attacks of the Allies,
did you not?

A. The defense of German cities against Allied bomb attacks—I
will try to give you a picture of the possibility.

Q. Can you not answer my question? Time may not mean quite
as much to you as it does to the rest of us. Can you not answer yes
or no? Did you then know, at the same time that you knew that the
war was lost, that the German cities could not successfully be defended against air attack by the enemy? Can you not tell us yes or
no?

A. I can say that I knew that at that period of time it was not possible.

Q. And after that time, the air attacks which were continued against England were well known to you that they could not turn the tide of war and were designed solely to effect a prolongation of what you then knew was a hopeless conflict?

A. I believe you are mistaken. After January there were no attacks, except perhaps a plane at a time, because at that time I needed all of my fighters for defense. If I had had any bombers and oil, then, of course, I would have used them up until the last minute to attack as reprisals for attacks which were being carried out on German cities. It would not have had anything to do with our chances.

Q. What about robot attacks? Were there any robot attacks after January 1945?

A. Thank heavens, we still had weapons—one weapon—that we could use. I have just set forth that as long as the fight was going on, we had to give return blows and as a soldier I can only regret that we did not have enough of these V-1's and V-2's, for this was the only means which perhaps would bring about an easing of the situation of the enemy attacks on our cities, if we were able to use reprisals against them.

Q. And there was no way to prevent the war going on as long as Hitler was the head of the German government, was there?

A. As long as Hitler was the Führer of the German people, he determined solely and alone the war leadership. As long as the enemy threatened us with the fact that he would accept only unconditional capitulation, I fought up until the last breath, for that was the only thing that was left to me to perhaps have a chance to turn fate, even though it looked hopeless.

Q. Well, the people of Germany who thought it was time for the slaughter to stop had no means to stop it except revolution or assassination of Hitler, did they?

A. A revolution changes a situation—that is, if the revolution is successful. The murder or assassination of Hitler at that period of time, say January 1945, would have brought about my succession. If the opponent had given me the same answer, an unconditional surrender, and those terrible conditions which had been handed out, I would have continued fighting under all circumstances.

Q. There was an attack on Hitler's life on July 20, 1944?

A. Unfortunately, yes.

Q. And there came a time in 1945 when Hitler made a will in Berlin whereby he turned over the presidency to your codefendant Admiral Dönitz. You know about that?

A. That is correct. I read of this testament here.

Q. And in so making his will and turning over the government of Germany to Admiral Dönitz, I call your attention to this statement:

> *Göring and Himmler, quite apart from their disloyalty to my person, have done immeasurable harm to the country and the whole nation by secret negotiations with the enemy which they conducted without my knowledge and against my wishes and by illegally attempting to seize power in the state for themselves.*

And by that will he expelled you and Himmler from the Party and from all offices of the state.

A. I can only reply for myself. What Himmler did I do not know. I neither betrayed the Führer nor did I at that period of time negotiate with even one foreign soldier. This will, or this document, of the Führer's rests on an unfortunate mistake and a mistake which grieves me: that the Führer could believe in his last hours that I would ever be disloyal to him. It all rests on a mistake of the transmission and perhaps on a wrong picture which Bormann gave to the Führer. I never thought for a minute to take over power illegally or to act against the Führer in any way.

Q. In any event you were arrested and expected to be shot?

A. That is correct. . . .

Q. When you met Hitler, as I understand your testimony, you found a man with a serious and definite aim, as you said, in that he was not content with the defeat of Germany in the previous war and was not content with the Versailles Treaty.

A. I believe you did not quite understand me correctly, for I did not say things in that order. I did set forth that I noted that Hitler had a definite view of the impotency of protest; and as a second point that he was of the opinion that Germany should be freed from the peace of Versailles. It was not only Adolf Hitler—every German, every patriotic German had the same feeling, and since I was a glowing patriot, as a glowing patriot I felt that the shame of Versailles was unbearable; and I identified myself with the man who thought the same as I, who saw the results which would come through Versailles, and that he perhaps would take the right way to set this Treaty of Versailles aside. But everything that was said in the Treaty of Versailles, if I may say so, was just empty chatter.

Q. So that if I understand you, from the very beginning, publicly and notoriously, it was the position of the Nazi Party that the Versailles Treaty must be set aside and that protest was impotent for that purpose?

A. From the beginning, it was the aim of Adolf Hitler, and for those of us in his movement, to free Germany of the shock of Versailles; by that we meant, not from the total Treaty but from those terms which were strangling Germany and which were to strangle Germany in the future.

Q. And to do it by war, if necessary?

A. We did not even debate about those things at that time. We debated only about the first condition; whether everyone else talked about the peace of Versailles, but we Germans always speak about the Dictate of Versailles. The first question was to achieve and establish a different political structure for Germany which would enable Germany to object against the Dictate, and not only a protest—an objection—but objection of such a nature that it would actually be considered.

Q. That is, the means was the reorganization of the German state, but your aim was to get rid of what you call the Dictate of Versailles?

A. The freeing from those terms of the Dictate of Versailles which for a continued period of time would make German life impossible and that was the aim; and in that connection, we did not say we shall have to have a war and defeat our enemies; this was the aim, and the methods had to be adapted to the political situation. . . .

III THE CASE FOR THE DEFENSE

MOTION ADOPTED BY ALL DEFENSE COUNSEL, NOVEMBER 19, 1945

This motion, which was submitted by Dr. Stahmer as a collective statement for the Nazis, outlined the basis of the defense's position throughout the trial—that the prosecution stood in violation of international law by holding the Germans guilty for crimes not on the books at the time they were committed. The defense argued that at no time in history had the waging of aggressive war been a recognized violation of international law. Within two days the Tribunal had rejected the Germans' motion, citing Article 3 of the Charter.

Two frightful world wars and the violent collisions by which peace among the states was violated during the period between these enormous and world embracing conflicts caused the tortured peoples to realize that a true order among the states is not possible as long as such state, by virtue of its sovereignty, has the right to wage war at any time and for any purpose. During the last decades public opinion in the world challenged with ever-increasing emphasis the thesis that the decision of waging war is beyond good and evil. A distinction is being made between just and unjust wars and it is asked that the community of states call to account the state which wages an unjust war and deny it, should it be victorious, the fruits of its outrage. More than that, it is demanded that not only should the guilty state be condemned and its liability be established, but that furthermore those men who are responsible for unleashing the unjust war be tried and sentenced by an International Tribunal. In that respect one goes nowadays further than even the strictest jurists since the early Middle Ages. This thought is at the basis of the first three counts of the Indictment which have been put forward in this Trial, to wit, the Indictment for Crimes against Peace. Humanity insists that this idea should in the future be more than a demand, that it should be valid international law.

However, today it is not as yet valid international law. Neither in the statute of the League of Nations, world organization against war, nor in the Kellogg-Briand Pact, nor in any other of the treaties which were concluded after 1918 in that first upsurge of attempts to ban

From International Military Tribunal, *Trial of the Major War Criminals before the International Military Tribunal,* 42 vols. [Blue Series] (Nuremberg, 1949), 1:168–170.

aggressive warfare, has this idea been realized. But above all the practice of the League of Nations has, up to the very recent past, been quite unambiguous in that regard. On several occasions the League had to decide upon the lawfulness or unlawfulness of action by force of one member against another member, but it always condemned such action by force merely as a violation of international law by the state, and never thought of bringing up for trial the statesmen, generals, and industrialists of the state which recurred to force. And when the new organization for world peace was set up last summer in San Francisco, no new legal maxim was created under which an international tribunal would inflict punishment upon those who unleashed an unjust war. The present Trial can, therefore, as far as Crimes against Peace shall be avenged, not invoke existing international law, it is rather a proceeding pursuant to a new penal law, a penal law enacted only after the crime. This is repugnant to a principle of jurisprudence sacred to the civilized world, the partial violation of which by Hitler's Germany has been vehemently discountenanced outside and inside the Reich. This principle is to the effect that only he can be punished who offended against a law in existence at the time of the commission of the act and imposing a penalty. This maxim is one of the great fundamental principles of the political systems of the Signatories of the Charter of this Tribunal themselves, to wit, of England since the Middle Ages, of the United States since their creation, of France since its great revolution, and the Soviet Union. And recently when the Control Council for Germany enacted a law to assure the return to a just administration of penal law in Germany, it decreed in the first place the restoration of the maxim, "No punishment without a penal law in force at the time of the commission of the act." This maxim is precisely not a rule of expedience but it derives from the recognition of the fact that any defendant must needs consider himself unjustly treated if he is punished under an ex post facto law.

The Defense of all defendants would be neglectful of their duty if they acquiesced silently in a deviation from existing international law and in disregard of a commonly recognized principle of modern penal jurisprudence and if they suppressed doubts which are openly expressed today outside Germany, all the more so as it is the unanimous conviction of the Defense that this Trial could serve in a high degree the progress of world order even if, nay in the very instance where it did not depart from existing international law. Wherever the Indictment charges acts which were not punishable at the time, the Tribunal would have to confine itself to a thorough examination and findings as to what acts were committed, for which purposes the Defense would cooperate to the best of their ability as true assistants of the Court. Under the impact of these findings of the Tribunal the states of the international legal community would then create a new law under which those who in the future would be guilty of starting an unjust war would be threatened with punishment by an International Tribunal.

The Defense are also of the opinion that other principles of a penal character contained in the Charter are in contradiction with the maxim, *"nulla poena sine lege."*

Finally, the Defense consider it their duty to point out at this juncture another peculiarity of this Trial which departs from the commonly recognized principles of modern jurisprudence. The Judges have been appointed exclusively by states which were the one party in this war. This one party to the proceeding is all in one: creator of the statute of the Tribunal and of the rules of law, prosecutor and judge. It used to be until now the common legal conception that this should not be so; just as the United States of America, as the champion for the institution of international arbitration and jurisdiction, always demanded that neutrals, or neutrals and representatives of all parties, should be called to the Bench. This principle has been realized in an exemplary manner in the case of the Permanent Court of International Justice at The Hague.

In view of the variety and difficulty of these questions of law the Defense hereby pray:

That the Tribunal direct that an opinion be submitted by internationally recognized authorities on international law on the legal elements of this Trial under the Charter of the Tribunal.

On behalf of the attorneys for all defendants who are present.

Dr. Stahmer

Dr. Hermann Jahrreiss

STATEMENT BEFORE THE NUREMBERG TRIBUNAL

Professor Jahrreiss is one of the leading figures in international law on the Continent. A prolific writer, he has taught at Leipzig, Greifswald, and Cologne, and holds both the French Legion of Honor and the Bundesverdienstkreuz as well as several honorary doctorates. At Nuremberg he was assigned to the defense of General Jodl. In the following selection from the court transcript, Jahrreiss took the prosecution to task on the criminality of aggression charge and buttressed his case with an analysis of the fluid international scene of the 1930s. He further attacked the principle of holding individuals guilty for acts of state which, he argued, denies a nation its basic right of sovereignty.

. . . If I understood the British chief prosecutor correctly, he is asserting that since the conclusion of the Pact of Paris there exists a clear legal order based on the entire world's uniform conviction as to what is right. Since 1927 the United States have negotiated first with France, then with the remaining Great Powers, with the exception of the Soviet Union, and also with some of the smaller powers concerning the conclusion of a treaty intended to abolish war. Secretary of State Kellogg stated (in a note to the French Ambassador, 27 February 1928) with memorable impressiveness what the Government in Washington were striving for, namely:

The powers should renounce war as an instrument of national policy, waiving all legal definitions and acting from a practical point of view, plainly, simply, and unambiguously, without qualifications or reservations. Otherwise the object desired would not be attained: to abolish war as an institution, that is, as an institution of international law.

After the negotiations had been concluded, Aristide Briand, the other of the two statesmen from whose initiative springs that pact which in Germany is often called the "Pact to Outlaw War," declared, when it was signed in Paris:

From the statement by counsel for the defendant Jodl, reprinted from *Trial of the Major War Criminals before the International Military Tribunal,* 42 vols. [Blue Series] (Nuremberg, 1949), 17:458–494.

Formerly deemed a divine right and remaining in international law as a prerogative of sovereignty, such a war has now at last been legally stripped of that which constituted its greatest danger: its legitimacy. Branded henceforth as illegal, it is truly outlawed by agreement. . . .

According to the conception of both leading statesmen, the Paris Pact amounted to a change of the world order at its very roots, if only all, or almost all, nations of the world—and particularly all the great powers—signed the pact or adhered to it later on, which did actually happen.

The change was to be based on the following conception: Up to the time of the Kellogg-Briand Pact, war had been an institution of international law. After the Kellogg-Briand Pact, war was high treason against the order created by international law.

Many politicians and scholars all over the world shared this conception. . . . It is also the basic conception of the Indictment at Nuremberg. . . .

Even for the members of the League of Nations war remained a means for settling disputes, prohibited in individual cases, but normal on the whole. Jean Ray, as late as 1930, said:

The League of Nations did not prove to be a guide to the true order of peace, indeed it did not even prove to be a sufficient brake to prevent a complete backward movement into the former state. For the world did in fact slide back entirely. . . .

Before the commencement of the Second World War the whole system of collective security, even in such scanty beginnings as it had made, had collapsed; and this collapse was acknowledged and declared expressly, or by equivalent action, by three world powers—and, in fact, declared with full justification. Great Britain clearly stated this at the beginning of the war to the League of Nations. . . .

The Soviet Union treated the German-Polish conflict simply according to the rules of classical international law concerning *debellatio*. . . .

The United States declared their strict neutrality. I shall also explain the import of this declaration.

The system of collective security has been the subject of much dispute. In this matter involving the world's conscience, which is of fundamental importance in this very Trial, it cannot be a matter of indifference that the system, rightly or wrongly, appeared in 1938 to such a prominent specialist on international law as the American, Edwin Borchard, to be absolutely inimical to peace and the offspring of the hysteria of our age. The collapse may have had various causes; it is certain that the above-mentioned three world powers testified at the beginning of September 1939 to the collapse—the complete collapse—and that they did not, in fact, do so as a consequence of the German-Polish war.

To begin with, on 7 September 1939, the British Foreign Office told the Secretary General of the League of Nations that the British Government had assumed the obligation, on 5 February 1930, to answer before the Permanent International Court of Justice at The Hague whenever a complaint was filed against Great Britain, which would include all cases of complaints which other states might lodge on account of conduct whereby Great Britain in a war had, in the opinion of the plaintiff, violated international law. The British Government had accepted this regulation because they had relied on the functioning of the machinery of collective security created by the League of Nations Covenant and the Pact of Paris—because, if it did function properly, and since Britain would certainly not conduct any forbidden wars, her opponent on the contrary being the aggressor, no collision between Britain and those states that were faithful to the security machinery could possibly be caused by any action of Britain as a seapower. However, the British Government had been disappointed in this confidence: ever since the League Assembly of 1938 it had no longer been possible to doubt that the security machinery would not function; on the contrary it had, in fact, collapsed completely. A number of members of the League had already declared their strict neutrality before the outbreak of war: "The entire machinery intended to maintain peace has broken down."

I will proceed to show how right the British Government were in the conclusions they drew. It should not be forgotten that the British Premier, Mr. Neville Chamberlain, had already proclaimed, on 22 February 1938 in the House of Commons, that is, before the so-called Austrian Anschluss, the complete inefficiency of the system of collective security. He said:

> *At the last election it was still possible to hope that the League might afford collective security. I believed it myself. I do not believe it now. I would say more: If I am right, as I am confident I am, in saying that the League as constituted today is unable to provide collective security for anybody, then I say we must not delude ourselves, and, still more, we must not try to delude small weak nations into thinking that they will be protected by the League against aggression and acting accordingly, when we know that nothing of the kind can be expected.*

The Geneva League of Nations was "neutralized," as Noel Baker politely expressed it later in the House of Commons.

Secondly, in view of the correct conclusions drawn by the British Government and expressed in their note of 7 September 1939 to the League of Nations, it is no wonder that the Soviet Union treated the German-Polish conflict in accordance with the old rules of power politics. In the German-Russian Frontier and Friendship Pact of 28 September 1939 and in the declaration made on the same day in common with the Reich Government, the Moscow Government bases its stand on the conception of the *debellatio* of Poland, that is, the liquidation of Poland's government and armed forces; no mention is made of the Pact of Paris or the League of Nations Covenant. The Soviet Union takes note of the liquidation of the Polish state machinery by means of war, and from this fact draws the conclusions which it deems right, agreeing with the Reich Government that the new order of things is exclusively a matter for the two powers.

It was therefore only logical that in the Finnish conflict, during the winter of 1939–1940, the Soviet Union should have taken its stand on classical international law. It disregarded the reactions of the League of Nations when, without even considering the application of the machinery of sanctions and merely pretending to apply an article of the Covenant referring to quite different matters, that body resolved that the Soviet Union had as an aggressor, placed itself outside the League. The report of the Swiss Federal Council of 30 January 1940 to the Federal Assembly endeavored to save the face of the League which was excluded from all political realities.

Thirdly, the President of the United States stated on 5 September 1939 that there existed a state of war between several states with whom the United States lived in peace and friendship, namely, Germany on the one hand, and Great Britain, France, Poland, India, and two of the British dominions on the other. Everyone in the United States was required to conform with neutrality regulations in the strictest manner.

Since the time of the preliminary negotiations, it was a well-known fact in the United States that Europe, and particularly Great Britain and France, saw the main value of the Pact to Outlaw War in the fact that the United States would take action in case of a breach of the pact. The British Foreign Secretary stated this on 30 July 1928, that is, four weeks previous to the signing of the pact. During the deliberations of the American Senate on the ratification of the pact, Senator Moses drew particular attention to this. Senator Borah affirmed at the time that it was utterly impossible to imagine that the United States would calmly stand by. After the discredit resulting from the failure of the policy of collective security in the case of Manchuria and Abyssinia the world had come to understand the now famous "quarantine" speech of President Franklin D. Roosevelt on 5 October 1937 and his "Stop Hitler!" warnings before and after Munich to mean that the United States would act on the next occasion. The declaration of neutrality of 5 September 1939 could therefore only mean: like Great Britain and the Soviet Union, the United States accepts as a fact the collapse of the system of collective security.

This declaration of neutrality has often been looked upon as the death blow to the system. The Washington government would be entitled to reject such a reproach as unjustified. For the system had already been dead for years, provided one is prepared to believe that it was ever actually alive. But many did not realize the fact that it was no longer alive until it was brought into relief by the American declaration of neutrality.

By 1 September 1939 the various experiments, which had been tried since the First World War with a view to replace the "anarchic world order" of classical international law by a better, a genuine, order of peace, were over, that is, to create in the community of states a general statute according to which there would be wars which are forbidden by law and others which are countenanced. These experiments, in the opinion of the major powers of the time, had failed. The greatest military powers of the earth clashed in a struggle in which they pitted their full strength against one another. For the proponents of a materialistic conception of history this meant the second phase in a process developing according to inexorable laws, whereby history swept away all diplomatic and judicial artifices with supreme indifference.

The majority of international lawyers throughout the world maintained that in universal international law as at present applied, there exists no distinction as to forbidden and nonforbidden wars. . . .

If the Reich did attack, in some specific case, in breach of a nonaggression pact which was still valid, it committed an offense in international law and is responsible therefore according to the rules of international law regarding such offenses.

But only the Reich—not the individual, even if he were the head of the state. This is beyond all doubt, according to existing international law. It is unnecessary even to speak about this. . . .

Of course, acts of state are acts of men. Yet they are in fact acts of state, that is, acts of the state carried out by its organs and not the private acts of Mr. Smith or Mr. Muller.

What the prosecution is doing when, in the name of the world community as a legal entity, it desires to have individuals legally sentenced for their decisions regarding war and peace, is, when facing the issue from the angle of European history, to look upon the state as one would look upon a private individual; indeed, more than that: what it is doing is destroying the spirit of the state. Such an indictment, the moral justification of which is not my concern— such an indictment is, as we have already shown, incompatible with the very nature of sovereignty. . . .

The Prosecution breaks up in its own mind the German state at a time when it stood upright in its full strength and acted through its organs. It must do so if it desires to prosecute individual persons for a breach of the peace between states. It must turn the defendants into private individuals. Then again the defendants—as it were, on the private level—are strung together into a conspiracy by legal concepts rooted in Anglo-Saxon law and alien to us. They are placed on a pedestal provided by the many millions of members of organizations and groups which are designated as criminal, thereby once more allowing them to appear as an "ultra-individual" value.

Insofar as the Charter supports all this by its regulations, it is laying down fundamentally new law, if—concurring with the British chief prosecutor—one measures against existing international law. That which, originating in Europe, has finally spread to the whole world and is called international law is, in essence, a law of the coordination of sovereign states. Measuring the regulations of the Charter against this law, we shall have to say: the regulations of the Charter deny the basis of this law; they anticipate the law of a world state. . . .

A lawyer . . . will merely have to establish that they are new— revolutionarily new. The laws regarding war and peace between states provided no room for them and could not do so. Thus they are criminal laws with retroactive force. . . .

We must now measure the regulations of the Charter not only against the international law which was valid for Germany and was recast into national law, as we say, but also against that national criminal law which was binding on the defendants at the time of the deed. . . .

Here we have the fundamental question in this Trial: What position did Hitler's orders occupy in the general order of Germany? Did they belong to the type of orders which were disallowed by the Charter of this Court as grounds for the exclusion of punishment? . . .

In a state in which the entire power to make final decisions is concentrated in the hands of a single individual, the orders of this one man are absolutely binding on the members of the hierarchy. This individual is their sovereign. . . . From the time when Hitler became head of the state, practice quickly resulted in Hitler heading both the hierarchy and the whole people as the undisputed and indisputable possessor of all competency. The result of the development was, at any rate, that Hitler became the supreme legislator as well as the supreme author of individual orders. . . .

The functionaries had neither the right nor the duty to examine the orders of the monocrat to determine their legality. For them these orders could never be illegal at all. . . .

Hitler's will was the final authority for their considerations on what to do and what not to do. The Führer's order cut off every discussion. Thus a person who as a functionary of the hierarchy invokes an order by the Führer is not trying to claim exemption from punishment for an illegal action but opposes the assertion that his conduct was illegal; for it is his contention that the order with which he complied was legally unassailable.

Only a person with full comprehension of this can have a conception of the hard inner struggles which so many German officials had to fight out in these years in the face of many a decree or resolution of Hitler's. For them such cases were not a question or a conflict between right and wrong; disputes about legality sank into insignificance. For them the problem was one of legitimacy; as time went on, human and divine law opposed each other ever more strongly and frequently. . . .

Hitler himself, at any rate, did not recognize this boundary line of inhumanity, of nonhumanity, as a limit to obedience in his relations with his subordinates; and here again opposition would have been considered a crime worthy of death in the eyes and judgment of this man, invested as he was with limitless power and controlling an irresistible machine. What should a man who received an order exceeding the line have done? What a terrible situation! The reply given in Greek tragedy, the reply by Antigone, in such a conflict cannot be imposed. It would show scant knowledge of the world to expect it, let alone demand it, as a mass phenomenon. . . .

Sheldon Glueck

THE NUREMBERG TRIAL AND AGGRESSIVE WAR

Sheldon Glueck, one of the nation's leading criminologists, taught at the Harvard Law School from 1929 to 1963, where he was the Roscoe Pound

Reprinted by permission of the author and publisher from the *Harvard Law Review* 59 (February 1946): 396–456. Copyright 1946 by The Harvard Law Review Association. (Footnotes omitted.)

Professor of Criminal Law. He had a profound influence on the formulation of the prosecution's case at Nuremberg. In the first instance, it was his pioneering work War Criminals: Their Prosecution and Punishment *which laid the theoretical foundation for declaring aggressive war illegal. Secondly, Professor Glueck was instrumental in determining the content of Nuremberg law as an advisor to Justice Jackson in 1945 and 1946. The following article summarizing the prosecution's case contends that aggressive war was implicitly recognized in international law before it was codified in the London Agreement. Further, it is the most comprehensive refutation available of the position argued by the defense that Germany was not guilty of aggression.*

Is there a rational and just basis for regarding a war of aggression (i.e., one not clearly justifiable on the grounds of self-defense or as an executive act of punishment by the community of law-abiding states against a law-violating member) as an international crime? And if the launching of an aggressive war is to be deemed a criminal offense, who is the criminal? The aggressive state? Its responsible (i.e., policy-making) statesmen? Its responsible military leaders, such as members of its General Staff?

Judging from available published data, this idea of including the launching of an aggressive war—a "crime against peace"—among the offenses for which the Axis Powers were to be held liable had its origin, so far as American policy is concerned, in a report to the President made on June 7, 1945 by the American Chief of Counsel for the prosecution of major war criminals. Justice Robert H. Jackson there said:

> *It is high time that we act on the juridical principle that aggressive war-making is illegal and criminal.*

Speaking of the alleged "retroactive" nature of a trial and punishment for the launching of legally prohibited (i.e., aggressive) warfare, Justice Jackson argued:

> *International Law is more than a scholarly collection of abstract and immutable principles. It is an outgrowth of treaties or agreements between nations and of accepted customs. But every custom has its origin in some single act, and every agreement has to be initiated by the action of some state. Unless we are prepared to abandon every principle of growth for International Law, we cannot deny that our own day has its right to institute customs and to conclude agreements that will themselves be-*

*come sources of a newer and strengthened International Law. . . . Hence
I am not disturbed by the lack of precedent for the inquiry we propose to
conduct.*

Nevertheless, the case for prosecuting individuals and states for
the "crime" of launching an aggressive war is not as strong as the
case for holding them responsible for violations of the recognized
laws and customs of legitimate warfare.

Is it strong enough to support the relevant count in the Nuremberg indictment? . . .

The Commission of Fifteen appointed by the Preliminary Peace
Conference at the end of World War I to examine the responsibility
for starting that war and for atrocities committed during its conduct
went into the question whether "acts which provoked the World War
and accompanied its inception," such as the invasion of Luxemburg
by the Germans in violation of the Treaty of London of 1867 and
their invasion of Belgium in violation of the Treaties of 1839, were
criminal. . . .

But while recoiling from the charge of *crime* and from trial before a court, the Commission nevertheless recommended that "it
would be right for the Peace Conference, in a matter so unprecedented, to adopt special measures, and even to create a special
organ in order to deal as they deserve with the authors of such
acts," and declared it to be "desirable that, *for the future, penal
sanctions* should be provided for such grave outrages against the
elementary principles of international law."

However, throughout the quarter-century between the two world
wars nothing so specific was done by the nations of the world to
implement the Commission's recommendation. The treaty for the
Renunciation of War (Briand-Kellogg Pact or "Pact of Paris"),
signed in Paris on August 27, 1928, to which Germany was a party
(and, ironically, the first signatory), condemned recourse to war for
the solution of international controversies, renounced it as an instrument of national policy, and bound the signatories to seek the settlement of all disputes by pacific means only. But that historic pact,
too, failed to make violation of its terms an international crime
punishable either by an international tribunal or by national courts.
Therefore, the technical legal basis for prosecution for violations

of the Pact of Paris as international crimes may be said to be still open to some question, though the moral grounds are crystal clear.
. . .

Thus we are back to the major question—whether aggressive war can be denominated an international crime—with the additional question, whether individuals comprising the Government and General Staff of an aggressor state may be prosecuted as liable for such crime. . . . It is . . . valuable to examine the issues involved, for the sake of those lawyers who insist that it is "illegal" and "ex post facto" to regard aggressive war as a crime and to hold individual members of a government responsible for such a crime. . . .

As to the first question, when one passes in review the numerous expressions of multinational agreement and opinion—to many of which Germany herself was a party—solemnly promising nonaggression toward neighboring states, condemning aggressive war as an instrument of national policy, and, in several instances, specifically declaring it to be an international crime, one may reasonably conclude that the time has arrived in the life of civilized nations when an international custom has developed to hold aggressive war to be an international crime.

It is familiar law in the international field that custom may, in the words of Article 38 of the Statute of the Permanent Court of International Justice, be considered "as evidence of a general practice accepted as law." . . .

All the solemn expressions of the conviction of civilized states regarding the need for conciliation, for the settlement of international disputes by pacific means only, for the renunciation of war as an instrument of national policy, and, logically for the recognition that aggressive war is an international crime, greatly re-enforce whatever inference to that effect is derivable from the Briand-Kellogg Pact itself. They may be regarded as powerful evidence of the existence of a widely prevalent juristic climate which has energized a spreading *custom* among civilized peoples to regard a war of aggression as not simply "unjust" or "illegal" but downright criminal.
. . .

The prosecution at Nuremberg under Count Two of the historic indictment, "Crimes Against Peace," for the crimes of "planning, preparation, initiation and waging wars of aggression, which were also in violation of international treaties, agreements and assurances," is, then, strictly speaking, not based upon proof of the breach of any specific provision of any particular one or more of the above-mentioned international treaties or conventions. It is rather based upon violation of customary international law—a system of law that is as obviously subject to growth as has been the law of any other developing legal order, by the crystallization of generally prevailing opinion and practice into law under the impact of common consent and the demands of general world security. Acquiescence of all members of the Family of Nations is not necessary for this purpose. All that is needed is reasonable proof of the existence of a widespread custom; and the numerous multilateral antiwar treaties, agreements and resolutions, as well as the statements and writings of experts in connection with such international pronouncements, comprise such proof.

The claim that in the absence of a specific, detailed, pre-existing *code* of international penal law to which all states have previously subscribed, prosecution for the international crime of aggressive war is necessarily ex post facto because no world legislature has previously spoken is specious. . . .

In the international field, then, as in the domestic, part of the system of prohibitions implemented by penal sanctions consists of customary or common law. In assuming that an act of aggressive war is not merely lawless but also criminal, the Nuremberg court would merely be following the age-old precedent of courts which enforce not only the specific published provisions of a systematic code enacted by a legislature, but also "unwritten" law. During the early stage (or a particularly disturbed stage) of any system of law —and international law is still in a relatively undeveloped state— the courts must rely a great deal upon nonlegislative law, and thereby run the risk of an accusation that they are indulging in legislation under the guise of decision, and are doing so ex post facto.

So is it with modern international common law, in prohibiting aggressive war on pain of punishment. . . .

Assuming modern aggressive war to be a crime, i.e., an offense against the Family of Nations and its international law, then the defendant must normally be the implicated state. A familiar analogy is the prosecution of a business corporation. In both cases, of course, the punishment upon conviction can only be in terms of a fine or deprivation of certain rights or privileges. But, as experience has shown, action against a state must necessarily be ineffective in reducing international criminalism, compared to the imposition of penal sanctions upon members of a cabinet, heads of a general staff, or other persons in authority in a government who have led a state into aggressive war and the breach of basic treaties designed for the security of all states.

As indicated, Article 6 of the Charter of the International Military Tribunal recognizes this fact. By implication, also, Article 1 of the Agreement for the Establishment of an International Military Tribunal, of which the Charter is an integral part, provides for personal rather than state liability:

> *There shall be established after consultation with the Control Council for Germany an International Military Tribunal for the trial of war criminals whose offenses have no particular geographical location whether they be accused individually or in their capacity as members of organizations or groups or in both capacities.*

So also the numerous solemn warnings to the Axis leaders by statesmen of the chief Member-States of the United Nations during the conduct of the war implied a plan to hold them personally responsible for their crimes.

These were all manifestations of the power of the victor, which could be the sole "law" to govern the treatment of the Nazi ringleaders. But assuming the application of normal legal principles, conservative international lawyers and publicists have pointed to two fundamental obstacles to the prosecution and punishment of the Nazi leaders for the crime of waging a war of aggression; namely, the doctrine of "acts of state," and the related principle that international law obligates and binds only states, not individual human beings.

Taking up the first objection, it is argued that international law forbids a state to make a subject of another state responsible for an act committed by him upon direction or with approval and ratification of his state, even if that act is a flagrant war crime and as such clearly contrary to international law itself. Responsibility for such a breach, It Is claimed, rests not on the individual, who acted as a mere instrument or "organ" of his state, but only upon the "collectivity of individuals," the corporate entity, which comprises the state. The reason assigned for this principle is that since the act of the individual must be "imputed" to the state, "prosecution of an individual by courts of the injured State for an act which, according to international law, is the act of another State, amounts to exercising jurisdiction over another State; and this is a violation of the rule of general international law that no State is subject to the jurisdiction of another State." It is, moreover, claimed that "there is no sufficient reason to assume that the rule of general customary law under which no State can claim jurisdiction over the acts of another State is suspended by the outbreak of war, and consequently that it is not applicable to the relationship between belligerents." . . .

It is perfectly obvious that the application of a universal principle of non-responsibility of a state's agents could easily render the entire body of international law a dead letter. For any group of criminally minded persons comprising the temporary government that has seized power in a state could readily arrange to declare all of its violations of the law of nations—either in initiating an illegal war or in conducting it contrary to the laws and customs of recognizedly legitimate warfare—to be "acts of state." Thus all its treaty obligations and international law generally could be rendered nugatory; and thus the least law-abiding member of the Family of Nations could always have a weapon with which to emasculate the very law of nations itself. The result would be that the most lawless and unscrupulous leaders and agents of a state could never be brought to account. If such a state won an aggressive war, the politicians, militarists and industrialists who had planned, ordered or executed even the most flagrant atrocities and cynical breaches of international and municipal law, would of course not subject themselves to prosecution in their own courts. And if they happened to lose— as Germany and its chronic militarists have in our day happened twice to do—they would again be assured of personal immunity through application of an irrational technicality. Only the state would have to pay reparations; and that would mean that either the war-impoverished losing state would gradually wriggle out of its obligation, and even transform it into a loss to the people of the victor state (as was true of Germany vis-à-vis the United States after the First World War); or many ordinary citizens of the losing state, who had had nothing to do with initiating or conducting an unjust and ruthless war, would be penalized through heavy taxation to meet the fine imposed upon their nation. The scoundrels at the top, who had actually plotted and carried out the breaches of international and municipal law, would conveniently escape with their lives and fortunes and conserve their strength for still another try at world domination—a process in which they have nothing to lose and everything to gain.

If a doctrine so contrary to reason and justice has indeed been accepted as unconditionally valid international law, it is high time the error were remedied. "It is an universal principle of jurisprudence through cases otherwise doubtful the rule or interpretation which gives the most reasonable results [is] to be applied; and the law of nations is as much entitled to the benefit of that principle as any other kind of law." Since law is supposed to embody the rule of reason in the interests of justice, and the unqualified act-of-state doctrine emasculates both reason and justice, it cannot be regarded as sound law.

There was therefore ample justification for the disavowal of the act-of-state doctrine in both the report to the President (June 7, 1945) by the American Chief of Counsel and the Charter of the International Military Tribunal. The idea that the act-of-state doctrine is universally and unconditionally operative is simply bad law; and bad law should be replaced with good law.

IV THE MEANING OF NUREMBERG

The editors of Fortune
THE NÜRNBERG NOVELTY

The Nuremberg Trial had scarcely begun when criticism of both the procedural and legal foundations of the Tribunal began to be voiced, often in the most unexpected quarters. The editors of Fortune *were among the first to state their diametrical opposition to the proceedings with criticism which ran the entire spectrum of controversial questions of international law related to the trial.*

More than two years ago in a statement issued in Moscow, President Roosevelt and Messrs. Churchill and Stalin passed judgment on the major Nazis, those criminals "whose offenses have no particular geographical localization." The Moscow declaration promised that these malefactors would "be punished by the joint decision of the governments of the Allies." The three spoke for the civilized world. And eventually most of the condemned, Hitler's immediate gang, turned up as prisoners.

As the Nürnberg process unfolds, laymen may wonder about the legal theory underlying it. What kind of trial is this? What creative force may international law look for here? And what dangers are involved? For there is a danger of startling developments. Let us contemplate this novel institution.

The Moscow declaration of 1943 promised that minor Nazis charged with local crimes would be tried where the crimes were committed. Such trials have been held and doubtless there will be many more. But in discussing the *major* criminals, the Moscow declaration refrained from speaking of courts or trials. It spoke rather of governments and government decisions. Some read in it a promise that the criminals would be expeditiously punished— perhaps immediately on capture, not by lynching or court order, but formally on the basis of the political decision.

Such summary judgments have precedents. At Waterloo the Allies defeated the power that had kept Europe in turmoil. Its chief was never tried. The Allies outlawed Napoleon, made him subject to "public vengeance," and isolated him on St. Helena. He did no further harm. And when in 1918 the German armies were beaten and the Kaiser fled to the Netherlands, he was not tried. The Dutch Government, in view of the institution of political asylum, refused to deliver the Kaiser. And the Allies—despite obvious power to do so—decided not to force the Netherlands' hand. The Kaiser, ridiculed and largely isolated (he could not quit Doorn), did not become even an irritating legend.

The crimes with which the Nazis are charged at Nürnberg, while worse in degree and broader in scope, resemble in nature those most historians attribute to Napoleon and the Kaiser—crimes against peace, humanity, and the laws of war. And just as the decisions concerning Napoleon and the Kaiser were political decisions about criminals made not by courts but by political authorities, so the decision made at Moscow by the Allied political leaders to punish the major Nazi criminals was a political decision. Lord Wright, Chairman of the United Nations War Crimes Commission, indicated as late as last June that the Allied governments might in the end punish the major Nazi criminals "by executive action" and not try them at all. Thus far there was no novelty.

But in the same month, when Lord Wright could still think in terms of the Moscow decision, there met in London four Allied delegations, British, French, Russian, and, for the U.S., Supreme Court Justice Robert H. Jackson. They created an International Military Tribunal, representing the four Allied governments. Before it were indicted the chief surviving Nazi criminals. A staff representing the four Allies recited a list of charges. And then another staff (including former Attorney General Francis Biddle) representing the same powers gave instructions for the prisoners to retain attorneys and prepare answers to the charges.

This revealed a novelty. The two Allied staffs were called prosecutors and judges, the tribunal a court. This time the political decision to punish was to be carried out by an institution judicial in form. Yet the mere fact that this tribunal is the implement of policy makes it a peculiar court. Like a court it has judges, prosecutors, bailiffs, lawyers, witnesses, defendants. To conduct a trial is the mandate of the charter drawn by Mr. Jackson's group, which created the tribunal.

But how can this tribunal fulfill the purpose of a court in holding a trial, which, in our law at any rate, is supposed to determine guilt or innocence? Even to suggest that these men's guilt is an open question is to open the question of whether the Allies should have made war upon them. If there was doubt about their guilt after they invaded Poland, why were they not tried *in absentia* by an international court and war against them postponed until guilt had been established? After our soldiers have laid down their lives, it is a little late to examine the question of guilt. And obviously we shall not open that question. For these are self-convicted men who announced intent (as in *Mein Kampf*) to commit the crimes all know they committed.

Indeed, were the Allied peoples to believe that this trial could result in acquittals, they would clamor for the dissolution of the tribunal and for immediate punishment. An acquittal would be the greatest crime of the age against the living and against those who died in battle against the Nazi criminals. What is appropriate to the Nazis, guilty beyond any reasonable doubt, is not a verdict. Only a sentence is appropriate. And there is no chance of acquittal. The verdict was written in Moscow in 1943. Hence there is logic, if not an iota of judiciousness, in the recent statement of Attorney General Tom Clark that he hopes the Nürnberg court "will deal out what we in Texas call 'law west of the Pecos'—fast justice, particularly fast."

Now, in American trials it is always possible for the accused, through a plea of self-defense, drunkenness, or insanity, or even some trick or mishap, to escape conviction. Our principle is that it is better for nine men who should have been convicted to go free than for one innocent Bertram Campbell to be convicted. A trial means that a real possibility of acquittal exists.

But nobody expects the Nürnberg judges to do anything but convict as a preliminary to announcing the exact form of the punishment, which was ordered in outline in 1943. The judgment is fixed in advance. That is true of any political trial and one may better describe this body as a political tribunal than as a court of justice or even a military one. And political tribunals make poor law, if any.

Respect for the tribunal as a court is not fortified by a look at details of the indictments. The first count charges conspiracy. The second charges crimes against peace. Its theory is that, regardless of the causes of World War II, to begin it was a violation of international agreements signed by the German Government, particularly the Briand-Kellogg Pact, and that Germany's responsible government

Von Papen, Schacht, and Fritzsche host a jubilant press conference following their acquittal. (*Photo no. 238-NT–812 in the National Archives*)

heads are personally liable for the breach of the treaties and the peace and therefore subject to punishment. But none of the pacts involved speaks of individual liability or sanctions or punishments. International law provides for no punishment of persons. Perhaps it should—but thus far only the charter of the Nürnberg novelty and the indictments based thereon make such a provision. And since they were written after the deeds, the "law" underlying the "trial" is in part ex post facto. Our legal tradition wisely frowns upon such law.

The second count, to which one of the four nations represented on the Nürnberg bench was long opposed, has an additional defect.

When the prosecution rises to prove the crime of making aggressive war, the Russian judge—a general of that Red Army which invaded Finland and the Baltic countries and, simultaneously with the Nazi Army, Poland—will be sitting on something less comfortable than a woolsack. To try a man for aggression when on the bench sits another aggressor is strange. True, Mr. Jackson has said that "there seems to be no way of doing anything about the crimes against peace and humanity except that the victors judge the vanquished." Does this mean that might makes right? It appears that the second count can have a destructive effect, possibly on U.S. law, surely upon international law.

The fourth count charges crimes against humanity. In part it refers to atrocities committed by the Nazis against minorities in Germany beginning in 1933. The tribunal's charter provides that such acts be considered criminal, even if done *before the war* and even if *not* in violation of German law. The theory is that if one state's legal system permits treatment of its population in what other states regard as a criminal fashion, there is a violation of international law and the heads of the state are personally liable. According to this theory, when the Army arbitrarily interned the Nisei the hostile Japanese Government acquired a legal right to try General DeWitt and others of our officials in an Axis court. According to this theory, if Stalin holds great numbers of people in concentration camps without what we regard as due process, we acquire a right to try him in some court of our choice. Quite obviously neither we nor he admit any such rights. In fact, we really reject the underlying theory on grounds of national sovereignty. And the count based on it is not based on international law. It is not based on *any* true legal concept, which must necessarily be universal, respecting neither persons nor nations, neither victor nor vanquished. Thus this count has a destructive effect both on national government and on international law.

The third count charges crimes against the laws of war. Unlike the others, it may not have a destructive effect on law. Rather it is based on a theory that has itself been pretty well destroyed by the atomic bomb: that there are legal and proper as against illegal and improper ways of waging war; that there could, in other words, be a clean war. The atomic bomb lends new force to the point of view that what is needed is not rules for clean wars but the abolition of wars. This count at best futilely tries to bolster collapsing law and thus has a retarding effect.

These points suffice to suggest the possibility that the defendants, if they do not simply choose to stand mute on the ground that they were convicted in the Moscow declaration of 1943, may give the tribunal an unpleasant time. To do so they need not equal the traitorous Laval's embarrassing brilliance. If the Nazis prove half as embarrassing to this peculiar tribunal as the guilty Laval was to the French court, they might further one of their oldest and most basic aims—to weaken and destroy the sense of justice that they have always despised.

Indeed, there are many ways in which this trial might weaken the sense of justice. We might next be urged to forget our constitutional ban on ex post facto laws. We might be urged to discard our sovereignty and open our domestic affairs to intervention not by a world body of which we could be a part but by any foreign power that cared to intervene. Many people want to outlaw atomic bombs, a move that, to be serious, would entail international inspection by a world body. And while disarmament and a world government may be indispensable for the survival of civilization, it would be hard to progress in that direction by punishing some for their past war crimes while ignoring the violations of others.

However one looks at it, there is a wide gap between the theory of the Nürnberg indictment and the theory on which we conduct our affairs. Hence, while the trial can strengthen respect for the relation of victor to vanquished—i.e., for power—it cannot strengthen law, the relation called justice. It can only weaken that.

Can no good come of the trial? Let us see what is hoped for. Some hope that out of the trial will come more than a fixing of the punishment, which was decided on in general in 1943. They hope that evidence will be put in against the Nazi leaders which, if not refuted, will throw on their conduct an even sharper light than now glares on it. They hope, too, that if some prisoners disagree among themselves, new bloody secrets may come out.

In short, many hope that Nürnberg may spread upon the record, in the words of the Nazi leaders themselves, a picture of guilt and horror that may uniquely strike the conscience of the German people. They hope also that as a consequence of Nürnberg's confidently expected condemnation of these men, future men will be deterred from similar crimes.

For any of these hopes to be realized will require exceedingly skillful management to give every appearance of being fair to the criminals. But any credit the court may acquire will at best apply to its function in casting light upon the already well-lighted crimes of the past. And what of the future, when wars can be so much more destructive than ever before? Alas, when it comes to the grandest hope of all, enrichment of that international law which all mankind so urgently requires—that seems entirely beyond the capacity of this court. Indeed, the very concept of international *justice* is being endangered by the Nürnberg novelty.

In the end, the prisoners will presumably be punished. Would it have been less effective as punishment if, soon after they were captured, a solemn assemblage of the heads of all the United Nations had proclaimed a sentence of immediate capital punishment as the sequel to the verdict of 1943? Such an assemblage would have spoken for a world that aches to be rid of the organizers of Nazi criminality. In history, Nürnberg's voice can have no such authority.

The Nürnberg trial will go to its conclusion. The spectator, aware that this is not an ordinary court of justice but rather a political organ, will better understand the process as it unfolds.

Senator Robert A. Taft
EQUAL JUSTICE UNDER LAW

Senator Robert A. Taft of Ohio (1889–1953) became well known for the independence and integrity he invariably displayed as one of the leading spokesmen for the Republican party during the Roosevelt and Truman years.

"Equal Justice under Law: The Heritage of the English-Speaking Peoples and Their Responsibility," address delivered at Kenyon College, Gambier, Ohio, October 5, 1946. Reprinted with permission from *Vital Speeches* (City News Publishing Co., Southold, Long Island), Vol. 13, No. 2, November 1, 1946, pp. 44–48.

*The public position Taft espoused on the Nuremberg Trials was an out-
standing example of his predilection for following the dictates of his personal
convictions, not the popular positions of the moment, and his courage was
celebrated by President Kennedy in his book* Profiles *in Courage. The following selection is taken from his speech at Kenyon College in which he
attacked the Nuremberg Trials as a miscarriage of justice and the due
process of law.*

Mr. Chairman and Members of the Conference: It gives me special
pleasure to come to Kenyon College and I feel greatly honored by
being invited to join in this Conference with the distinguished men
who have come from all parts of the world to join in this discussion.
The Conference could not have been more timely, for now, if ever, we
must re-examine the basis of our thinking if civilization is to be pre-
served.

I wish to speak of the heritage of the English-speaking peoples in
the field of government, and their responsibility to carry on that heritage, and to apply its tried principles to the entire world as rapidly as
that can be done. The very basis of the government of the United
States, derived through the colonies from principles of British government, was the liberty of the individual and the assurance to him of
equal treatment and equal justice. We cannot claim that these principles were original with the English-speaking peoples, because, of
course, they existed in Greece and in the Roman Republic and in
other nations before England became a nation. But to a large extent
they disappeared during the Middle Ages and their revival was most
marked in Great Britain, and even more in the establishment of the
American Republic.

I desire today to speak particularly of equal justice, because it is
an essential of individual liberty. Unless there is law, and unless there
is an impartial tribunal to administer that law, no man can be really
free. Without them only force can determine controversy, as in the
international field today, and those who have not sufficient force
cannot remain free. Without law and an appeal to a just and independent court to interpret that law, every man must be subject to
the arbitrary discretion of his ruler or of some subordinate government official.

Over the portal of the great Supreme Court building in Washington
are written the words "Equal Justice Under Law." The Declaration of

Independence, the Constitution of the United States and every pronouncement of the founders of the government stated the same principle in one form or another. Thomas Jefferson in his first inaugural emphasized above everything the necessity for "equal and exact justice to all men of whatever state or persuasion, religious or political."

In England the progress towards a definite law, administered by efficient and impartial courts or tribunals, was slow and uncertain. The common law developed slowly and only became clear and definite after many centuries. . . .

However slowly it developed, there developed with it something even more important, namely a public reverence for law and a public acceptance of the verdict, even though it might be felt to be wrong. As James Truslow Adams says in his analysis of the British people, "Connected with many of the points we have mentioned is that feeling for law and order which strikes almost every visitor to England. It is a trait with a long history behind it, but seems to have become deeply embedded in the race." I cannot overemphasize the importance of this attitude, the willingness to accept the decision of an impartial tribunal made in accordance with the law, even if that decision is thought to be wrong. Until we reach such a universal acceptance in the world at large, we cannot hope that any international organization can prevent a resort to force, and the war which must follow it.

Unfortunately, the philosophy of equal justice under law, and acceptance of decisions made in accordance with respected institutions, has steadily lost strength during recent years. It is utterly denied in totalitarian states. There the law and the courts are instruments of state policy. It is inconceivable to the people of such a state that a court would concern itself to be fair to those individuals who appear before it when the state has an adverse interest. Nor do they feel any need of being fair between one man and another. Therefore they see no reason for presenting logical argument to justify a position. Nothing is more typical of the Communist or the Fascist than to assert and re-assert an argument which has been completely answered and disproved, in order to create public opinion by propaganda to the ignorant.

The totalitarian idea has spread throughout many nations where, in the nineteenth century, the ideals of liberty and justice were accepted. Even in this country, the theory that the state is finally responsible for every condition, and that every problem must be cured by giving the government arbitrary power to act, has been increasingly the philosophy of the twentieth century. It infects men who still profess complete adherence to individual liberty and individual justice, so that we find them willing to sacrifice both to accomplish some economic or social purpose. There is none of the burning devotion to liberty which characterized Patrick Henry and even the conservative leaders of the American Revolution.

Even before the war we had drifted far from justice at home. Expedience has been the key to the legislation of recent years and many of the existing bureaus administer the law without any belief in the principle that the government should be fair to every individual according to a written law. . . .

But even more discouraging is the attitude of the people and the press. Government action which twenty-five years ago would have excited a sense of outrage in thousands, is reported in a few lines and if disapproved at all, is disapproved with a shrug of the shoulders and a hopeless feeling that nothing can be done about it.

To a large extent this feeling has been promoted by the attack on the Supreme Court, and the effort to make the courts instruments of executive policy. The old court may have been too conservative, but the judges believed they were interpreting the laws and Constitution as they were written, and most of the country believed that they were honestly impartial. Today the Court regards itself as the maker of policy—no maker of policy can command respect for impartial dispensation of justice.

I believe more strongly than I can say that if we would maintain progress and liberty in America, it is our responsibility to see not only that laws be rewritten to substitute law for arbitrary discretion but that the whole attitude of the people be educated to a deep devotion to law, impartiality and equal justice.

It is even more important to the entire world that these principles be established as the guide for international action. In my opinion they afford the only hope of future peace. Not only must there be a more definite law to govern the relations between nations, not only must there be tribunals to decide controversies under that law, but the peoples of the world must be so imbued with respect for law and the tribunals established that they will accept their decisions without an appeal to force.

Whether we have a league of sovereign nations like the United Nations, or a World State, there cannot be an end of war if any important people refuse to accept freely the principle of abiding by law, or if truly impartial tribunals are not established.

Unfortunately, I believe we Americans have also in recent foreign policy been affected by principles of expediency and supposed necessity, and abandoned largely the principle of justice. We have drifted into the acceptance of the idea that the world is to be ruled by the power and policy of the great nations and a police force established by them rather than by international law.

I felt very strongly that we should join the United Nations organization, but it was not because I approved of the principles established in the Charter. Those who drafted the original Dumbarton Oaks proposals apparently had little knowledge of the heritage of the English-speaking peoples, for in those proposals there was no reference to justice and very little to liberty. At San Francisco a good many declarations were inserted emphasizing the importance of law and justice, but they were not permitted to interfere with the original set-up of the Security Council. The Security Council is the very heart of the United Nations, the only body with power to act. The Charter gives it the power to adopt any measure, economic or military, which it considers necessary to maintain or restore international peace and security. The heritage of the English-speaking peoples has always emphasized liberty over peace and justice over security. I believe that liberty and justice are the only channel to permanent peace and security. . . .

The Atlantic Charter professed a belief in liberty and justice for all nations, but at Teheran, at Yalta, at Moscow, we forgot law and justice. Nothing could be further from a rule of law than the making of secret agreements distributing the territory of the earth in accordance with power and expediency. We cannot excuse ourselves by declining territorial acquisition ourselves, or subjecting ourselves to unreasonable and illogical restriction on our sovereignty over uninhabited Pacific Islands. We are just as much to blame if we acquiesce in unjustified acquisition of territory by others, such as the handing over of the Kurile Islands to Russia without trusteeship of any kind.

Without a word of protest, we have agreed to the acquisition of Lithuania, Estonia and Latvia by the USSR. There is little justice to the people of Poland in the boundaries assigned to them. The extending of justice throughout the world may be and is beyond our powers, but certainly we need not join in the principles by which force and national policy is permitted to dominate the world.

During the war, and since, I have felt that there has been little justice in our treatment of the neutral countries. We took the position in effect that no nation had the right to remain neutral, and bullied these countries to an extreme restrained only by consideration of policy, but not of justice.

The treatment of enemy countries has seldom been just after any war, but only now are we beginning to get some justice into our treatment of Germany. Our treatment has been harsh in the American Zone as a deliberate matter of government policy, and has offended Americans who saw it, and felt that it was completely at variance with American instincts. We gave countenance to the revengeful and impracticable Morgenthau plan which would have reduced the Germans to economic poverty. We have fooled ourselves in the belief that we could teach another nation democratic principles by force. Why we can't even teach our own people sound principles of government. We cannot teach liberty and justice in Germany by suppressing liberty and justice.

I believe that most Americans view with discomfort the war trials which have just been concluded in Germany and are proceeding in Japan. They violate that fundamental principle of American law that a man cannot be tried under an ex post facto statute.

The trial of the vanquished by the victors cannot be impartial no matter how it is hedged about with the forms of justice. I question whether the hanging of those, who, however despicable, were the leaders of the German people, will ever discourage the making of aggressive war, for no one makes aggressive war unless he expects to win. About this whole judgment there is the spirit of vengeance, and vengeance is seldom justice. The hanging of the eleven men convicted will be a blot on the American record which we shall long regret.

In these trials we have accepted the Russian idea of the purpose of trials—government policy and not justice—with little relation to

Anglo-Saxon heritage. By clothing policy in the forms of legal procedure, we may discredit the whole idea of justice in Europe for years to come. In the last analysis, even at the end of a frightful war, we should view the future with more hope if even our enemies believed that we had treated them justly in our English-speaking concept of law, in the provision of relief and in the final disposal of territory. I pray that we do not repeat this procedure in Japan, where the justification on grounds of vengeance is much less than in Germany.

Our whole attitude in the world, for a year after V-E Day, including the use of the atomic bomb at Hiroshima and Nagasaki, seems to me a departure from the principles of fair and equal treatment which has made America respected throughout the world before this second World War. Today we are cordially hated in many countries. I am delighted that Secretary Byrnes and Senator Vandenburg have reversed our policy in many of the respects I have referred to. But abroad as at home we have a long way to go to restore again to the American people our full heritage of an ingrained belief in fairness, impartiality and justice.

Peace in the world can only come if a law is agreed to relating to international relations, if there is a tribunal which can interpret that law and decide disputes between nations, and if the nations are willing to submit their disputes to impartial decision regardless of the outcome. There can be no peace until the public opinion of the world accepts, as a matter of course, the decisions of an international tribunal.

War has always set back temporarily the ideals of the world. This time, because of the tremendous scope of the war, the increased barbarism of its methods and the general prevalence of the doctrine of force and expediency even before the war, the effect today is even worse and the duration of the postwar period of disillusionment may be longer.

As I see it, the English-speaking peoples have one great responsibility. That is to restore to the minds of men a devotion to equal justice under law.

Henry L. Stimson

THE NUREMBERG TRIAL: LANDMARK IN LAW

Henry L. Stimson (1867–1950) enjoyed a long and influential governmental career which he celebrated in an autobiography entitled On Active Service in Peace and War. *He served President Hoover as Secretary of State and in 1940 President Roosevelt named him Secretary of War, the post he held until 1945. As a result of his close association with Roosevelt and Truman, he was a firm supporter of the United States' commitment to the Nuremberg principles, and in January 1947 he answered the critics of the Tribunal in perhaps the leading forum of the government establishment, the journal* Foreign Affairs. *In this article Secretary Stimson gave eloquent testimony to the contention that Nuremberg did indeed further the cause of justice and world order.*

In the confusion and disquiet of the war's first aftermath, there has been at least one great event from which we may properly take hope. The surviving leaders of the Nazi conspiracy against mankind have been indicted, tried, and judged in a proceeding whose magnitude and quality make it a landmark in the history of international law. The great undertaking at Nuremberg can live and grow in meaning, however, only if its principles are rightly understood and accepted. It is therefore disturbing to find that its work is criticized and even challenged as lawless by many who should know better. In the deep conviction that this trial deserves to be known and valued as a long step ahead on the only upward road, I venture to set down my general view of its nature and accomplishment.

The defendants at Nuremberg were leaders of the most highly organized and extensive wickedness in history. It was not a trick of the law which brought them to the bar; it was the "massed angered forces of common humanity." There were three different courses open to us when the Nazi leaders were captured: release, summary punishment, or trial. Release was unthinkable; it would have been taken as an admission that there was here no crime. Summary punishment was widely recommended. It would have satisfied the immediate requirement of the emotions, and in its own roughhewn way it would have been fair enough, for this was precisely the type of justice that the Nazis themselves had so often used. But this fact was in reality the best reason for rejecting such a solution. The whole moral position of the victorious Powers must collapse if their judgments could be enforced only by Nazi methods. Our anger, as righteous anger, must be subject to the law. We therefore took the third course and tried the captive criminals by a judicial proceeding. We gave to the Nazis what they had denied their own opponents—the protection of the law. The Nuremberg Tribunal was thus in no sense an instrument of vengeance but the reverse. It was, as Mr. Justice Jackson said in opening the case for the prosecution, "one of the most significant tributes that Power has ever paid to Reason."

The function of the law here, as everywhere, has been to insure fair judgment. By preventing abuse and minimizing error, proceedings under law give dignity and method to the ordinary conscience of mankind. For this purpose the law demands three things: that the defendant be charged with a punishable crime; that he have full opportunity for defense; and that he be judged fairly on the evidence by a proper judicial authority. Should it fail to meet any one of these three requirements, a trial would not be justice. Against these standards, therefore, the judgment of Nuremberg must itself be judged.

I. Punishable Crimes

In our modern domestic law, a man can be penalized only when he has done something which was authoritatively recognized as punishable when he did it. This is the well-known principle that forbids *ex post facto* law, and it accords entirely with our standards of fair play. A mistaken appeal to this principle has been the cause of much confusion about the Nuremberg trial. It is argued that parts of the Tribunal's Charter, written in 1945, make crimes out of what before were activities beyond the scope of national and international law. Were this an exact statement of the situation we might well be concerned, but it is not. It rests on a misconception of the whole nature of the law of nations. International law is not a body of authoritative codes or statutes; it is the gradual expression, case by case, of the moral judgments of the civilized world. As such, it corresponds precisely to the common law of Anglo-American tradition. We can understand the law of Nuremberg only if we see it for what it is—a great new case in the book of international law, and not a formal enforcement of codified statutes. A look at the charges will show what I mean.

The Charter of the Tribunal recognizes three kinds of crime, all of which were charged in the indictment: crimes against peace, war crimes, and crimes against humanity. There was a fourth charge, of conspiracy to commit one or all of these crimes. To me personally this fourth charge is the most realistic of them all, for the Nazi crime is in the end indivisible. Each of the myriad transgressions was an interlocking part of the whole gigantic barbarity. But basically it is the first three that we must consider. The fourth is built on them.

Of the three charges, only one has been seriously criticized. War crimes have not greatly concerned the Tribunal's critics; these are offenses well understood and long generally recognized in the law or rules of war. The charge of crimes against humanity has not aroused much comment in this country, perhaps because this part of the indictment was not of central concern to the American prosecutor. The Tribunal's findings on this charge are significant, but not such as to raise much question of their legal validity, so I defer my comment to a later section of this article.

There remains the charge of crimes against peace, which has been the chief target of most of the honest critics of Nuremberg. It is under this charge that a penalty has been asked, for the first time, against the individual leaders in a war of aggression. It is this that well-intentioned critics have called "ex post facto law."

It is clear that until quite recently any legal judgment against a warmaker would have been absurd. Throughout the centuries, until after World War I, the choice between war and peace remained entirely in the hands of each sovereign state, and neither the law nor the ordinary conscience of humanity ventured to deny that right. The concept of just and unjust wars is of course as old at least as Plato. But in the anarchy of individual sovereignties, the right to fight was denied to no ruler. For the loser in a war, punishment was certain. But this was not a matter of law; it was simply a matter of course. At the best it was like the early law of the blood feud, in which the punishment of a murderer was the responsibility of the victim's family alone and not of the whole community. Even in 1914 the German violation of Belgian neutrality was regarded as a matter for action only by those nations directly concerned in the Treaties of 1839. So far indeed was this sovereign right of war-making accepted that it was frequently extended to include the barbarous notion that a sovereign ruler is not subject to the law.

In the face of this acceptance of war as a proper instrument of sovereign national policy, the only field for the early development of international law lay in restricting so far as possible the brutalities of warfare. In obedience to age-long instincts of chivalry and magnanimity, there were gradually developed international standards for the conduct of war. Civilians and neutrals were given protecting rights and privileges, the treatment of prisoners was prescribed, and certain weapons were outlawed. It is these long-established and universally accepted standards, most of them formally included in the internal law of Germany, that are covered by the charge of war crimes in the Nuremberg indictment.

The attempt to moderate the excesses of war without controlling war itself was doomed to failure by the extraordinary scientific and industrial developments of the nineteenth and twentieth centuries. By 1914 the world had been intertwined into a single unit and weapons had been so far developed that a major war could shake the whole structure of civilization. No rules of warfare were sufficient to limit the vast new destructive powers of belligerents, and the First World War made it clear that old notions must be abandoned; the world must attack the problem at its root. Thus after 1918 repeated efforts were made to eliminate aggressive war as a legal national undertaking. These efforts reached their climax in the Kellogg-Briand Pact of 1928, in which 63 nations, including Germany, Japan and Italy, renounced aggressive warfare. This pact was not an isolated incident of the postwar era. During that period the whole world was at one in its opinion of aggressive war. In repeated resolutions in the League of Nations and elsewhere, aggression was roundly denounced as criminal. In the judgment of the peoples of the world the once proud title of "conqueror" was replaced by the criminal epithet "aggressor."

The progress made from 1918 to 1931 was halting and incomplete, but its direction was clear; the mandate for peace was over-

whelming. Most tragically, the people who had renounced war were
not sufficiently alert to their danger when in the following years the
ruling groups of three great nations, in wanton denial of every principle of peace and civilization, launched a conspiracy against the
rest of the world. Thus it happened that in the ten years which began
with the invasion of Manchuria the principles of the Kellogg Pact
were steadily under attack, and only as the danger came slowly
home to each one of them individually did the peace-loving nations
take action against aggression. In early 1945, as it became apparent
that the long-delayed victory was at hand, the question posed itself
directly: Has there been a war of aggression and are its leaders
punishable? There were many then, as there are some now, who
argued that there was no law for this offense, and they found their
justification in the feebleness and acquiescence of other nations in
the early aggression of the Axis. Other counsels prevailed, however,
and by the Charter of the Nuremberg Tribunal the responsible leaders
of aggressive war were subjected to trial and conviction on the
charge of crimes against peace.

Here we come to the heart of the matter. Able lawyers and honest
men have cried out that this aggressive war was not a crime. They
have argued that the Nuremberg defendants were not properly fore-
warned when they made war that what they did was criminal.

Now in one sense the concept of ex post facto law is a strange one
to apply here, because this concept relates to a state of mind on the
part of the defendants that in this case was wholly absent. That concept is based on the assumption that if the defendant had known
that the proposed act was criminal he would have refrained from
committing it. Nothing in the attitude of the Nazi leaders corresponds
to this assumption; their minds were wholly untroubled by the question of their guilt or innocence. Not in their aggression only but in
their whole philosophy, they excluded the very concept of law. They
deliberately put themselves below such a concept. To international
law—as to the law of Germany—they paid only such respect as they
found politic, and in the end they had smashed its every rule. Their
attitude toward aggressive war was exactly like their attitude toward
murder—both were useful instruments in a great design. It is therefore impossible to get any light on the validity of this charge of
aggressive war by inspecting the Nazi mind. We must study rather

the minds of the rest of the world, which is at once a less revolting and a more fruitful labor.

What did the rest of us think about aggressive war at the time of the Nazi attacks? This question is complex, but to that part of it which affects the legality of the Nuremberg trial we can give a simple answer. That we considered aggressive war wicked is clear; that we considered the leaders of an aggressive war wicked is equally clear. These opinions, in large part formally embodied in the Kellogg Pact, are the basis for the law of Nuremberg. With the detailed reasoning by which the prosecution has supported the law set forth in the Charter of the International Military Tribunal, we cannot here concern ourselves. The proposition sustained by the Tribunal is simple: if a man plans aggression when aggression has been formally renounced by his nation, he is a criminal. Those who are concerned with the law of this proposition cannot do better than to read the pertinent passages in the opening address of Mr. Justice Jackson, the closing address of Sir Hartley Shawcross, and the opinion of the Tribunal itself.

What really troubles the critics of Nuremberg is that they see no evidence that before 1945 we considered the capture and conviction of such aggressors to be our legal duty. In this view they are in the main correct, but it is vitally important to remember that a legal right is not lost merely because temporarily it is not used. What happened before World War II was that we lacked the courage to enforce the authoritative decision of the international world. We agreed with the Kellogg Pact that aggressive war must end. We renounced it, and we condemned those who might use it. But it was a moral condemnation only. We thus did not reach the second half of the question: What will you do to an aggressor when you catch him? If we *had* reached it, we should easily have found the right answer. But that answer escaped us, for it implied a duty to catch the criminal, and such a chase meant war. It was the Nazi confidence that we would never chase and catch them, and not a misunderstanding of our opinion of them, that led them to commit their crimes. Our offense was thus that of the man who passed by on the other side. That we have finally recognized our negligence and named the criminals for what they are is a piece of righteousness too long delayed by fear.

We did not ask ourselves, in 1939 or 1940, or even in 1941, what punishment, if any, Hitler and his chief assistants deserved. We asked simply two questions: How do we avoid war, and how do we keep this wickedness from overwhelming us? These seemed larger questions to us than the guilt or innocence of individuals. In the end we found an answer to the second question, but none to the first. The crime of the Nazis, against *us,* lay in this very fact: that their making of aggressive war made peace here impossible. We have now seen again, in hard and deadly terms, what had been proved in 1917—that "peace is indivisible." The man who makes aggressive war at all makes war against mankind. That is an exact, not a rhetorical, description of the crime of aggressive war.

Thus the Second World War brought it home to us that our repugnance to aggressive war was incomplete without a judgment of its leaders. What we had called a crime demanded punishment; we must bring our law in balance with the universal moral judgment of mankind. The wickedness of aggression must be punished by a trial and judgment. This is what has been done at Nuremberg.

Now this is a new judicial process, but it is not ex post facto law. It is the enforcement of a moral judgment which dates back a generation. It is a growth in the application of law that any student of our common law should recognize as natural and proper, for it is in just this manner that the common law grew up. There was, somewhere in our distant past, a first case of murder, a first case where the tribe replaced the victim's family as judge of the offender. The tribe had learned that the deliberate and malicious killing of any human being was, and must be treated as, an offense against the whole community. The analogy is exact. All case law grows by new decisions, and where those new decisions match the conscience of the community, they are law as truly as the law of murder. They do not become ex post facto law merely because until the first decision and punishment comes, a man's only warning that he offends is in the general sense and feeling of his fellow men.

The charge of aggressive war is unsound, therefore, only if the community of nations did not believe in 1939 that aggressive war was an offense. Merely to make such a suggestion, however, is to discard it. Aggression is an offense, and we all know it; we have known it for a generation. It is an offense so deep and heinous that we cannot endure its repetition.

The law made effective by the trial at Nuremberg is righteous law long overdue. It is in just such cases as this one that the law becomes more nearly what Mr. Justice Holmes called it: "the witness and external deposit of our moral life."

With the judgment of Nuremberg we at last reach to the very core of international strife, and we set a penalty not merely for war crimes, but for the very act of war itself, except in self-defense. If a man will argue that this is bad law, untrue to our ideals, I will listen. But I feel only pity for the casuist who would dismiss the Nazi leaders because "they were not warned it was a crime." They were warned, and they sneered contempt. Our shame is that their contempt was so nearly justified, not that we have in the end made good our warning.

II. Fair Trial

Next after its assertion of the criminality of aggressive war, the triumph of Nuremberg rests in the manner and degree to which it has discharged with honor the true functions of a legal instrument. The crimes charged were punishable as we have seen—so clearly punishable that the only important suggested alternative to a trial was summary execution of the accused. It is in its pursuit of a different course that the Nuremberg Tribunal has demonstrated at once the dignity and the value of the law, and students of law everywhere will find inspiration and enlightenment in close study of its work. In its skilful development of a procedure satisfying every traditional and material safeguard of the varying legal forms of the prosecuting nations, it represents a signal success in the field of international negotiation, and in its rigid fidelity to the fundamental principles of fair play it has insured the lasting value of its work.

In their insistence on fairness to the defendants, the Charter and the Tribunal leaned over backwards. Each defendant was allowed to testify for himself, a right denied by Continental law. At the conclusion of the trial, each defendant was allowed to address the Tribunal, at great length, a right denied by Anglo-American law. The difference between Continental and Anglo-American law was thus adjusted by allowing to the defendant his rights under both. Counsel for the defendants were leading German lawyers and professors from the German universities, some of them ardent and unrepentant Nazis.

Counsel were paid, fed, sheltered and transported at the expense of the Allies, and were furnished offices and secretarial help. The defense had full access to all documents. Every attempt was made to produce desired witnesses when the Tribunal believed that they had any relevant evidence to offer. In the summation of the trial the defense had 20 days and the prosecution three, and the defense case as a whole occupied considerably more time than the prosecution.

The record of the Nuremberg trial thus becomes one of the foundation stones of the peace. Under the most rigid safeguards of jurisprudence, subject to challenge, denial and disproof by men on trial for their lives and assisted by counsel of their own choosing, the great conspiracy has been unmasked. In documents unchallenged by the defense and often in the words of the defendants themselves, there is recorded the whole black history of murder, enslavement and aggression. This record, so established, will stand as a demonstration, on a wholly new level of validity and strength, of the true character of the Nazi regime. And this is so not in spite of our insistence upon law, but because of it.

In this connection it is worth noting that the trial has totally exploded many of the strange notions that seem to lurk in the minds of some who have expressed their doubts about Nuremberg. Some of the doubters are not basically concerned with "ex post facto law" or with "vengeance." Their real trouble is that they did not think the Nazis could be proved guilty. To these gentlemen I earnestly commend a reading of the record. If after reading it they do not think there was in fact aggressive war, in its most naked form, then I shall be constrained to believe that they do not think any such thing exists or can exist.

III. Fair Judgment

Not having made a study of the evidence presented in the case with special reference to each defendant, I am not qualified to pass judgment on the verdicts and sentences of the Tribunal against individuals and criminal groups. I have, however, heard no claim that these sentences were too severe. The Tribunal's findings as to the law are on the whole encouraging. The charge of aggressive war was accepted and ably explained. The charge of war crimes was sustained almost without comment. The charge of crimes against humanity was limited by the Tribunal to include only activities pursued in connection with the crime of war. The Tribunal eliminated from its jurisdiction the question of the criminal accountability of those responsible for wholesale persecution before the outbreak of the war in 1939. With this decision I do not here venture to quarrel, but its effect appears to me to involve a reduction of the meaning of crimes against humanity to a point where they become practically synonymous with war crimes.

If there is a weakness in the Tribunal's findings, I believe it lies in its very limited construction of the legal concept of conspiracy. That only eight of the twenty-two defendants should have been found guilty on the count of conspiracy to commit the various crimes involved in the indictment seems to me surprising. I believe that the Tribunal would have been justified in a broader construction of the law of conspiracy, and under such a construction it might well have found a different verdict in a case like that of Schacht.

In this first great international trial, however, it is perhaps as well that the Tribunal has very rigidly interpreted both the law and the evidence. In this connection we may observe that only in the case of Rudolf Hess, sentenced to life imprisonment, does the punishment of any of the defendants depend solely on the count of aggressive war. All of those who have been hanged were convicted of war crimes or crimes against humanity, and all but one were convicted of both. Certainly, then, the charge of aggressive war has not been established in international law at the expense of any innocent lives.

The judgment of the Tribunal is thus, in its findings of guilt, beyond challenge. We may regret that some of the charges were not regarded as proven and some of the defendants not found clearly guilty. But we may take pride in the restraint of a tribunal which has so clearly insisted upon certain proof of guilt. It is far better that a Schacht should go free than that a judge should compromise his conscience.

IV. The Meaning of Nuremberg

A single landmark of justice and honor does not make a world of peace. The Nazi leaders are not the only ones who have renounced and denied the principles of western civilization. They are unique only in the degree and violence of their offenses. In every nation which acquiesced even for a time in their offense, there were offenders. There have been still more culpable offenders in nations which joined before or after in the brutal business of aggression. If we claimed for Nuremberg that it was final justice, or that only these criminals were guilty, we might well be criticized as being swayed by vengeance and not justice. But this is not the claim. The American prosecutor has explicitly stated that he looks uneasily and with great regret upon certain brutalities that have occurred since the ending of the war. He speaks for us all when he says that there has been enough bloodletting in Europe. But the sins of others do not make the Nazi leaders less guilty, and the importance of Nuremberg lies not in any claim that by itself it clears the board, but rather in the pattern it has set. The four nations prosecuting, and the nineteen others subscribing to the Charter of the International Military Tribunal, have firmly bound themselves to the principle that aggressive war is a personal and punishable crime.

It is this principle upon which we must henceforth rely for our legal protection against the horrors of war. We must never forget that under modern conditions of life, science and technology, all war has become greatly brutalized, and that no one who joins in it, even in self-defense, can escape becoming also in a measure brutalized. Modern war cannot be limited in its destructive methods and in the inevitable debasement of all participants. A fair scrutiny of the last two world wars makes clear the steady intensification in the inhumanity of the weapons and methods employed by both the aggressors and the victors. In order to defeat Japanese aggression, we were forced, as Admiral Nimitz has stated, to employ a technique of unrestricted submarine warfare not unlike that which 25 years ago was the proximate cause of our entry into World War I. In the use of strategic air power, the Allies took the lives of hundreds of thousands of civilians in Germany, and in Japan the destruction of civilian life wreaked by our B-29s, even before the final blow of the atomic bombs, was at least proportionately great. It is true that our use of this destructive power, particularly of the atomic bomb, was for the purpose of winning a quick victory over aggressors, so as to minimize the loss of life, not only of our troops but of the civilian populations of our enemies as well, and that this purpose in the case of Japan was clearly effected. But even so, we as well as our enemies have contributed to the proof that the central moral problem is war and not its methods, and that a continuance of war will in all probability end with the destruction of our civilization.

International law is still limited by international politics, and we must not pretend that either can live and grow without the other. But in the judgment of Nuremberg there is affirmed the central principle of peace—that the man who makes or plans to make aggressive war is a criminal. A standard has been raised to which Americans, at least, must repair; for it is only as this standard is accepted, supported and enforced that we can move onward to a world of law and peace.

Herbert Wechsler
THE ISSUES OF THE NUREMBERG TRIAL

Herbert Wechsler, the Harlan Fiske Stone Professor of Constitutional Law at the Columbia Law School, is a distinguished figure in the field of legal scholarship. Among other works he is known for The Federal Courts and the Federal System *and* Principles, Politics, and Fundamental Law. *His knowledge of the legal issues of the Nuremberg Trial is widely recognized as well; he served as a technical adviser to the United States' delegation at Nuremberg. Soon after the conclusion of the trial, he countered the adversaries of the proceedings with the following significant article in* Political Science Quarterly.

One may say without impertinence to historians that the judgment that history will render upon a legal proceeding is not usually a matter of acute concern either to counsel or to the court. In this respect, at least, the Nuremberg trial was a highly exceptional affair; for the perspective of most of the participants, and even that of the defendants, was focused very much on the future, distant and problem-

Reprinted with permission from *Political Science Quarterly*, Vol. 62 (March 1947), pp. 11–26. (Footnotes deleted.)

atical as it is. The dominant mood was put in words by Justice Jackson, in opening the case for the prosecution: "We must never forget that the record on which we judge these defendants today is the record on which history will judge us tomorrow."

The verdict of history will not be rendered for a long time, but we may be certain that the process of deliberation will be active and that the debate has already begun. The trial is extolled as a crucial achievement in the development of international law, a triumph of reason and justice in the bitter wake of the war. But voices have been raised from the beginning to proclaim the battle cry of the attack: novelty and confusion, error and pretense, a peril to essential liberties safeguarded by domestic law. What are the issues that challenge examination as this active critique unfolds? What are the factors to be weighed in the balance by those who will record for the judgment of posterity the history of our turbulent time? . . .

The issues that are important are those presented by the Charter in its substantive aspects, as interpreted and applied by the Nuremberg Court. The Charter was, of course, binding upon the Tribunal in the same way that a constitutional statute would bind a domestic court. But the generalizations set forth in the Agreement demanded, as legislation always does, creative interpretation in its application to the challenging facts of a particular case. . . .

Should the United States—and the question may be put with equal validity for each of the victors—have cast its influence against any punitive proceedings, declining to participate and refusing to surrender the persons of its prisoners to other countries clamoring to proceed? Such a course would have forsaken the pledges and the warnings issued as an instrument of war and would have responded with a blanket *nolumus* to the demand for retribution that rose like a plaintive chant from all the desolated lands. Certainly only the firmest conviction that punishment in this situation could serve no adequate temporal purpose would have sanctioned dismissal of the millions of complainants with the admonition that "vengeance belongs to God." In truth, the volume of accumulated passion sufficed in itself to establish such a temporal purpose—for who can doubt that indiscriminate violence, a bloodbath beyond power of control, would have followed an announcement by the responsible governments that they were unwilling to proceed? If nothing else was to be accomplished, it was essential that some institutional mechanism be provided that would reserve the application of violence to the public force, to cases in which punishment might serve a constructive purpose and in which reason would conclude that it was deserved.

It is not to be conceded, however, that this negative function, whatever its importance, is the only purpose that was to be served. The assumption of domestic society that punishment is a preventive weapon is not as irrelevant to international behavior as some persons seem disposed to affirm. Insofar as the penalty eliminates a danger presented by the particular individual—hardly an objective of indifference to a military occupation—the function is no less plain in this situation than it is in municipal affairs. But the dominant justification of punishment, especially of the punishment of death, is usually felt to be the deterrence of others; and here it has been asserted that the justification must fail because victory carries immunity whether or not the victor was the aggressor and whatever the measures by which victory was attained.

The argument has a degree of validity but it does not prove enough to prevail. Treason, too, is punishable only when it is abortive; when "it prospers," as the old verse goes, "none dare call it treason"; it is the traitors who call the turn. With respect to war and the manner in which it is conducted, as with respect to treason, there are men who, valuing personal survival, will take account of the contingency of failure. It is to them that the threats are addressed. Moreover, the threat of punishment is not limited in the mode of its operation to the weight that it carries as a factor in decision at the climactic moment of choice. It also operates, and perhaps more significantly, at anterior stages in the patterns of conduct, the dark shadow of organized disapproval eliminating from the ambit of consideration alternatives that might otherwise present themselves in the final competition of choice. These considerations point to some deterrent efficacy; that, and not the assurance of prevention, is all that we can claim for punishment as an instrument of domestic law. It is deemed to be sufficient in municipal affairs, not because of a mathematical calculation of its efficiency, but rather because society, so desperately in need of instrumentalities of prevention, cannot dispense with such potency as condemnation and punishment have. . . .

If punishment cannot be dismissed as intrinsically ineffective in the situation with which we are dealing, we must consider whether it was in fact conditioned upon proper grounds.

Putting aside for the moment any special conception of legality, who will assert that the conditions of punishability prescribed by the London Charter are not accurately addressed to the evils incident to war that international society should seek to prevent? The greatest evil is, of course, the initiation of war itself. Once the evil of war has been precipitated, nothing remains but the fragile effort, embodied for the most part in the conventions, to limit the cruelty by which it is conducted. These are the two major branches of the Charter: crimes against peace and violations of the laws and customs of war. Of these two challenges to life and to all that makes life worth living, who will deny that the larger offense is the unjustified initation of a war?

Goering, having admitted organizing the Nazi program of slave labor—a plain violation of the conventions and a traditional war crime—defended himself, in effect, by attacking the Hague Conventions as inapplicable to modern war. It would be a mistake to suppose that his point is entirely without substance—though no conception of modern military necessity could have justified what the evidence showed. But is it not clear that the attention that would be accorded to a complaint of this order fails when it is remembered that the military necessity asserted was at best that of his own creation? One who viewed as the basic question for Germany—and I quote Hitler's words—"where the greatest possible conquest could be made at the lowest cost," had hardly the same position to justify extremes in the use of force as his victims might have, acting in an honest estimate of what was necessary in their own defense. But this is only to demonstrate that the Tribunal was right in declaring that the initiation of a war of aggression "is the supreme international crime."

There are, of course, problems, and difficult ones indeed, in the ultimate definition of aggression—at least under conditions of world organization as they have obtained in the last years. There may be difficult issues in defining the scope of national authority to act in what it conceives to be necessary self-defense—one of the points of our reservation on the Kellogg-Briand Pact. But those issues were not involved in Nuremberg—for not even Hitler, had he stood in the dock, could have asserted against the verified minutes of his own meetings that when he gave the marching orders against Poland he was acting in self-defense. Measured by the Nuremberg evidence the problem of the conditions of punishment did not inhere in the general character of the rules laid down in the London Charter, but rather in the extent of the liability of individuals that those rules undertook to prescribe.

We cannot canvass all the problems of this order, but they can be illustrated by references to the case.

1. Article 6 (a) of the Charter defines as a crime against peace not only the preparation and initiation of a war of aggression but also the "waging" of such a war. Does this mean that, once it is established that the German war was, in fact, one of aggression, everyone who participated in waging it has committed an international crime? If so, every soldier who fought in the Wehrmacht in the field, everyone who participated in war production would, at the least, be brought within the rule. To be sure, the prosecution disclaimed any such sweeping contention, insisting, especially in the case of the military men, that it was for their part in fomenting and initiating the war and in the perpetration of war crimes that the charges against them had been filed. Common sense would, indeed, rebel at any conception of liability that failed to take adequate account of the actual choice open to particular individuals living within a national state or, to state the same point in a different way, of the compulsions to support a national policy that they may be wholly unable to influence or to change. The point would perhaps be best met if it were recognized that there are cases in which, so far as international sanctions are concerned, justice may require that superior orders be recognized as a complete defense. Whether such orders should constitute a defense or only a mitigation, or neither, would, in this view, depend on the actual freedom of choice open to individuals in the society of nations as it exists at the particular time. Since the Charter provision barred such orders as a defense in any case, the Tribunal was forced to deal with the issue in other terms. The conviction of Doenitz of waging a war of aggression, compared with the acquittal of Fritzsche, who functioned as a propagandist during the war, suggests that the Tribunal, extremely sensitive to problems of this kind, actually drew the line in terms of the significance of the role played by the particular individual

and the extent of his opportunity for ascertaining the underlying facts about the character of the war.

2.   A similar problem is posed by the affirmation, under the Charter, of liability for conspiracy to wage aggressive war—both as a crime in itself and as a basis of responsibility for substantive offenses committed pursuant to the common plan.

It was, in effect, the submission of the prosecution that the Nazi leaders and their associates were engaged from the start in the furtherance of a program having for its specific objective the attainment of large territorial gains at least in Europe; that from the beginning they were committed to the attainment of those ends by any necessary means—including aggressive wars; that the development of the Nazi Party, the seizure of power, the suppression of free labor, the attack on the Church, the regimentation of youth, the persecution of the Jews and other minorities, the reorganization of the state, rearmament, reoccupation of the Rhineland, Austria, Czechoslovakia and ultimately Poland, and the general war were all contemplated steps in the unfolding of the conspiratorial plan; that after the war began, the plan developed to embrace, as systematic objectives, deportation, pillage and extermination in general disregard of the laws of war; and, finally, that these objectives were so widely publicized and otherwise generally understood that anyone who occupied an important position in party or government or otherwise rendered significant aid to the Nazi cause would necessarily be guilty of criminal participation.

This position, however valid it might be as to Hitler or Goering or even others, was rejected by the Tribunal insofar as it swept everyone into the net. For conspiracy to be criminal under the Charter, "it must not be too far removed from the time of decision and action"; the Tribunal must find evidence of a specific "concrete plan" and "determine the participants in that concrete plan." Everyone who supports a political program is not to be labeled a criminal conspirator merely because, in the perspective of history, the program seems a coherent unity leading to criminal ends. It is for this reason that eleven of the defendants were acquitted on the charge of conspiracy, leading to the total acquittal of Fritzsche, von Papen and Schacht. Shocking it was to give support to Hitler's regime, and repulsive to men of our persuasion, but measured, as it should be, by the standards we would apply to ourselves, more was required to establish complicity in the criminal conspiracy alleged.

It was not enough that von Papen supported the Nazi accession to power, that he aided the Austrian venture (which, being before Munich, was not charged as an aggressive war) or that he served during the war at Ankara—for it was not shown that he was privy to any of the planning that launched the series of aggressive wars. Schacht was in charge of rearmament until 1937, of the Reichsbank until 1939, and not finally dismissed from the government until 1943 —but a majority of the Tribunal was not satisfied that he was privy to the specific purpose of utilizing those armaments for aggressive war. These conclusions involved, of course, the inferences to be drawn from the evidence, and anyone who knows the record will attest the vitality in the judgment of the Tribunal of the principle of reasonable doubt. The point would be indicated less controversially by suggesting a clear case: a welfare officer who concluded that social service was a good even in a Nazi environment, and who did not delude himself as to what Hitler was about, could not have been convicted of criminal participation merely by proving that welfare services contributed to the maintenance of the Nazi hold.

The necessity of such limiting principles is particularly apparent when a charge of criminality pierces the insulation of the national state and the defendants rely heavily on national patriotism to justify their participation in government affairs. It is apparent also for another reason. If liability were asserted in such broad terms that practically everyone within the offending state would sense himself as subject to it, once the die were cast by the initiation of war, the sanctions of the laws of war would have no field of operation. There would, in short, be no incentive for anyone within the country to mitigate the rigors of the conflict or, indeed, to help bring it to an end.

3. Points such as these apply with special force to the charges leveled against the six organizations. The extraordinary provisions of the Charter on which these charges were based were formulated in the view that it would be practically impossible to enforce responsibility under generally accepted theories of accessorial liability if it were necessary to repeat in every individual case the necessarily elaborate proof of the criminal character of particular organizations and groups. It was concluded, accordingly, that a procedure should

be employed to permit the issue of the culpability of organizations to be determined in a single trial in which their leaders would be individual defendants, reserving to particular members the opportunity, should they be prosecuted for their membership, of adducing any evidence that might free them from personal culpability despite their membership in the criminal group. The justification for the device was that it could work no essential injustice since, on the assumptions made, if the evidence in the major trial had been repeated in any of the individual proceedings, the state of the evidence would be such that the defendant would, in any event, be put to his proof.

However plausible in conception, this aspect of the Nuremberg proceeding proved to be a doubtful element. Two million persons at least were included within the scope of the charges and, as the organizations were defined by the indictment, there were inescapable ambiguities in the measure of their actual scope. More than this, the underlying theory faced procedural difficulties of major moment as thousands of members of the challenged organizations offered to testify that they were unaware of the criminal purposes alleged and innocent of any criminal acts. Was the Tribunal to try the issues thus presented, and could it undertake to do so without protracting the main proceeding to wholly impossible lengths?

The problem was resolved, in substance, by the criteria employed by the Tribunal to determine criminality. In the first place, it was held to be essential that the organization charged have actual existence as a group entity, so that individuals when they became members understood that they were identifying themselves with a collective purpose. In the second place, it was required that criminal objectives be shown to be the pervasive purpose of the group as a whole and not merely the secret intentions of its leaders or of some isolated portion of the whole. In the third place, in estimating the criminality of group objectives, the Tribunal employed the same limiting conceptions that were addressed to the conspiracy charge as a whole.

The consequence was not only denial of the declaration of criminality as to three of the accused organizations but rigorous limitations of the declarations made with respect to the Gestapo, the S.S. and the Leadership Corps. Some categories of membership were excluded entirely, notably those which terminated prior to 1939. Even more significantly, the membership to be included was re-defined in the declaration to comprise only those persons who became or remained members voluntarily with knowledge of the criminal objectives, or who themselves participated in the formulation or execution of criminal plans. In the final result, therefore, the declaration of criminality is all but deprived of significance, for in any subsequent proceeding against individual members it will be necessary for the prosecution to establish guilty knowledge or participation; and the proof that will suffice for this purpose would, under ordinary circumstances, suffice to make out an individual case. And this, I submit, is as it should be, for in actual fact, in the present state of knowledge in Germany, there is little excuse for prosecuting anyone if the evidence will not establish an individual case. The denazification program applies, of course, to all Germans and is more than sufficient for other situations—but its justification inheres less in punitive considerations than in the simple premise that the Nazis are least eligible to participate in the reconstruction of Germany and most eligible to perform the disagreeable labor involved in cleaning up the debris of the war. Indeed, the Tribunal recommended, in terms that the Control Council will undoubtedly accept, that anyone convicted only of membership in an organization declared crimlnal should, in any event, be treated no more severely than the denazification law would allow.

I have said enough, I trust, to indicate the type of problem involved in the application of the Charter that seems to me to warrant the closest attention as the process of historical inquiry proceeds. Issues of this kind are inherent in any effort to apply international sanctions to individuals; they find their parallel within the nations in the surprisingly universal conceptions of culpability embodied in municipal penal law.

It will be said that I have spoken of the Nuremberg trial in terms that ignore the entire controversy and, in a genuine sense, my critic will be right. I have not addressed myself to whether a tribunal of the victors could be impartial, to whether the law of the Charter is ex post facto or whether it is "law" at all. These are, indeed, the issues that are currently mooted. But there are elements in the debate that should lead us to be suspicious of the issues as they are drawn in these terms. For, most of those who mount the attack on one or another of these contentions hasten to assure us that their plea is not one of immunity for the defendants; they argue only that they should have been disposed of politically, that is, dispatched out of hand. This is a curious position indeed. A punitive enterprise launched on the basis of general rules, administered in an adversary proceeding under a separation of prosecutive and adjudicative powers is, in the name of law and justice, asserted to be less desirable than an ex parte execution list or a drumhead court-martial constituted in the immediate aftermath of the war. I state my view reservedly when I say that history will accept no conception of law, politics or justice that supports a submission in these terms. Those who choose to do so may view the Nuremberg proceeding as "political" rather than "legal" —a program calling for the judicial application of principles of liability politically defined. They cannot view it as less civilized an institution than a program of organized violence against prisoners, whether directed from the respective capitals or by military commanders in the field.

I will go further, however, and assert that history would have granted short shrift to a program of summary execution, for such a program is intrinsically unreasonable and could not have been carried out without mistake. Moreover, despite the controversy as to whether the Geneva Convention survives unconditional surrender, when no army remains in the field, I cannot conceive for myself that such a program comports with the Convention's demands. If the execution of prisoners without trial is a war crime while hostilities are in progress, I do not see why it is in any better position when hostilities have come to an end. In my view, Justice Jackson was wrong in arguing that the defendants could point to no other law than the London Charter to assure them any hearing at all. They could point to the Geneva Convention. But the substance of his argument was right. Those who relied upon a treaty for their protection could not argue that treaties were without significance as a basis of liability, if their punishment was otherwise just.

No one who examines the record and the judgment, as most of the commentators have not, will question the disinterestedness of the Tribunal; and those who argue that distinterestedness is inherently impossible in this situation may ask themselves why nations that can produce such impartial critics should be intrinsically incapable of producing equally impartial judges. The fact is that the judgment of the Tribunal was mainly a judgment of limitation, its principal operation more significantly that of protecting innocence than that of declaring and punishing guilt. When I speak of "innocence" I mean not only a technical freedom from responsibility under the rules laid down; I mean, more deeply, the exculpation of those who could not justly be declared to be guilty under rules of liability that we would be prepared to apply to ourselves.

No one who is satisfied that the conditions of punishment laid down by the Charter and the Tribunal are essentially just and constructive, in the terms I have previously advanced, will in the end deny them his endorsement on the ground that they are retroactively defined. There is, indeed, too large a disposition among the defenders of Nuremberg to look for stray tags of international pronouncements and reason therefrom that the law of Nuremberg was previously fully laid down. If the Kellogg-Briand Pact or a general conception of international obligation sufficed to authorize England, and would have authorized us, to declare war on Germany in defense of Poland—and in this enterprise to kill countless thousands of German soldiers and civilians—can it be possible that it failed to authorize punitive action against individual Germans judicially determined to be responsible for the Polish attack? To be sure, we would demand a more explicit authorization for punishment in domestic law, for we have adopted for the protection of individuals a prophylactic principle absolutely forbidding retroactivity that we can afford to carry to that extreme. International society, being less stable, can afford less luxury. We admit that in other respects. Why should we deny it here?

There is, however, one point in the current debate that we cannot summarily dismiss. It is the point that the punitive enterprise we have undertaken applies only to the enemy. My concern on this score is not with the contention that sanctions must for this reason be ineffective, a point that I have previously met. Nor is it with the argument that we have established a precedent that some future victor may invoke against us. If we are guilty of aggression we shall merit its invocation; if we are not, we can ask for no more—not alone for ourselves but for our cause—than the opportunity to establish our innocence that the Nuremberg defendants received. My concern is with the point of equality itself, so important an element of justice—

equality in the sense that the sanctions do not apply either to our allies or to ourselves. The Russians cannot be put to their defense in relation to Finland or to Poland. We are obliged to present to no Tribunal the considerations we would advance to justify the manner in which we exhibited to Japan the power of the atom bomb. This is a genuine difficulty—to which the Tribunal indicated its sensitivity in various ways, such as refusing to assess a penalty against Doenitz for submarine violations that did not differ significantly from our own practice in the Pacific, as attested by Admiral Nimitz. To be sure, the depravity of our enemies and the fact that theirs was the aggression accord us such large leeway in this connection that our relative moral position is secure. But this is a mitigation rather than a defense to the inequity that Nuremberg involves.

I do not think that the difficulty argues that we should have abstained from the Nuremberg venture and accorded immunity to the guilty defendants, the only terms on which abstinence would have been real. It argues rather that Nuremberg, far more than San Francisco, was the assumption of an irrevocable obligation—to build a world of just law that shall apply to all, with institutions strong enough to carry it into effect. It is, moreover, as Justice Jackson has so properly reiterated, an obligation assumed as well by those of our allies who participated in the trial or gave it their sanction by adhering to the Charter. If we succeed in that great venture—and no nation can succeed alone—Nuremberg will stand as a cornerstone in the house of peace. If we fail, we shall hear from the German ruins an attack on the Nuremberg judgment as the second "diktat" of Versailles; and, notwithstanding the goodness of our intentions, we may have no sufficient answer.

V FROM YAMASHITA TO EICHMANN

Charles Lyon
THE CASE OF GENERAL YAMASHITA

Charles Lyon, who served on the staff of the prosecution at Nuremberg, clearly and dispassionately surveyed the issues involved in the controversy concerning General Yamashita in his review of A. Frank Reel's The Case of General Yamashita. *One gains from reading it an appreciation of the difficulties which arise for a victor nation when universal standards of justice join battle with the passions aroused by war. The reader will have to assess for himself the validity of General MacArthur's remark about Yamashita: "This officer . . . has failed his duty to his troops, to his country, to his enemy, and to mankind. He has failed utterly his soldier's faith. His life was a blot on the military profession."*

Review of A. Frank Reel, *The Case of General Yamashita* (Chicago: University of Chicago Press, 1949)

This book, which might well be entitled "The Ordeal of General Yamashita," is a highly critical account of the war crimes trial of that Japanese general, written by one of the ten U.S. officers appointed to the staff of defense counsel.

Since the trial took place more than four years ago, a reminder of the basic events is perhaps in order. In the last year of the war Yamashita, once known in the American press as "the tiger of Malaya," became the top Japanese army commander in the Philippine theater; and shortly after the capitulation he was tried before a U.S. military commission composed of American army officers on charges of responsibility for the widespread atrocities by Japanese troops in the final battle for the Philippines. (The trial was not concerned with earlier events, such as the Bataan death march, since Yamashita was not in the Philippines at that time.) A finding of guilty was rendered and sentence of death by hanging imposed by the military commission on December 7, 1945. Review was denied by the Supreme Court of the United States on jurisdictional grounds on February 4, 1946, with notable dissenting opinions by the late Justices Rutledge and Murphy,

Reprinted by permission of the author and publisher from "Review of A. Frank Reel, *The Case of General Yamashita*," *Columbia Law Review* 50 (1950): 394–402. (Footnotes omitted.)

who delivered stinging indictments of the proceedings before the military commission. Clemency was thereupon denied by General MacArthur; and the sentence of hanging thus confirmed was promptly carried out.

Reel's book is, in large part, an elaboration of the bitter criticisms of the trial made by Justices Murphy and Rutledge. The book disclaims any pretensions of being a comprehensive and exhaustive legal analysis of the trial or of the jurisdictional questions presented before the Supreme Court. Written in popular, nonlegalistic style, it tells a vivid, dramatic story of the trial as seen through the eyes of a defense attorney who obviously worked with great zeal, devotion and energy for the client who had so recently been his enemy. Clearly the book was intended to be readable by laymen as well as lawyers, and in this respect it is an eminent success. It is also obviously designed to convey, with shocking impact, a sense of outrage at apparent violations of our ideals of justice and fair play. In this respect, too, the book seems to have been a marked success.

At this point the book presents problems for a conscientious reviewer. Ordinarily a reviewer in these pages deals with a book covering a field or subject matter with which he has some special familiarity, and he thus feels free to express views as to the accuracy or competence of the author's treatment. Here the subject matter is an extremely voluminous trial record available only in Washington, which this reviewer, like others, has not read. In view of this handicap and in view of Reel's sweeping charges of unfairness practiced by the Yamashita military commission and by General MacArthur and his top associates, official comments upon the book have been obtained from General MacArthur's headquarters; and in the interests of fairness these are set forth in [appendixes] to this review.

Reel indicts the Yamashita trial on two main counts, one substantive and one procedural. On the substantive side, Reel freely admits that murder, rape and other atrocities of sadistic cruelty were committed on a very wide scale by Japanese troops during the time Yamashita was in the Philippines; and that these atrocities were practiced on civilian men, women, and children as well as men in uniform. But Reel argues that there was insufficient evidence to hold Yamashita responsible for these acts of his troops. The basic theory of the prosecution and of the military commission's findings was that Yama-

General Yamashita prepares his defense with the counsel assigned to him by the United States Army. (*Reproduced from the collections of the Library of Congress.*)

shita failed to discharge his duty to restrain his troops from committing these wholesale atrocities. The defense contended that, by reason of interservice rivalries in the Japanese command and breakdowns in his communications, Yamashita was not in a position to know of the atrocities charged, particularly those in Manila, much less to prevent them. Reel also deals with some of the prosecution's efforts to link his client with actual orders to commit atrocities or to show direct specific knowledge of their occurrence, and tells quite persuasively why such evidence should not have been believed. (One cannot tell whether such evidence was in fact credited by the commission because its findings, like the verdict of a jury, did not discuss the evidence in detail.)

It is difficult to appraise the net effect of what Reel has to say concerning the substantive side of the case. No one can judge without reading the entire record whether or not it contained evidence to support a finding that Yamashita knew of at least some of the atrocities charged and had the power, in at least some instances, to control the conduct of the troops committing them. Also, it would seem that a large part of Reel's complaint goes to the failure of the commission to believe the bulk of the defendant's own testimony. At the same time he argues that no weight should have been given to Yamashita's statement on cross-examination that "I believe that I did control my troops."

Reel's account of the procedural side of the trial seems the more persuasive part of his book, since many of his criticisms on this head are supported by detailed quotations or references from the record, which presumably speak for themselves. One gathers that the major theme throughout the trial was speed; and the basic dates alone would seem to support this claim. Yamashita surrendered on September 2, 1945. The military commission was designated and defense counsel appointed by October 1st. An arraignment was held on October 8th and the trial commenced on October 29th. (The Nuremberg trials had not yet started, though the German collapse had taken place several months earlier.) The trial was concluded December 5th and—most interesting of all—the commission delivered its findings within less than forty-eight hours, on December 7th, the fateful anniversary date. At the arraignment the prosecution furnished, after some protest, a bill of particulars listing no less than sixty-four sets of crimes committed by Japanese troops. A supplemental bill of particulars, furnished only three days before the trial, added fifty-nine further items. The defense asked for more time to prepare to meet these additional charges and the commission stated that such request would be considered at the close of the prosecution's case. But when that point was reached on November 20th, a motion for continuance was denied; the most the commission would grant was a recess of half a day.

Reel tells us, with impressive references to the record, that speed was sought by the commission in numerous other ways; for example, through widespread use of affidavits alone, with the affiants not made available for cross-examination; narrow limitations by the commission on the scope or length of defense cross-examination; frequent admonishment of defense counsel to cease their procedural objections; browbeating defense witnesses called to establish translation errors; etc.

One also gathers from Reel's book that the commission and other military authorities tried to discourage any resort by the defense to civil courts. The area commander, Lt. General Styer, apparently behaved like an ordinary process-dodger when a copy of a petition for writ of habeas corpus to the Philippine Supreme Court was delivered to his office. And the commission refused to provide the defense with the sixteen copies of the mimeographed record which they were required to supply to that Court.

There are still other matters in Reel's book, which, unlike these basic charges of unfairness, are not found in the record of the case nor in the opinions of Justices Rutledge and Murphy. These matters relate to the role of General MacArthur in the whole affair. Reel tells us that shortly before the commission decided not to grant the defense a continuance, defense counsel accidentally discovered that a cable had been sent from MacArthur's headquarters in Tokyo to the representatives of that headquarters in Manila. Reel's account of the cable is as follows:

> General MacArthur was "disturbed," said the wire, at "reports of a possible continuance" in the Yamashita case; General MacArthur "doubted" the "need of defense for more time"; General MacArthur "urged" haste.

Reel has still more to say about General MacArthur, again purportedly based on some kind of unexplained access to official cables. He says that when defense counsel filed petitions for habeas corpus and certiorari to the Supreme Court of the United States, the War Department "suggested" to the General that he stay execution pending action by the Court; that this suggestion the General declined to follow; and that an outright order from the War Department was necessary. We are also told that, after the Supreme Court had wired, the General affirmed the death sentence without waiting to receive the Supreme Court opinion, including the dissents by the only two justices who discussed the merits of the trial. A portion of General MacArthur's public statement on that occasion is quoted by Reel as follows: "I have reviewed the proceedings in vain search for some mitigating circumstances on his behalf. I can find none . . . . The results are beyond challenge."

These events concerning, or allegedly concerning, General Mac-Arthur, were dealt with in the questions addressed by this reviewer to the Department of the Army. The questions and the response from Brig. Gen. Courtney Whitney of General MacArthur's headquarters appear in the appendix hereto. General Whitney's letter, read literally, does not seem necessarily to constitute a denial of Reel's cablegram stories, though it was evidently meant as such.

Reel's account of the Yamashita trial offers an almost irresistible temptation to pass judgment on war-crimes trials in general, including, of course, the thirteen trials of some two hundred German defendants at Nuremberg. Reel has surrendered to this temptation in a final chapter, which runs largely to such generalizations as "trials by the victor of the vanquished" and "ex post facto" law, a type of discussion in which Reel is no more of an oracle—though perhaps no less —than various other people who have expressed themselves in print in such fashion. A good deal could be said concerning the short-comings of this last chapter, but it is perhaps enough to say that they should not prejudice the reader in assessing the rest of the book. The real strength of Reel's book lies in its very readable account, based on detailed knowledge of the record, of what happened in the Yamashita trial—or at least a very readable version of a part of what happened. A similar knowledge of the Nuremberg record would have disclosed that, happily, the features of the Yamashita case that outraged him find sharp contrasts at Nuremberg.

Indeed, in discussing his substantive charge that Yamashita was convicted without any real evidence of personal responsibility for the acts of his troops, Reel himself states, "Here we find a fundamental difference between the German war-crimes trials in Nuremberg and the Yamashita case," and "Nowhere in the record of the Nuremberg trials can there be found the cavalier disregard of that touchstone of our criminal law—the element of personal culpability—that signalizes the Yamashita case." In fact, a detailed examination of the Nuremberg cases woud have permitted Reel to go still further. He would have found a searching inquiry into the personal position of each defendant, which took into account his actual effective power and authority as well as limitations placed on his freedom of choice; and he would have found a substantial percentage of defendants acquitted, many on a plea of "necessity" or duress, which was given far wider scope than it ever had been in Anglo-American domestic criminal law.

Such an examination of the records would also have shown Reel a striking contrast with the procedures which he tells us were employed in the Yamashita trial. He would have found nothing remotely resembling the speed of his trial, or the various handicaps which he says were placed on his defense, or the response to the defense motion for a continuance. He would have discovered trials that ran from ten months to over a year, in which most of the time was given to the defense. Instead of a one-sentence charge supplemented by a bill of particulars supplied three days before trial, he would have seen lengthy indictments, more detailed than bills of particulars, filed long before trial. If Reel had observed the actual proceedings (as this reviewer did for two years as a prosecutor) he would have seen on the bench not Army officers but judges trained in the traditions of our jurisprudence most of whom were drawn from the highest state courts of this country; and he would have found these courts placing no such limitations on the defense in cross-examination or otherwise, as he tells us he encountered in the Yamashita trial. Reel's book tells us nothing as to the procedures actually employed at Nuremberg, and this omission hardly lends credit to his easy assumption that "all these war-crimes trials . . . are not really trials in the sense that there is an honest possibility of acquittal."

Thus nothing in Reel's book demonstrates that war-crimes trials are generally unfair any more than the Sacco and Vanzetti trial proves that Americans cannot or do not get fair trials in this country. If generalizations are to be drawn, the one most naturally suggested by the entire thrust of his book is that, unhappily, justice can become strongly diluted with expediency in Army trial proceedings. (This, of course, in no way excuses the Yamashita proceedings, although Reel at one point seems to employ such a line of reasoning when he states that Japanese "trials" of Philippine guerillas were the same sort of trials given Japanese enlisted men.)

Reel's book thus stands as a sharp indictment (though perhaps not conviction) of Army justice, and more particularly of those of our military who were concerned with this case. With all reservations that one should make who has not read the full record, it is still difficult to see how Reel's charges can be completely explained away, at least as to the procedural lapses he enumerates. We find no such complete explanation, at any rate, in the lengthy memorandum issued by General MacArthur's headquarters, which relies heavily on the majority opinion of the Supreme Court. For example, we are told:

> *The book is essentially an attack upon our American system of jurisprudence—indeed, it might better be said upon our American system—in the refusal of the author, a practicing attorney, to accept the judgment of the United States Supreme Court, acting through a majority thereof, on issues both argued before that tribunal and discussed in the book. . . . The author but shows himself unable to accept the ethical base establishing in our country the primacy of majority decision.*

Of course, the fact is that the majority opinion did not discuss, much less approve, the procedural conduct of the Yamashita trial, because it decided it had no jurisdiction to inquire into the matter; and the only two members of the Court, Rutledge and Murphy, who felt they should make this inquiry criticized the trial in the strongest possible terms.

Beyond that, any charge that it is un-American to question the wisdom of a majority opinion of the Supreme Court would impeach not only Mr. Reel but also the entire American bar and bench as well as the Supreme Court itself.

Appendix A. Brig. Gen. Courtney Whitney, Chief, Government Section, General Headquarters, Supreme Commander for the Allied Powers, The Case of General Yamashita, A Memorandum 21 (1949)

. . . Highly questionable as much that the author has said may be, his right to say it is not here in issue. What is in issue is the translation of his book into the Japanese language and its dissemination among the Japanese people. The interest of the United States in the security of the American forces occupying the country render it so. To protect that interest and preserve that security it is essential to guard against inflammatory material designed to arouse irresponsible Japanese elements into active opposition. The book contains just such inflammatory material in its biased and shameless distortion and suppression of the facts in the effort to secure Yamashita's vindication in the minds of its readers. The common sense of the great majority of the Japanese people would reject the false concept it is intended to propagate as they have witnessed at first hand the spiritual qualities of the American soldier and the moral strength and righteousness of American justice. But it is of the irresponsible elements and opposition minorities with which we must concern ourselves. The trial of Yamashita and entire detail of the legal proceedings leading to his execution were widely carried at the time in the Japanese press without the slightest restriction—hence there is no mere question of censorship involved. Far more than that is involved; the question of American prestige, American dignity, and American security.

Appendix B. Letter, Brig. Gen. Courtney Whitney, to Charles S. Lyon, January 7, 1950

The questions you recently submitted to the Department of the Army with respect to the trial of General Yamashita have been referred to this headquarters. In general, the answers may be found in the accompanying memorandum prepared in view of the inspired publicity attending efforts by the publishers of "The Case of General Yamashita" to secure its sale among the Japanese people in the Japanese language.

The specific references you cite to illustrate the alleged admonishment of defense counsel by the Military Commission are confined to undocumented generalities by the book's author, despite the availability to him of the trial record for detailed specification. Admonishment of counsel is of course no more a novelty in military than in civil jurisprudence, but the undocumented pleading thereof, years after final adjudication of the issues, hardly merits serious consideration.

As to the other allegations you mention, similarly general and undocumented, you should understand in the first place that the military commisssion which heard the Yamashita case was appointed by the Commanding General, Philippine-Ryukyus Command, Lieutenant General Wilhelm D. Styer, with headquarters in Manila, which officer thereafter had exclusive jurisdiction over the subject matter until jurisdiction passed to General MacArthur as the Theater Commander upon and solely by virtue of the former's approval of a sentence involving death. Had any lesser sentence been adjudged, this headquarters would in all probability not even have received a copy of the trial record.

There is indeed little in the book itself which partakes of the character of a legal discussion, susceptible to clear analysis or detailed rebuttal, as the author obviously writes as a novelist making frequent calls upon literary license.

While General MacArthur, as the Theater Commander, in the exercise of his overall responsibility for the apprehension and trial of war criminals, issued the orders establishing the broad procedures to be followed, he at no time personally intervened either in the Yamashita trial or any other war crimes proceedings, except such as had been, because of the nature of the sentence involved, formally referred for his review. Supported by ample legal precedent, he did consistently adhere to the view that neither the civil courts of the Philippines nor of the United States could lawfully assume jurisdiction over cases duly referred for trial to military courts. As you know, this view was fully sustained by both the Philippine and United States Supreme Courts. Despite this, at no time, even as to the major war criminals whose cases were adjudged by the International Military Tribunal for the Far East, was any move made toward the execution of a sentence of death while any appellate procedure was pending before the United States Supreme Court.

The author's contention that General MacArthur should have awaited formal receipt of the minority dissent to Chief Justice Stone's majority opinion on the Yamashita case before himself taking action thereon, defies both reason and logic. At once officially advised by radio of the Supreme Court's judgment, the General had no alternative, repugnant as the duty was, than to proceed in the discharge of his own responsibility. By what strange process of reasoning can it be argued that, to the contrary, he was bound in duty or propriety to stay his action until informed of the rejected dictum of a minority dissent? But apart from this, it so happens that the minority opinion was widely carried, along with the majority, by the news services, giving General MacArthur full information thereon before acting upon the Yamashita case.

The book in reference first came to the attention of this headquarters through efforts made to market it in Japan in the Japanese language. This is discussed at length in the accompanying memorandum, but briefly in effect such a move would be to propagate among the Japanese people the theses, among others, that (1) Yamashita had been denied elementary justice by General MacArthur and our highest civil and military tribunals, and (2) that "the cruel Japanese Kempeitai (special military police) were essentially clever imitators" of historic American example. The proceedings in the trial of Yamashita, including those on appeal before the Philippine and United States Supreme Courts, were widely reported in the Japanese press without the slightest censorship or restriction. At this late date, when public memory of the related facts in the case has necessarily grown dim, the effort to propagate such theses, in the sensitive atmosphere of an occupied country, could obviously have a dangerously unsettling effect upon the less informed among the Japanese through its use as a coercive propaganda weapon by subversive minority elements.

These theses, of course, have no basis in truth, but it is shocking indeed on this delicately balanced outpost constantly facing formidable subversive propaganda from the Asiatic mainland, to see Americans join in the campaign of vilification, adding their weight to existing pressures directed at undermining Japanese faith in American justice and morality.

As a member of the legal profession, I am sure that so distinguished a journal as the Columbia Law Review would not undertake a review of a book of the character involved without careful examination of the trial record, voluminous as it is, to distinguish between fact and fiction. Even more, if discussion of the Yamashita trial incidents is indeed considered contributory to the knowledge and development of jurisprudence, objectivity would seem to demand that such trial record be the locus of inquiry rather than the obviously biased viewpoint of an attorney unable, even at this late date, to accept the due and final decisions under the judicial process.

Robert K. Woetzel

THE EICHMANN CASE IN INTERNATIONAL LAW

Robert K. Woetzel is a recognized authority on the Nuremberg trials. He is President, Foundation for the Establishment of an International Criminal Court, professor of international law and politics at Boston College, and Secretary-General of the International Criminal Law Commission. His work analyzing the legal problems of Nuremberg appeared under the title The Nuremberg Trials in International Law. *He also entered the lists on the* Eichmann *case which not only raised many old issues but inspired a bitter controversy along entirely new lines as well. Professor Woetzel treats the following points in his article: that Eichmann was abducted from Argentina in violation of international law; that the state of Israel, acting as the prosecution, was not in existence at the time Eichmann's crimes were committed and therefore had no jurisdiction in the case; and finally, that the Geneva Convention on Genocide of 1948 calls for a trial either by the country where the crimes were perpetrated or by an international tribunal. Israel, he argues, met neither of these requirements.*

Since the Nuremberg trials ended, a number of similar proceedings have taken place. One of the most important of these is the trial of Adolf Eichmann, former Chief of the Jewish Affairs Section of the Reich Security Head Office who was entrusted with the so-called "final solution of the Jewish question." In this capacity Eichmann assisted in the liquidation of several million Jews at Auschwitz and other Nazi extermination camps. He also participated in the famous Wannsee Conference in Berlin in 1942 where plans were discussed for the "final solution." He was both an architect and chief executor of the policy which led to the death of almost six million persons. For fifteen years after the war he managed to evade justice, until in 1960 he was abducted by agents of the State of Israel from his hiding place in Argentina. He was brought to Jerusalem for trial before an Israeli court on charges of "crimes against the Jewish people," crimes against humanity, war crimes and membership in a hostile organization as defined in the Israeli Nazi and Nazi Collaborators (Punishment) Law of 1950.

The Nuremberg and Eichmann trials differed in many respects. The

From *Criminal Law Review* [London] (October 1962), pp. 671–682. Reprinted by permission of the author and the publisher, Sweet & Maxwell Ltd. (Footnotes omitted.)

150

basis of jurisdiction of the court in the *Eichmann* case was not the same as that of the International Military Tribunal at Nuremberg, and the legal character of the law applied in these cases was also different. The basis of jurisdiction of the IMT at Nuremberg was the endorsement of the "quasi-totality of civilized states" acting through the United Nations War Crimes Commission before the trial, and confirmed by the U.N. General Assembly afterwards; it can, therefore, be considered an international court convened *ad hoc* for the prosecution of the German war criminals. It also applied international law as laid down in the Charter of the IMT and elaborated in the judgment of the Court which received the unanimous confirmation of the international community acting through the United Nations in the General Assembly Resolution 1 (95) of December 11, 1946, and has since been formulated by the International Law Commission in a report which was accepted as of December 12, 1950.

The international basis of the succeeding Nuremberg trials was less clear: they were based on Allied Control Council Law No. 10 of December 20, 1945, but were held under American auspices; the international character of the trials has, therefore, been denied by some writers. They resembled the IMT in the law that was applied, as did the International Military Tribunal at Tokyo and other war crimes trials held after the Second World War; but neither Control Council Law No. 10 on which they were based, nor the judgments, were confirmed by the international community, which is very different from the case of the IMT.

The Israeli court which tried Eichmann did not lay claim to being international in its legal character or representing the international community. Its jurisdiction in the case was initially challenged on several counts. In view of the abduction of Eichmann from Argentina, which was censured by the Security Council of the United Nations, in a resolution of June 23, 1960, denouncing it as a "violation of the sovereignty of a Member State . . . incompatible with the Charter of the United Nations," it was contended that an Israeli court should not take jurisdiction over him: *ex injuria jus non oritur*. Furthermore, according to the principle known in the United States as the doctrine of the "fruit of the poisonous tree," a thing acquired by illegal means, such as an unlawful search and seizure, must be restored to its original owner.

Counsel for the defense at the trial, Dr. Servatius, also submitted that the fact that the judges on the tribunal were of the Jewish nation and the State of Israel might prejudice them against the accused, in view of the charges involved. Finally, counsel contended that the court was not competent to try the deeds, since they were acts of state committed before the existence of the State of Israel.

Judge Landau, speaking for the court, rejected these claims in a ruling of April 17, 1961, and declared that it was immaterial how the accused had been brought to Israel as long as he was within the jurisdiction of Israel; courts had assumed jurisdiction in similar cases before. The official character of the actions charged to Eichmann did not invalidate the competence of the court. Furthermore, the court applied Israel law not international law, which is one of the main distinguishing marks between national and international tribunals. The court repeated these arguments in its judgment and contended further that Israeli law was not in conflict with international law on these points.

The issue of abduction is of particular importance in the *Eichmann* case. The position of the Israeli court on the abduction issue has been supported by certain writers on the grounds that " 'morality' overrides 'other' rules of 'positive law.' " It has been contended that the special circumstances in the *Eichmann* case justified Israel's action. It is clear that particularly grave charges were involved in the *Eichmann* case both from a moral and legal standpoint, but arguments based on morality can easily be stretched and the limits of action are often difficult to define, so that they are controversial and must be used sparingly.

It is true, however, as the Israeli tribunal indicated, that courts had assumed jurisdiction over similar cases involving criminal offenses, although the accused had been brought into their territorial jurisdiction by unlawful means. Among the most important of these were *Ex. p. Elliott, Ker* v. *Illinois* and *Frisbie* v. *Collins*; in the *Ker* case an abduction was committed in Peru which was in violation of a treaty between the United States and that country. These few precedents would not necessarily confirm a principle of customary international law, even if in a particular situation the obligation of bringing a person to justice might have seemed more important from a moral standpoint than other considerations. According to the rule *ex injuria jus non oritur,* Israel would not ordinarily have been entitled to assume jurisdiction over Eichmann upon having him abducted.

Furthermore, Eichmann's actions did not take place on Israeli territory nor were citizens of Israel affected by them, since they occurred several years before the establishment of the State of Israel. An Israeli court would not, therefore, ordinarily have jurisdiction in such a case under the territoriality principle or an extension of it to cover actions affecting citizens of a prosecuting state outside of its territorial boundaries as in the *Lotus* case. On the other hand, it must be pointed out that the territoriality principle has been breached in various instances, thus in cases covered by the universal principle of jurisdiction, according to which international crimes like piracy or trade in slaves can be punished in any state regardless of where or when they were committed, since they affect the common interest of mankind. Furthermore, positive international law does not contain express rules limiting the development of the international criminal law of the various nations. But the practice of states shows that certain norms like the territoriality principle have evolved which do not form a general body of rules, but which have been construed as limiting the nations in their right to prosecute foreign nationals.

The same can be said for the nationality principle, according to which a country may take jurisdiction in a case involving one or more of its nationals. Eichmann was not a national of Israel, and the court was, therefore, not justified in trying him under this principle. The argument that "quasi-nationality" or the "link" between Israel and the Jews who suffered from Eichmann's deeds justified the court's action in assuming jurisdiction will be examined later in this discussion.

Next the argument must be considered that the Israeli tribunal could not try Eichmann, because his deeds amounted to acts of state committed in the name of the German government. While it is correct that the principle of the equality of sovereign nations does not allow for the prosecution by one government of the acts of another government, it is generally recognized that this applies only to those acts of state which are within the competence of the government authorizing them and within its sphere of jurisdiction. Insofar as Eichmann's actions were violations of the sovereign rights of another state and outside of the competence of the German government, the defense of act-of-state would not apply. Countries whose citizens suffered harm from Eichmann's actions could, therefore, assume jurisdiction over him. But serious objections might still be raised against an Israeli court, since Israeli citizens were not involved at the time the actions were committed. Furthermore, arguments might also be made on the basis of the territoriality and nationality principles against an Israeli court assuming jurisdiction over actions by German authorities affecting German citizens.

The court in the *Eichmann* case has also been criticized for applying ex post facto law, especially with regard to the delict of "crimes against the Jewish people." Furthermore, the fact that the death penalty can be administered for such acts, while it has been generally abolished in the state of Israel, adds to the exceptional character of the law under which Eichmann was tried. It is undeniable, of course, that the charges against Eichmann were exceptionally grave. The special delict of "crimes against the Jewish people" is novel, both in national and international law; insofar as ordinary war crimes and crimes against humanity were involved—and the charges tended to overlap—as well as in the case of the rather more controversial delict of membership in a criminal or hostile organization, which resembles the Anglo-Saxon concept of conspiracy, it is clear that given proper jurisdiction of the court a person might be tried for such actions under national and international law. They had been tried before the IMT at Nuremberg; the judgment of the court was unanimously confirmed by the United Nations and the principles have been codified in international law. The objection against ex post facto legislation would, therefore, not apply to such acts. The arguments, however, that Israel was not a belligerent state in the Second World War, that the crimes were not committed on its territory, and that Eichmann did not as a German national fall under its jurisdiction must still be considered serious challenges to the competence of the Jerusalem court.

It has been contended that universal jurisdiction exists for the actions charged, since they amounted to genocide. The Israeli tribunal based its authority as the *forum deprehensionis* or court of the country in which the accused is actually held in custody on various cases in which the towns of northern Italy had during the Middle Ages tried certain types of criminals ("banditi, vagabundi, assassini") who happened to be within their jurisdiction, regardless of where their actions had been committed. It mentioned that the basis of authority of such a court had been referred to in the *Corpus Juris Civilis*, *"ubi de criminibus agi oportet."* The tribunal further maintained that Grotius had approved of the right of states to try crimes committed outside of their sphere of jurisdiction, if "these violate in extreme form, in relation to any persons, the law of nature or the law of nations." Finally, it stated that the crime of genocide could be tried under the universal principle of jurisdiction like piracy, and it cited various authorities, including Vattel, Blackstone, and Wheaton, to prove that courts of any country could assume jurisdiction over pirates, since they were *hostis humani generis.*

It is clear that certain acts like piracy can be tried under the universal principle of jurisdiction. The issue involved in the *Eichmann* case is whether the offenses with which he was charged fell into this category of actions. The precedents cited by the Israeli tribunal from the Middle Ages as well as the statements by Grotius would not necessarily establish a basis for assuming jurisdiction over actions which had not been tried previously under the universal principle. The Italian cases took place within a different framework of international law prior to the establishment of nation states and modern international law after 1648, and the opinions of writers do not necessarily establish principles of international law. It must be determined, therefore, whether or not there existed a practice to try such cases, any agreements between nations, or laws like the Israeli Nazi and Nazi Collaborators ((Punishment) Law in other countries which would provide a basis for the jurisdiction of the tribunal in the *Eichmann* case according to customary or conventional international law, or the "general principles of law recognized by civilized nations," referred to in Article 38 of the Statute of the International Court of Justice. Needless to say, the Jerusalem court was not bound to apply international law, but Israeli law. Nevertheless, its contention that the offenses defined in the Israeli law were also international crimes must be tested according to standards of international law.

Crimes against humanity involving genocide were tried by the IMT at Nuremberg. The Israeli court stated, therefore, that ". . . all that has been said in the Nuremberg principles on the 'crime against

humanity' applies *a fortiori* to the 'crime against the Jewish people'."
The tribunal also compared the other crimes with which Eichmann
was charged to the delicts defined in the Charter of the IMT and
Control Council Law No. 10. But the IMT was an international court,
and the intervention of the Allies in sponsoring a trial of such acts
committed by Germans against their fellow citizens as crimes against
humanity was justified by the exceptional conditions prevailing in
Germany at the time and the endorsement of the quasi-totality of
civilized states. Other Allied tribunals, which were not necessarily
international in character, tried similar acts under Control Council
Law No. 10. Their basis of jurisdiction is controversial, as has been
indicated previously, and they have not been confirmed by the international community, in contrast to the IMT. If they are considered
national tribunals, they might be regarded as limited precedents for
the trial of Eichmann before a national Israeli court for crimes against
humanity. This could be disputed, however, since the subsequent
Nuremberg proceedings were based on multinational or inter-Allied
agreement, which was not the case in the Eichmann trial. There seems
to be little basis in customary international law and the practice of
states for the assumption of the Israeli tribunal that crimes against
humanity involving genocide can be tried under the universal principle
of jurisdiction.

As far as conventional international law is concerned, the Genocide
Convention of 1948 is based on the territoriality principle. While the
Geneva Convention on Prisoners of War of 1949 established the
universal principle of jurisdiction for ordinary war crimes, Article
6 of the Genocide Convention provides that "Persons charged with
genocide or any of the other acts enumerated in article III shall be
tried by a competent tribunal of the states in the territory of which
the act was committed, or by such international penal tribunal as may
have jurisdiction with respect to those contracting parties which
shall have accepted its jurisdiction."

The court in the *Eichmann* case argued that the Convention fulfills
two roles: in the sphere of customary international law it re-affirms
the principle that "genocide, whether in times of peace or in times of
war, is a crime under international law"; in the sphere of conventional
international law it establishes obligations between the contracting
parties for the prevention and punishment of crimes of genocide in

the future. According to an Advisory Opinion of the International Court of Justice of May 28, 1951, given at the request of the United Nations General Assembly on the question of the reservations to the Convention, "the principles inherent in the convention are acknowledged by the civilized nations as binding on the country even without a conventional obligation"; the Court further stated that "The Genocide Convention was . . . intended by the General Assembly and by the contracting parties to be definitely universal in scope. It was in fact approved on December 9, 1948, by a resolution [No. 96 (1)] which was unanimously adopted by fifty-six States."

The Israeli tribunal maintained, therefore, that the conventional obligation established by Article 6 applied *ex nunc* and not *ex tunc*. Since the offenses with which Eichmann was charged were violations of principles of international law even without a conventional obligation, and since they were committed *before* the acceptance of the Genocide Convention by the General Assembly, the court concluded that Article 6 did not apply in his case.

The court is correct in stating that a conventional obligation need not apply *ex tunc*, unless this is specifically provided for as part of the agreement, and that the crime of genocide could, according to the International Court of Justice, be considered a violation of a principle of customary international law even before the Genocide Convention. But this would not necessarily establish the universal principle of jurisdiction for crimes of genocide; nor would the assumption that the provisions of Article 6 of the Genocide Convention are not exhaustive. Further basis for such a conclusion would have to be sought in the practice of states, conventional international law, general principles of law, judicial decisions, and the writings of eminent authorities. It has been indicated, however, that very little basis exists in customary international law for the extension of the universal principle to crimes of genocide. At the time of the conclusion of the Eichmann trial there were no further international agreements or pronouncements of the United Nations, nor decisions of national or international tribunals, aside from certain trials which followed the IMT at Nuremberg, that would support such an extension. There is also no overwhelming consensus of opinion among lawyers in favor of the basis claimed for the trial. While the territoriality and nationality principles have been breached in the laws of some countries, they are generally recognized as safeguards of justice. It is impossible, therefore, to conclude that the provisions of the Israeli Nazi and Nazi Collaborators (Punishment) Law which establishes the jurisdiction of Israeli courts over certain crimes regardless of the place where they were committed or the nationality of the defendant represent "general principles of law recognized by civilized nations."

It must be concluded, therefore, that the court in the *Eichmann* case was not justified in claiming a basis in customary international law for the extension of the universal principle of jurisdiction to crimes against humanity involving genocide. The same would hold true for the delict of membership in a criminal organization. As far as ordinary war crimes are concerned, it is true that the Geneva Convention of 1949 established the universal principle of jurisdiction for such offenses, but it is controversial whether it would apply *ex tunc*. There are few precedents to support the jurisdiction of a state to try war crimes which were committed by another national against citizens of a third state, if the act did not take place on its territory.

The argument that Israel has a moral right to try crimes against Jews regardless of where or when they were committed does not have much basis in law. Jews who are not citizens of Israel do not fall under the jurisdiction of the State of Israel, and an extension of jurisdiction of the courts of Israel to cover actions committed outside of the territorial limits of that state and involving injury to aliens who may have a connection with persons in Israel and other countries on account of their race or religion, would amount to an unwarranted extension of the nationality principle. The Israeli Prime Minister Ben-Gurion made such a claim for jurisdiction at the time of the Eichmann trial, on the grounds that Israel as the Jewish state represented world Jewry and had a right to protect Jews everywhere from injury; and the Israeli court also refers to the right of a victim nation to try those who assault its existence. But Israel as a state did not exist at the time the acts charged were committed and the "very striking connection" between the Jewish people and the State of Israel which the court mentions in its judgment is not covered under any extension of the nationality principle or the "passive personality principle" as it has also been called, according to which a nation may assume criminal jurisdiction when one of its citizens is the victim of a crime. No unilateral action by the Israeli Government or an Israeli court could make it a principle of international law without the consent of the community of states through practice or agreement. The competence of the Israeli court in trying crimes against the Jewish people, therefore, clearly derived from national law and not from international law or practice.

In conclusion, it should be pointed out that many of the criticisms concerning the jurisdiction of the tribunal in the *Eichmann* case could have been avoided through the institution of an international trial. The IMT at Nuremberg would have been sufficient precedent for such a proceeding, and the occasion might have afforded an ideal opportunity to have the law of Nuremberg applied by an international tribunal appointed by the United Nations acting for the international community.

VI THE LEGAL DEBATE OVER AGGRESSION IN VIETNAM

Office of the Legal Adviser, U.S. Department of State

THE LEGALITY OF UNITED STATES PARTICIPATION IN THE DEFENSE OF VIETNAM

In response to both congressional and public criticism of the American involvement in Vietnam, the Office of the Legal Adviser of the Department of State undertook in 1966 to draw up an official defense of the Administration's policies. The object was to demonstrate that the United States had acted in complete accord with international law. This position embraced the following points of law: that both individual and collective defense is sanctioned in the face of aggression; that North Vietnam had violated the Geneva Accords of 1954; and that by intervening the President of the United States was within his rights both because of his constitutional authority, and Washington's SEATO treaty commitments.

March 4, 1966

1. THE UNITED STATES AND SOUTH VIETNAM HAVE THE RIGHT UNDER INTERNATIONAL LAW TO PARTICIPATE IN THE COLLECTIVE DEFENSE OF SOUTH VIETNAM AGAINST ARMED ATTACK

In response to requests from the Government of South Vietnam, the United States has been assisting that country in defending itself against armed attack from the Communist North. This attack has taken the forms of externally supported subversion, clandestine supply of arms, infiltration of armed personnel, and most recently the sending of regular units of the North Vietnamese army into the South.

International law has long recognized the right of individual and collective self-defense against armed attack. South Vietnam and the United States are engaging in such collective defense consistent with international law and with United States obligations under the United Nations Charter.

From "The Legality of United States Participation In the Defense of Viet-Nam," *Department of State Bulletin* 54:1396 (March 28, 1966): 474–489. (Footnotes omitted.)

A. South Vietnam Is Being Subjected to Armed Attack by Communist North Vietnam

The Geneva accords of 1954 established a demarcation line between North Vietnam and South Vietnam. They provided for withdrawals of military forces into the respective zones north and south of this line. The accords prohibited the use of either zone for the resumption of hostilities or to "further an aggressive policy."

During the five years following the Geneva conference of 1954, the Hanoi regime developed a covert political-military organization in South Vietnam based on Communist cadres it had ordered to stay in the South, contrary to the provisions of the Geneva accords. The activities of this covert organization were directed toward the kidnaping and assassination of civilian officials—acts of terrorism that were perpetrated in increasing numbers.

In the three-year period from 1959 to 1961, the North Vietnam regime infiltrated an estimated 10,000 men into the South. It is estimated that 13,000 additional personnel were infiltrated in 1962, and, by the end of 1964, North Vietnam may well have moved over 40,000 armed and unarmed guerrillas into South Vietnam.

The International Control Commission reported in 1962 the findings of its Legal Committee:

> . . . there is evidence to show that arms, armed and unarmed personnel, munitions and other supplies have been sent from the Zone in the North to the Zone in the South with the objective of supporting, organizing and carrying out hostile activities, including armed attacks, directed against the Armed Forces and Administration of the Zone in the South.
>
> . . . there is evidence that the PAVN [People's Army of Vietnam] has allowed the Zone in the North to be used for inciting, encouraging and supporting hostile activities in the Zone in the South, aimed at the overthrow of the Administration in the South.

Beginning in 1964, the Communists apparently exhausted their reservoir of Southerners who had gone North. Since then the greater number of men infiltrated into the South have been native-born North Vietnamese. Most recently, Hanoi has begun to infiltrate elements of the North Vietnamese army in increasingly large numbers. Today, there is evidence that nine regiments of regular North Vietnamese forces are fighting in organized units in the South.

In the guerrilla war in Vietnam, the external aggression from the North is the critical military element of the insurgency, although it is unacknowledged by North Vietnam. In these circumstances, an "armed attack" is not as easily fixed by date and hour as in the case of traditional warfare. However, the infiltration of thousands of armed men clearly constitutes an "armed attack" under any reasonable definition. There may be some question as to the exact date at which North Vietnam's aggression grew into an "armed attack," but there can be no doubt that it had occurred before February 1965.

B. International Law Recognizes the Right of Individual and Collective Self-Defense against Armed Attack

International law has traditionally recognized the right of self-defense against armed attack. This proposition has been asserted by writers on international law through the several centuries in which the modern law of nations has developed. The proposition has been acted on numerous times by governments throughout modern history. Today the principle of self-defense against armed attack is universally recognized and accepted.

The Charter of the United Nations, concluded at the end of World War II, imposed an important limitation on the use of force by United Nations members. Article 2, paragraph 4, provides:

> *All Members shall refrain in their international relations from the threat or use of force against the territorial integrity or political independence of any state, or in any other manner inconsistent with the Purposes of the United Nations.*

In addition, the charter embodied a system of international peace-keeping through the organs of the United Nations. Article 24 summarizes these structural arrangements in stating that the United Nations members:

> . . . confer on the Security Council primary responsibility for the maintenance of international peace and security, and agree that in carrying out its duties under this responsibility the Security Council acts on their behalf.

However, the charter expressly states in article 51 that the remaining provisions of the charter—including the limitation of article 2, paragraph 4, and the creation of United Nations machinery to keep the peace—in no way diminish the inherent right of self-defense against armed attack. Article 51 provides:

> Nothing in the present Charter shall impair the inherent right of individual or collective self-defense if an armed attack occurs against a Member of the United Nations, until the Security Council has taken the measures necessary to maintain international peace and security. Measures taken by Members in the exercise of this right of self-defense shall be immediately reported to the Security Council and shall not in any way affect the authority and responsibility of the Security Council under the present Charter to take at any time such action as it deems necessary in order to maintain or restore international peace and security.

Thus, article 51 restates and preserves, for member states in the situations covered by the article, a long-recognized principle of international law. The article is a "saving clause" designed to make clear that no other provision in the charter shall be interpreted to impair the inherent right of self-defense referred to in article 51.

Three principal objections have been raised against the availability of the right of individual and collective self-defense in the case of Vietnam: (1) that this right applies only in the case of an armed attack on a United Nations member; (2) that it does not apply in the case of South Vietnam because the latter is not an independent sovereign state; and (3) that collective self-defense may be undertaken only by a regional organization operating under chapter VIII of the United Nations Charter. These objections will now be considered in turn.

C. The Right of Individual and Collective Self-Defense Applies in the Case of South Vietnam Whether or Not That Country Is a Member of the United Nations

1. South Vietnam enjoys the right of self-defense. The argument that the right of self-defense is available only to members of the United Nations mistakes the nature of the right of self-defense and the relationship of the United Nations Charter to international law in this respect. As already shown, the right of self-defense against armed attack is an inherent right under international law. The right is not conferred by the charter, and, indeed, article 51 expressly recognizes that the right is inherent.

The charter nowhere contains any provision designed to deprive nonmembers of the right of self-defense against armed attack. Article 2, paragraph 6, does charge the United Nations with responsibility for insuring that nonmember states act in accordance with United Nations "principles so far as may be necessary for the maintenance of international peace and security." Protection against aggression and self-defense against armed attack are important elements in the whole charter scheme for the maintenance of international peace and security. To deprive nonmembers of their inherent right of self-defense would not accord with the principles of the organization, but would instead be prejudicial to the maintenance of peace. Thus article 2, paragraph 6—and, indeed, the rest of the charter— should certainly not be construed to nullify or diminish the inherent defensive rights of nonmembers.

2. The United States has the right to assist in the defense of South Vietnam although the latter is not a United Nations member. The cooperation of two or more international entities in the defense of one or both against armed attack is generally referred to as collective self-defense. United States participation in the defense of South Vietnam at the latter's request is an example of collective self-defense.

The United States is entitled to exercise the right of individual or collective self-defense against armed attack, as that right exists in international law, subject only to treaty limitations and obligations undertaken by this country.

It has been urged that the United States has no right to participate in the collective defense of South Vietnam because article 51 of the United Nations Charter speaks only of the situation "if an armed attack occurs *against a Member of the United Nations.*" This argument is without substance.

In the first place, article 51 does not impose restrictions or cut down the otherwise available rights of United Nations members. By its own terms, the article preserves an inherent right. It is, therefore, necessary to look elsewhere in the charter for any obligation of members restricting their participation in collective defense of an entity that is not a United Nations member.

Article 2, paragraph 4, is the principal provision of the charter imposing limitations on the use of force by members. It states that they:

> . . . *shall refrain in their international relations from the threat or use of force against the territorial integrity or political independence of any state, or in any other manner inconsistent with the Purposes of the United Nations.*

Action taken in defense against armed attack cannot be characterized as falling within this proscription. The record of the San Francisco conference makes clear that article 2, paragraph 4, was not intended to restrict the right of self-defense against armed attack.

One will search in vain for any other provision in the charter that would preclude United States participation in the collective defense of a nonmember. The fact that article 51 refers only to armed attack "against a Member of the United Nations" implies no intention to preclude members from participating in the defense of nonmembers. Any such result would have seriously detrimental consequences for international peace and security and would be inconsistent with the purposes of the United Nations as they are set forth in article 1 of the charter. The right of members to participate in the defense of nonmembers is upheld by leading authorities on international law.

D. The Right of Individual and Collective Self-Defense Applies Whether or Not South Vietnam Is Regarded as an Independent Sovereign State

1. South Vietnam enjoys the right of self-defense. It has been asserted that the conflict in Vietnam is "civil strife" in which foreign intervention is forbidden. Those who make this assertion have gone so far as to compare Ho Chi Minh's actions in Vietnam with the efforts of President Lincoln to preserve the Union during the American Civil War. Any such characterization is an entire fiction disregarding the actual situation in Vietnam. The Hanoi regime is anything but the legitimate government of a unified country in which the South is rebelling against lawful national authority.

The Geneva accords of 1954 provided for a division of Vietnam into two zones at the 17th parallel. Although this line of demarcation was intended to be temporary, it was established by international agreement, which specifically forbade aggression by one zone against the other.

The Republic of Vietnam in the South has been recognized as a separate international entity by approximately 60 governments the world over. It has been admitted as a member of a number of the specialized agencies of the United Nations. The United Nations General Assembly in 1957 voted to recommend South Vietnam for membership in the organization, and its admission was frustrated only by the veto of the Soviet Union in the Security Council.

In any event there is no warrant for the suggestion that one zone of a temporarily divided state—whether it be Germany, Korea, or Vietnam—can be legally overrun by armed forces from the other zone, crossing the internationally recognized line of demarcation between the two. Any such doctrine would subvert the international agreement establishing the line of demarcation, and would pose grave dangers to international peace.

The action of the United Nations in the Korean conflict of 1950 clearly established the principle that there is no greater license for one zone of a temporarily divided state to attack the other zone than there is for one state to attack another state. South Vietnam has the same right that South Korea had to defend itself and to organize collective defense against an armed attack from the North. A resolution of the Security Council dated June 25, 1950, noted "with grave concern the armed attack upon the Republic of Korea by forces from North Korea," and determined "that this action constitutes a breach of the peace."

2. The United States is entitled to participate in the collective defense of South Vietnam whether or not the latter is regarded as an independent sovereign state. As stated earlier, South Vietnam has been recognized as a separate international entity by approximately 60 governments. It has been admitted to membership in a number of the United Nations specialized agencies and has been excluded from the United Nations Organization only by the Soviet veto.

There is nothing in the charter to suggest that United Nations members are precluded from participating in the defense of a recognized international entity against armed attack merely because the entity may lack some of the attributes of an independent sovereign state. Any such result would have a destructive effect on the stability of international engagements such as the Geneva accords of 1954 and on internationally agreed lines of demarcation. Such a result, far from being in accord with the charter and the purposes of the United Nations, would undermine them and would create new dangers to international peace and security.

E. The United Nations Charter Does Not Limit the Right of Self-Defense to Regional Organizations

Some have argued that collective self-defense may be undertaken only by a regional arrangement or agency operating under chapter VIII of the United Nations Charter. Such an assertion ignores the structure of the charter and the practice followed in the more than 20 years since the founding of the United Nations.

The basic proposition that rights of self-defense are not impaired by the charter—as expressly stated in article 51—is not conditioned by any charter provision limiting the application of this proposition to collective defense by a regional arrangement or agency. The structure of the charter reinforces this conclusion. Article 51 appears in chapter VII of the charter, entitled "Action with Respect to Threats to the Peace, Breaches of the Peace, and Acts of Aggression," whereas chapter VIII, entitled "Regional Arrangements," begins with article 52 and embraces the two following articles. The records of the San Francisco conference show that article 51 was deliberately placed in chapter VII rather than chapter VIII, "where it would only have a bearing on the regional system."

Under article 51, the right of self-defense is available against any armed attack, whether or not the country attacked is a member of a regional arrangement and regardless of the source of the attack. Chapter VIII, on the other hand, deals with relations among members of a regional arrangement or agency, and authorizes regional action as appropriate for dealing with "local disputes." This distinction has been recognized ever since the founding of the United Nations in 1945.

For example, the North Atlantic Treaty has operated as a collective security arrangement, designed to take common measures in preparation against the eventuality of an armed attack for which collective defense under article 51 would be required. Similarly, the Southeast Asia Treaty Organization was designed as a collective defense arrangement under article 51. Secretary of State Dulles emphasized this in his testimony before the Senate Foreign Relations Committee in 1954.

By contrast, article 1 of the Charter of Bogotá (1948), establishing the Organization of American States, expressly declares that the organization is a regional agency within the United Nations. Indeed, chapter VIII of the United Nations Charter was included primarily to take account of the functioning of the inter-American system.

In sum, there is no basis in the United Nations Charter for contending that the right of self-defense against armed attack is limited to collective defense by a regional organization. . . .

*　*　*

CONCLUSION

South Vietnam is being subjected to armed attack by Communist North Vietnam, through the infiltration of armed personnel, military equipment, and regular combat units. International law recognizes the right of individual and collective self-defense against armed attack. South Vietnam, and the United States upon the request of South Vietnam, are engaged in such collective defense of the South. Their actions are in conformity with international law and with the Charter of the United Nations. The fact that South Vietnam has been precluded by Soviet veto from becoming a member of the United Nations and the fact that South Vietnam is a zone of a temporarily divided state in no way diminish the right of collective defense of South Vietnam.

The United States has commitments to assist South Vietnam in defending itself against Communist aggression from the North. The United States gave undertakings to this effect at the conclusion of the Geneva conference in 1954. Later that year the United States undertook an international obligation in the SEATO treaty to defend South Vietnam against Communist armed aggression. And during the past decade the United States has given additional assurances to the South Vietnamese Government.

The Geneva accords of 1954 provided for a cease-fire and re-groupment of contending forces, a division of Vietnam into two zones, and a prohibition on the use of either zone for the resumption of hostilities or to "further an aggressive policy." From the beginning, North Vietnam violated the Geneva accords through a systematic effort to gain control of South Vietnam by force. In the light of these progressive North Vietnamese violations, the introduction into South Vietnam beginning in late 1961 of substantial United States military equipment and personnel, to assist in the defense of the South, was fully justified; substantial breach of an international agreement by one side permits the other side to suspend performance of corresponding obligations under the agreement. South Vietnam was justified in refusing to implement the provisions of the Geneva accords calling for reunification through free elections throughout Vietnam since the Communist regime in North Vietnam created conditions in the North that made free elections entirely impossible.

The President of the United States has full authority to commit United States forces in the collective defense of South Vietnam. This authority stems from the constitutional powers of the President. However, it is not necessary to rely on the Constitution alone as the source of the President's authority, since the SEATO treaty —advised and consented to by the Senate and forming part of the law of the land—sets forth a United States commitment to defend South Vietnam against armed attack, and since the Congress—in the joint resolution of August 10, 1964, and in authorization and appropriations acts for support of the U. S. military effort in Vietnam —has given its approval and support to the President's actions.

United States actions in Vietnam, taken by the President and approved by the Congress, do not require any declaration of war, as shown by a long line of precedents for the use of United States armed forces abroad in the absence of any congressional declaration of war. . . .

Richard A. Falk

INTERNATIONAL LAW AND THE UNITED STATES' ROLE IN THE VIETNAM WAR

Richard A. Falk, Milbank Professor of International Law at the Woodrow Wilson School of International Affairs at Princeton, numbers among the leading figures in the legal field who have questioned the United States involvement in Vietnam. In the following selection he trains his legal arsenal on the State Department memorandum (see previous selection), stressing the following points: that the United States' interpretation of Hanoi's violation of the Geneva Accords is debatable; that the definition of aggression in the guerrilla, counterinsurgency context is unclear; that much of the United States' legalizing in the 1960s was a front while we sought victory in the field; and that Washington's SEATO obligation is questionable in the Vietnamese context.

. . . Civil strife can be analyzed in terms of three different types of violent conflict. A Type-I conflict involves the direct and massive use of military force by one political entity across a frontier of another—Korea, or Suez. To neutralize the invasion it may be necessary to act promptly and unilaterally, and it is appropriate either to use force in self-defense or to organize collective action under the auspices of a regional or global institution. A Type-II conflict involves substantial military participation by one or more foreign nations in an internal struggle for control, e.g., the Spanish Civil War. To neutralize this use of military power it may be necessary, and it is appropriate, to take offsetting military action confined to the in-

Reprinted by permission of the author, The Yale Law Journal Company and Fred B. Rothman & Company from *The Yale Law Journal*, Vol. 75 (1967), pp. 1095–1158. (Footnotes omitted.)

ternal arena, although only after seeking unsuccessful recourse to available procedures for peaceful settlement and machinery for collective security. A third type of conflict, Type III, is an internal struggle for control of a national society, the outcome of which is virtually independent of external participation. Of course, the outcome of a Type-III conflict may affect the relative power of many other countries. Hungary prior to Soviet intervention, Cuba (1958–1959), and the Dominican Republic prior to United States intervention, typify this class of struggle. It is inappropriate for a foreign nation to use military power to influence the outcome. The degree of inappropriateness will vary with the extent and duration of the military power used, and also with the explicitness of the foreign nation's role. Thus, the reliance on Cuban exiles to carry out the anti-Castro mission at the Bay of Pigs (1961) is somewhat less inappropriate than the use of United States Marines. Perhaps appreciating this distinction, North Vietnam relied almost exclusively on South Vietnamese exiles during the early years of the anti-Diem war.

These three models are analytical tools designed to clarify the nature and consequences of policy choices. Reasonable men may disagree on the proper classification of a particular war, especially if they cannot agree on the facts. An understanding of the controversy over the legality of United States participation in the war in Vietnam seems aided by keeping in mind these distinct models.

The United States is treating the war as a Type-I conflict. I would argue, for reasons set out in the next section, that the war belongs in Class III. But if this position entailing nonparticipation is rejected, then the maximum American response is counter-intervention as is permissible in a Type-II situation.

Two general issues bear on an interpretation of the rights and duties of states in regard to internal wars of either Type II or III. First, to what extent does the constituted elite—the incumbent regime—enjoy a privileged position to request outside help in suppressing internal challenges directed at its control? Traditional international law permits military assistance to the incumbent regime during early stages of an internal challenge. However, once the challenging faction demonstrates its capacity to gain control and administer a substantial portion of the society, most authorities hold that a duty of neutrality or nondiscrimination governs the relations of both factions to outside states. A state may act in favor of the incumbent to neutralize a Type-III conflict only until the challenge is validated as substantial. A crucial question is whether outside states can themselves determine the point at which the challenge is validated, or whether validation is controlled, or at least influenced, by international procedures and by objective criteria of validation. The United States' position stresses its continuing right to discriminate in favor of the incumbent regime and to deny even the political existence of the National Liberation Front (NLF), despite the de facto existence of the NLF over a long period and its effective control of a large portion of the disputed territory.

A second question partially applicable to Vietnam is whether it is ever permissible to discriminate in favor of the counter-elite. The Communist states and the ex-colonial states of Asia and Africa assume that there are occasions warranting external participation in support of the insurgent faction. The Afro-Asian states argue that political legitimacy is established by an international consensus expressed through the formal acts of international institutions, rather than by the mere control of the constituted government. This theory of legitimacy sanctions foreign military assistance to an "anticolonialist" struggle. The extent to which this new attitude alters traditional international law is at present unclear, as is its full relevance to the conflict in Vietnam. The argument for applicability to Vietnam would emphasize the continuity between the 1946–1954 anticolonial war in Vietnam and the present conflict. It would presuppose that the diplomatic recognition of South Vietnam by some sixty countries conferred only nominal sovereignty, and that the Saigon regime is a client government of the United States, which has succeeded to the imperialistic role of the French. This approach implies that external states such as North Vietnam, China, and the Soviet Union have "the right" to render support to the NLF.

These notions of permissible discrimination in favor of the constituted elite or the challenging counter-elite complicate considerably the legal analysis of participation in a Type-III conflict and blur the boundaries between Types II and III. Any adequate statement of the international law of internal war, must acknowledge this complexity, and admit along with it a certain degree of legal indeterminancy.

The vast and competent literature on the war in South Vietnam provides an essential factual background for an impartial approach to the legal issues presented in the Memorandum of Law prepared by the State Department. It is impossible to summarize all of the relevant facts, but it may be useful to indicate certain lines of reasoning that account for part of my disagreement with the official legal analysis. This disagreement reflects my interpretation of the internal war as primarily a consequence of indigenous forces. Even more, it stems from my concern for taking into account certain facts entirely excluded from the Memorandum, such as the pre-1954 war against the French and the repression of political opposition by the Diem regime.

It must be kept in mind that the present conflict in Vietnam originated in the war fought between the French and the Vietminh for control of *the whole* of Vietnam, which was "settled" at Geneva in 1954. Although the intentions of the participants at Geneva were somewhat ambiguous, the general view at the time was that the Geneva agreements anticipated reunification under the leadership of Ho Chi Minh by 1956 to coincide with the French departure. France came to Geneva a defeated nation; the Vietminh held two-thirds or more of the country. Had elections been held, it is generally agreed that reunification under Ho Chi Minh would have resulted, however one interprets the suppression of political opposition in the North or intimidation in the South. Independent observers also agree that the anticipation of the prospect of peaceful reunification led Hanoi to observe the Geneva arrangements during the two years immediately following 1954. The undoubted disappointment caused by the refusal of the French and the Americans to make Saigon go through with the elections helps explain the resumption of insurrectionary violence after 1956.

The Vietminh did leave a cadre of 5,000 or so elite guerrillas in the South, withdrawing others, as agreed, north of the Seventeenth Parallel. Those left in the South apparently went "underground," hiding weapons for possible future use. This action seems no more than a reasonable precaution on the part of Hanoi in light of Saigon's continuing objection to the Geneva terms, and in view of Washington's evident willingness from 1954 onward to give Saigon political and military support. Given the terms of conflict and the balance of forces in Vietnam prior to the Geneva Conference, French acceptance of a Vietnam-wide defeat, American reluctance to affirm the results of Geneva, and Saigon's repudiation of the settlement, it seems quite reasonable for Hanoi to regard a resumption of the civil war as a distinct contingency. Although a decade of de facto independence (affirmed by diplomatic recognition) now gives South Vietnam a strong claim to existence as a political entity, Hanoi certainly had no obligation in 1954 to respect claims of an independent political status for Saigon. To clarify the diplomatic context in Geneva, it is well to recall that the Vietminh was the sole negotiator on behalf of Vietnamese interests at Geneva in 1954.

Later in 1954 the Saigon regime under Premier Diem ruthlessly suppressed all political opposition. Observers agree that organization of an underground was an inevitable reaction to this suppression, and that the NLF at its inception included many non-Communist elements. It also appears that Saigon was unwilling to negotiate, or even consult, on questions affecting reunification, and was unwilling to normalize economic relations with Hanoi. The great economic strain imposed on North Vietnam forced it to use scarce foreign exchange to obtain part of its food supply from other countries.

Furthermore, the French military presence soon was replaced by an American military presence prior to the scheduled elections on reunification. The evolution of an American "commitment" to Saigon's permanence and legitimacy contrasts radically with both the expectations created at Geneva in 1954 and the subsequent attitudes of the French. United States involvement in the politics of South Vietnam increased constantly; it was no secret that the Diem government largely was constituted and sustained in its early months by the United States.

Despite the escalating American political, military, and economic assistance, the Saigon regime proved incapable of achieving political stability. Numerous regimes have come and gone. None has commanded the respect and allegiance of any significant segment of the population. Often in situations of civil war diverse factions are able to establish an expedient working unity during the period of common national emergency. The NLF seems to maintain substantial control over its heterogeneous followers while one Saigon regime after another collapses or totters on the brink. The United States recognized at an early stage that the Saigon regime had to transform its own feudal social structure before it could provide the basis for viable government in South Vietnam. This is a most unusual demand by an external ally; it bears witness to the fragile and dubious claim of each successive Saigon regime to govern even the parts of South Vietnam not held by the Vietcong.

In addition, Saigon and the United States seem to have neglected repeated opportunities for negotiations with Hanoi during earlier stages of the war. As late as February 1965, the United States government rebuked U Thant for engaging in unauthorized negotiations. Until the prospects for a military solution favorable to Saigon diminished to the vanishing point, the United States made no attempt to negotiate a peaceful settlement or to entrust responsibility for settlement to either the Security Council or the Co-Chairmen of the Geneva Conference. This reluctance, when added to the political losses suffered by Hanoi at Geneva in 1954, makes it easier to comprehend Hanoi's reluctance to negotiate now.

All of these considerations lead me to regard the war in South Vietnam primarily as a Type-III conflict, in which the United States ought not to have participated. Because of Hanoi's increasing participation on behalf of the Vietcong, it is arguable, although rather unpersuasive, that this war is properly categorized as an example of Type II, so that the United States could legitimately give military assistance to Saigon, but is obligated to limit the arena of violence to the territory of South Vietnam. The weakness of the Saigon regime compared to the NLF renders necessary a disproportionately large military commitment by the United States to neutralize the indigenous advantages of the Vietcong and the support of Hanoi. Our disproportionate commitment makes it appear that the United States rather than Hanoi is escalating the war. And this appearance undercuts any defense of our participation as necessary to offset participation on the other side, and thereby give "the true" balance of domestic forces a chance to control the outcome. The State Department Memorandum assumes that the war is a Type-I conflict, and argues that American participation is really collective self-defense in response to an armed attack by North Vietnam upon South Vietnam. But to characterize North Vietnam's participation in the struggle in the South as "an armed attack" is unwise as well as incorrect. Such a contention, if accepted as an authoritative precedent, goes a long way toward abolishing the distinction between international and civil war. The war in South Vietnam should be viewed as primarily between factions contending for control of the southern zone, whether or not the zone is considered a nation. A claim of self-defense by Saigon seems misplaced, and the exercise of rights of self-defense by committing violent acts against the territory of North Vietnam tends toward the establishment of an unfortunate precedent.

The Memorandum of the State Department was submitted by the Legal Adviser to the Senate Committee on Foreign Relations on March 8, 1966. In assessing it, we should keep in mind several considerations. First, the United States Government is the client of the Legal Adviser, and the Memorandum, as is entirely appropriate, is an adversary document. A legal adviser in Hanoi could prepare a comparable document. Adversary discourse in legal analysis should be sharply distinguished from an impartial determination of the merits of opposed positions.

Second, the Legal Memorandum was evidently framed as a response to the Memorandum of Law prepared by the Lawyers Committee on American Policy Toward Vietnam. The argument of the Lawyers Committee fails to raise sharply the crucial issue—namely, the discretion of the United States to delimit its legal rights and duties by treating the conflict in South Vietnam as an international war of aggression rather than as a civil war.

Third, the Legal Adviser's Memorandum implies that both the facts of aggression and the legal rules governing self-defense are clear. This is misleading. Except in instances of overt, massive aggression across an international frontier, international law offers very *indefinite* guidance about the permissible occasions for or extent of recourse to force in self-defense. Doctrinal ambiguity is greatest with respect to internal wars with significant external participation. International law offers very little authoritative guidance on the central issue of permissible assistance to the contending factions. To conclude that international law is indefinite is not to suggest that it is irrelevant. On the contrary, if rules are indefinite and procedures for their interpretation unavailable, prevailing national practice sets precedents for the future. In this light, American activity in Vietnam is particularly unfortunate for the future of doctrines aimed at limiting international violence.

In this section I propose to criticize the legal argument of the Memorandum, taking some issue with both inferences of fact and conclusions of law. I will analyze the consequences of characterizing international participation in Vietnam as intervention and counter-intervention in an ongoing civil war. Although I will call attention to the shortcomings in the legal position of the United States, my main intention is to approach this inquiry in the spirit of scholarly detachment rather than as an adversary critic. Such detachment is not value-free. I try to appraise the claims of national actors in light of the requirements of world order. My appraisal presupposes the desirability of narrowing the discretion of nations to determine for themselves the occasions on which violence is permissible or that an increase of the scale and scope of ongoing violence is appropriate. I am convinced that it is important for *any* country (including my own) to reconcile its foreign policy with the rules regulating the use of force in international affairs, and that, therefore, it does not serve *even* the national interest to accept a legal justification for our own recourse to violence that we would not be prepared to have invoked against us by other states similarly situated. The international legal order, predominantly decentralized, depends for effectiveness on the acceptance by principal states of the fundamental ordering notions of symmetry, reciprocity, and national precedent-setting.

In analyzing the Memorandum I will adhere to its outline of issues, concentrating on the most significant.

Collective Self-Defense.   The Memorandum argues that the United States may, at Saigon's request, participate in the collective self-defense of South Vietnam because North Vietnam has made a prior armed attack. But may indirect aggression be treated as an armed attack without the approval of an appropriate international institution? The United States rests its case on the role of Hanoi in the period between 1954 and 1959 in setting up "a covert political-military organization" and by its infiltration of "over 40,000 armed and unarmed guerrillas into South Vietnam" during the subsequent five years. The Memorandum concludes that "the external aggression from the North is the critical military element of the insurgency," that "the infiltration of thousands of armed men clearly constitutes an 'armed attack' under any reasonable definition," and that although there may be doubt as to "the exact date at which North Vietnam's aggression grew into an 'armed attack,' [it certainly] had occurred before February 1965."

This argument is questionable on its face, that is, without even criticizing its most selective presentation of the facts. Consider first the highly ideological character of prevailing attitudes toward the just use of force. The Communist countries favor support for wars of national liberation; the West—in particular, the United States—favors support for anti-Communist wars; and the Afro-Asian states favor support for anticolonialist and antiracist wars. Consider also the importance, acknowledged by the United States in other settings, of circumscribing the right of self-defense. The use of force on some other basis—for example, defensive intervention or regional security—moderates rather than escalates a conflict. But the invocation of self-defense as a rationale during a conflict perviously contained within a single state tends to enlarge the arena of conflict to include states that are claiming and counter-claiming that each other's intervention in the civil strife is an armed attack. If the infiltration constitutes an armed attack, the bombing of North Vietnam may be justified. But if North Vietnam had operative collective defense arrangements with China and the Soviet Union it is easy to project a scenario of escalation ending in global catastrophe. If, on the other hand, infiltration is merely intervention, and appropriate responses are limited to counter-intervention, the area of violence is restricted to the territory of South Vietnam and its magnitude is kept within more manageable limits.

The argument in the Memorandum also assumes that armed help to the insurgent faction is under all circumstances a violation of international law. As mentioned earlier, at some stage in civil strife it is permissible for outside states to regard the insurgent elite the equal of the incumbent regime and to render it equivalent assistance. Since no collective procedures are available to determine when an insurgency has proceeded far enough to warrant this status, outside states enjoy virtually unlimited discretion to determine the comparative legitimacy of competing elites. In effect, then, no rules of international law exist to distinguish clearly between permissible and impermissible intervention in civil strife. To call hostile intervention not only impermissible but an instance of the most serious illegality—an armed attack—seems very unfortunate. In addition to a tendency to escalate any particular conflict, the position that interventions are armed attacks so broadens the notion of armed attack that all nations will be able to make plausible claims of self-defense in almost every situation of protracted internal war. It therefore seems desirable to confine the armed attack/self-defense rationale to the Korea-type conflict (Type I) and to deny its applicability in Vietnam, whether the war in Vietnam is denominated Type II or Type III. The Memorandum's argument on self-defense is also deficient in that it relies upon a very selective presentation of the facts. It ignores Saigon's consistent opposition to the terms of the Geneva settlement, thereby casting in very different light Hanoi's motives for the steps it took in South Vietnam to assert its claims. It is essential to recall that the pre-1954 conflict was waged for control of *all* of Vietnam and that the settlement at Geneva was no more than "a cease-fire." President Diem's ruthless suppression of political opposition in South Vietnam from 1954 onward, in violation of the ban on political reprisals included in the Geneva Agreements, is also relevant.

Furthermore, the injection of an American political and military presence was, from the perspective of Hanoi, inconsistent with the whole spirit of Geneva. The United States decision to commit itself to maintaining a Western-oriented regime in South Vietnam upset the expectations regarding the Southeast Asian balance of power; in that respect, it was similar to the Soviet attempt to upset the Caribbean balance of power by installing intermediate-range missiles in Cuba in 1962.

The Memorandum seems to concede that until 1964 the bulk of infiltrated men were South Vietnamese who had come north after the cease-fire in 1954. The use of exiles to bolster an insurgent cause appears to be on the borderline between permissible and impermissible behavior in contemporary international politics. The role of the United States Government in sponsoring the unsuccessful invasion at the Bay of Pigs in 1961 was a far more flagrant example of the use of exiles to overthrow a constituted government in a neighboring country than the early role of Hanoi in fostering an uprising in the South. The claim by the United States to control political events in Cuba is far more tenuous than the claim by North Vietnam to exercise control (or at least remove the influence of a hostile superpower) over political life in the South. And Castro's regime was domestically viable in a manner that Saigon regimes have never been—suggesting that South Vietnam presents a more genuine revolutionary situation than does contemporary Cuba. It seems more destructive of world order to help overthrow a firmly established government than to assist an ongoing revolution against a regime incapable of governing.

African countries admit helping exiles overthrow governments under white control. American support for Captive Nations Week is still another form of support outside of the Communist bloc for exile aspirations. In short, international law neither attempts nor is able to regulate support given exile groups. The activities of Hanoi between 1954 and 1964 conform to patterns of tolerable conflict in contemporary international politics.

The Memorandum contends that subsequent to 1964, Hanoi has increasingly infiltrated regular elements of the North Vietnamese army until at present "there is evidence that nine regiments of regular North Vietnamese forces are fighting in the South." Arguably, the NLF was not eligible to receive external support in the early years of strife after 1954, as its challenge to the government amounted to no more than "a rebellion." But certainly after the Vietcong gained effective control over large portions of the countryside it was *permissible* for North Vietnam to treat the NLF as a "belligerent" with a right to conduct external relations. This area of international law is exceedingly vague; states have a wide range of discretion in establishing their relations with contending factions in a foreign country.

The remainder of the first section of the Memorandum responds to the Lawyers Committee Memorandum of Law, but is not relevant to the solution of the critical legal questions. It is persuasive but trivial for the State Department to demonstrate that international law recognizes the right of individual and collective self-defense against an armed attack; that nonmembers of the United Nations enjoy the same rights of self-defense as do members; that South Vietnam Is a political entity entitled to claim the right of self-defense despite its origin as a "temporary zone"; and that the right of collective self-defense may be exercised independent of a regional arrangement organized under Chapter VIII of the United Nations Charter. South Vietnam would have had the right to act in self-defense *if an armed attack had occurred,* and the United States would then have had the right to act in collective self-defense.

It is also important to determine whether the United States has complied with the reporting requirement contained in Article 51 of the United Nations Charter. The United States did encourage a limited Security Council debate during August 1964 of the Gulf of Tonkin "incidents." Furthermore, the United States submitted two reports to the Security Council during February 1965 concerning its recourse to bombing North Vietnam and the general character of the war. And in January 1966 the United States submitted the Vietnam question to the Security Council. It seems reasonable to conclude that the Security Council (or, for that matter, the General Assembly) is unwilling and unable to intervene in any *overt* manner in the conflict in Vietnam. This conclusion is reinforced by the hostility of the Communist states toward American proposals for a settlement. On the other hand, there is no evidence of formal initiative by the members of the United Nations to question the propriety of the United States policies. The very serious *procedural* question posed is whether the failure of the United Nations to act relieves the United States of its burden to submit claims of self-defense to review by the organized international community. A further question is whether any international legal limitations upon national discretion apply when the United Nations refrains from passing judgment on claims to use force in self-defense.

The Security Council failed to endorse American claims in Vietnam, and this failure was not merely a consequence of Soviet or Communist opposition. Therefore, if the burden of justification for recourse to self-defense is upon the claimant, inaction by the United Nations provides no legal comfort on the *substantive issue*—that is, the legality of proportional self-defense given "the facts" in Vietnam.

As to the *procedural issue*—that is, compliance with the reporting requirement of Article 51—the United States may be considered to have complied pro forma, but not in terms of the spirit of the Charter of the United Nations.

The overriding purpose of the Charter is to commit states to use force only as a last resort after the exhaustion of all other alternatives. In the early period after 1954 the United States relied heavily on its unilateral economic and military capability to protect the Saigon regime against the Vietcong. No *prior* attempt was made, in accordance with Article 33, to settle the dispute by peaceful means. Yet the spirit of the Charter requires that a nation claiming to undertake military action in collective self-defense must first invoke the collective review and responsibility of the United Nations. The United States did not call for United Nations review until January 1966, that is, until a time when the prospects for a favorable military solution at tolerable costs seemed dismal, many months subsequent to bombing North Vietnamese territory. As long as a military victory was anticipated, the United States resented any attempt to question its discretion to use force or to share its responsibility for obtaining a settlement. American recourse to procedures for peaceful settlement came as a last rather than a first resort. The United States had made no serious effort to complain about alleged North Vietnamese violations of the Geneva Agreements, nor to recommend a reconvening of a new Geneva Conference in the decade of escalating commitment after 1954. Saigon submitted complaints to the International Control Commission, but that body was neither constituted nor intended to deal with the resumption of a war for control of South Vietnam that was apparently provoked by Saigon's refusal to hold elections.

Further, not until 1965 did the United States welcome the independent efforts of the Secretary-General to act as a negotiating intermediary between Washington and Hanoi. Until it became evident that a military victory over the Vietcong was not forthcoming, the United States Government was hostile to suggestions emanating from either U Thant (or de Gaulle) that a negotiated settlement was both *appropriate* and *attainable*. The State Department's belated offer to negotiate must be discounted in light of its public relations overtones and our effort over the last decade to reverse the expectations of Geneva. The United States negotiating position is also made less credible by our failure to accord the NLF diplomatic status as a party in conflict. This failure is especially dramatic in light of the NLF's ability effectively to govern territory under its possession and Saigon's relative inability to do so.

The American approach to negotiations lends support to the conclusion that our sporadic attempts at a peaceful settlement are belated gestures, and that we seek "victory" at the negotiating table only when it becomes unattainable on the battlefield. The United States showed no willingness to subordinate national discretion to the collective will of the organized international community. In fact, Vietnam exemplifies the American global strategy of using military power whenever necessary to prevent Communist expansion and to determine these necessary occasions by national decisions. This militant anti-Communism represents the essence of unilateralism.

One must conclude that the United States was determined to use its military power as it saw fit in Vietnam in the long period from 1954 to January 1966. In 1966 at last a belated, if halfhearted, attempt to collectivize responsibility was made by appealing to the Security Council to obtain, in the words of the Memorandum, "discussions looking toward a peaceful settlement on the basis of the Geneva accords." The Memorandum goes on to observe that "Indeed, since the United States submission on January 1966, members of the Council have been notably reluctant to proceed with any consideration of the Vietnam question." Should this reluctance come as a surprise? Given the timing and magnitude of the American request it was inevitable that the United Nations would find itself unable to do anything constructive at that stage. United Nations inaction has deepened the awareness of the Organization's limited ability to safeguard world peace, whenever the nuclear superpowers take opposite sides of a violent conflict. Disputes must be submitted *prior* to deep involvement if the United Nations is to play a significant role. The war in Vietnam presented many appropriate opportunities—the various steps up the escalation ladder—for earlier, more effective, American recourse to the United Nations. But during the entire war in Vietnam, the United States has shown no significant disposition to limit discretionary control over its national military power by making constructive use of collective procedures of peaceful settlement. . . .

The Relevance of Commitments to Defend South Vietnam. . . .

Secretary Rusk has injected a further confusion into the debate by his stress on "the SEATO commitment" in the course of his testimony before the Senate Foreign Relations Committee in the early months of 1966. He said, for instance, in his prepared statement: "It is this fundamental SEATO obligation that has from the outset guided our actions in Vietnam." The notion of the obligation is derived from Article IV(1) of the SEATO treaty which says that "each party recognizes that aggression by means of armed attack . . . would endanger its own peace and safety, and agrees that it will in that event act to meet the common danger in accordance with its constitutional processes." It is somewhat doubtful that Article IV(1) can be properly invoked at all in Vietnam because of the difficulty of establishing "an armed attack." Secretary Rusk contends, however, that this provision not only *authorizes* but *obliges* the United States to act in the defense of South Vietnam.

Ambiguity again abounds. If the commitment to act in Vietnam is incorporated in a treaty, the United States is legally bound. Such an interpretation of Article IV(1) would apply equally to other states that have ratified the SEATO treaty. None of the other SEATO signatories acknowledge such "a commitment" to fulfill a duty of collective self-defense, nor does the United States contend they have one. France and Pakistan oppose altogether any military effort on behalf of the Saigon regime undertaken by outside states.

Secretary Rusk later softened his insistence that Article IV(1) imposed a legal commitment qua obligation upon the United States. In an exchange with Senator Fulbright during Senate hearings on Vietnam, Mr. Rusk offered the following explanation:

> The Chairman. . . .*do you maintain that we had an obligation under the Southeastern Asian Treaty to come to the assistance, all-out assistance of South Vietnam? Is that very clear?*
> Secretary Rusk. *It seems clear to me, sir, that this was an obligation—*
> The Chairman. *Unilateral.*
> Secretary Rusk. *An obligation of policy. It is rooted in the policy of the treaty. I am not now saying if we had decided we would not lift a finger about Southeast Asia that we could be sued in a court and be convicted of breaking a treaty.*

It seems evident if an armed attack has been established, the treaty imposes a legal obligation to engage in collective self-defense of the victim. But in the absence of a collective determination by the SEATO membership that an armed attack has taken place, it is difficult to maintain that Article IV(1) does more than authorize discretionary action in appropriate circumstances.

The Memorandum argues that "the treaty does not require a collective determination that an armed attack has occurred in order that the obligation of Article IV(1) become operative. Nor does the provision require collective decision on actions to be taken to meet the common danger. This interpretation of Article IV(1) is a blatant endorsement of extreme unilateralism, made more insidious by its pretense of "obligation" and its invocation of the multilateral or regional scaffolding of SEATO. Here the legal position of the State Department displays maximum cynicism, resorting to international law to obscure the national character of military action. In essence, the United States claims that it is under an obligation to determine for itself when an armed attack has occurred, and that once this determination is made there arises a further obligation to act in response. This justification for recourse to force is reminiscent of the international law of war prior to World War I, when states were free to decide for themselves when to go to war. The regressive tendency of this position is further intensified by applying it in a situation where there was a background of civil war and where the alleged aggression was low-scale, extended over time, and covert. Under "the Rusk Doctrine" a country alleging "armed attack" seems free to act in self-defense whenever it wishes. The rhetoric of commitment seems connected with the effort to make the policy of support for Saigon irreversible in domestic arenas and credible in external arenas, especially in Saigon and Hanoi, but it has little to do with an appreciation of the relevance of international law to United States action in Vietnam. . . .

The Authority of the President under the Constitution. I agree with the Legal Adviser's analysis that the President possesses the constitutional authority to use American military forces in Vietnam without a declaration of war. Past practice and present policy support this conclusion. To declare war against North Vietnam would further rigidify our own expectations about an acceptable outcome and it would almost certainly escalate the conflict. It might activate dormant collective defense arrangements between North Vietnam and its allies.

But the Constitution is relevant in another way not discussed by the Memorandum. The President is bound to act in accordance with governing law, including international law. The customary and treaty norms of international law enjoy the status of "the law of the land" and the President has no discretion to violate these norms in the course of pursuing objectives of foreign policy. An impartial determination of the compatibility of our action in Vietnam with international law is highly relevant to the constitutionality of the exercise of presidential authority in Vietnam.

The President has the constitutional authority to commit our armed services to the defense of South Vietnam without a declaration of war *provided* that such "a commitment" is otherwise in accord with international law. Whether all or part of the United States' action violates international law is also a constitutional question. International law offers no authoritative guidance as to the use of force *within* South Vietnam, but the bombing of North Vietnam appears to be an unconstitutional use of presidential authority as well as a violation of international law. . . .

The foregoing analysis points to the following set of conclusions:

1. The United States insistence upon treating North Vietnamese assistance to the Vietcong as "an armed attack" justifying recourse to "self-defense" goes a long way toward abolishing the legal significance of the distinction between civil war and international war. Without this distinction, we weaken a principal constraint upon the scope and scale of violence in international affairs—the confinement of violence associated with internal wars to the territory of a single political unit. Another adverse consequence of permitting "self-defense" in response to covert aggression is to entrust nations with very wide discretion to determine for themselves the occasions upon which recourse to *overt* violence across international boundaries is permissible. An extension of the doctrine of self-defense would defeat a principal purpose of the United Nations Charter—the delineation of fixed, narrow limits upon the use of overt violence by states in dispute with one another.

2. The United States made no serious attempt to exhaust international remedies prior to recourse to unilateral military power. The gradual unfolding of the conflict provided a long period during which attempts at negotiated settlement could have

taken place. Only belatedly and in a pro forma fashion did the United States refer the dispute to the United Nations. The United States made no attempt to comply with "the international law principle" alleged by footnote 10 of the Memorandum to govern the action of North Vietnam. Nor did it attempt during the early phases of the war to subordinate its discretion to the Geneva machinery. No use was made even of the consultative framework of SEATO, an organization inspired by United States initiative for the specific purpose of inhibiting Communist aggression in Southeast Asia. Policies of force were unilaterally adopted and put into execution; no account was taken of the procedural devices created to give a collective quality to decisions about the use of force. Yet the prospect for controlling violence in world affairs depends upon the growth of limiting procedural rules and principles.

3. By extending the scope of violence beyond the territory of South Vietnam the United States has created an unfortunate precedent in international affairs. Where international institutions fail to provide clear guidance as to the character of permissible action, national actions create quasi-legislative precedents. In view of the background of the conflict in Vietnam (including the expectation that South Vietnam would be incorporated into a unified Vietnam under the control of Hanoi after the French departure), the American decision to bomb North Vietnam sets an unfortunate precedent. If North Vietnam and its allies had the will and capability to employ equivalent military force, the precedent would even allow them to claim the right to bomb United States territory in reprisal.

4. The widespread domestic instability in the Afro-Asian world points up the need for an approach to internal war that aims above all to insulate this class of conflict from intervention by the great powers. The early use of peace observation forces, border control machinery, restraints on the introduction of foreign military personnel, and standby mediation appears possible and beneficial. Responses to allegations of "aggression" should be verified prior to the unilateral use of defensive force, especially when time is available. Claims of covert aggression might then be verified with sufficient authority and speed to mobilize support for community security actions.

5. In the last analysis, powerful nations have a responsibility to use defensive force to frustrate aggression when international

machinery is paralyzed. Vietnam, however, does not provide a good illustration of the proper discharge of this responsibility. North Vietnam's action does not seem to constitute "aggression." Available international machinery was not used in a proper fashion. The domestic conditions prevailing in South Vietnam were themselves so inconsistent with prevailing ideals of welfare, progress, and freedom that it is difficult to claim that the society would be better off as a result of a Saigon victory. The massive American presence has proved to be a net detriment, greatly escalating the war, tearing apart the fabric of Vietnamese society, and yet not likely to alter significantly the political outcome. The balance of domestic and area forces seems so favorable to the Vietcong that it is unlikely that the NLF can be kept forever from political control. The sacrifice of lives and property merely postpones what appears to be an inevitable result. The United States voluntarily assumed a political responsibility for the defense of South Vietnam that has been gradually converted into a political commitment and a self-proclaimed test of our devotion to the concept of collective self-defense. This responsibility is inconsistent with the requirements of world order to the extent that it depends upon unilateral prerogatives to use military power. The national interest of the United States would be better served by the embrace of *cosmopolitan isolationism*—either we act in conjunction with others or we withdraw. We are the most powerful nation in world history. It is hubris to suppose, however, that we are the policemen of the world. Our wasted efforts in Vietnam suggest the futility and frustration of the politics of overcommitment. We are not the only country in the world concerned with containing Communism. If we cannot find cooperative bases for action we will dissipate our moral and material energies in a series of Vietnams. The tragedy of Vietnam provides an occasion for rethinking the complex problems of use of military power in world affairs and calls for an examination of the increasingly imperial role of the United States in international society. Perhaps we will discover the relevance of international law to the *planning* and *execution* of foreign policy as well as to its *justification*. Certainly the talents of the State Department's Legal Adviser are wasted if he is to be merely an official apologist summoned long after our President has proclaimed "a solemn national commitment."

Telford Taylor

AGGRESSIVE WAR, VIETNAM AND THE COURTS

General Telford Taylor has enjoyed a distinguished career in government, law, the military, and teaching, but his finest hour came as head of the United States prosecution staff at Nuremberg. Most recently he published Nuremberg and Vietnam *in which he deals with the disputed points of law arising from the Nuremberg precedent. In the following selection from that work, Taylor probes the legal nuances of the charge that the United States was the aggressor in Vietnam and offers an explanation diametrically opposed to that of Richard Falk and the critics of American policy. He rejects the "Nuremberg defense"—that is, individuals refusing to serve in Vietnam or pay a "war tax" who cite Nuremberg law—basing his argument on Article VI of the Constitution.*

"At the time of the Nuremberg trials," wrote the late Thurman Arnold, eminent writer, judge and staunch defender of President Johnson's Vietnam policies, "those who write the think columns in our press, such as Walter Lippman, and independent organizations of intellectuals . . . and liberal professors on our campuses, acclaimed the principle of the outlawing of aggressive war as a great step forward in international law. Today they are bending every effort to prevent the enforcement of the principle that Nuremberg announced to the world. . . . They are encouraging Hanoi to believe that if it will only hang on the United States will abandon its attempt to enforce the Nuremberg principle in Asia." Official voices take up the same theme. "The indelible lesson . . . is that the time to stop aggression is at its very beginning," Secretary of State Dean Rusk told the American Society of International Law. "Surely we have learned over the past three decades that the acceptance of aggression leads only to a sure catastrophe. Surely we have learned that the aggressor must face the consequences of his action. . . ."

On what does this pro-United States invocation of Nuremberg and its principles rest? Essentially, it is a three-step proposition: (1) that North Vietnam attacked South Vietnam in violation of Article 2 of the

United Nations Charter, (2) that South Vietnam was entitled to use force to repel the unlawful attack, and (3) that the United States is justified in joining South Vietnam in "collective defense" under Article 51 of the Charter.

But among those opposed to our policy in Vietnam, Nuremberg is cited even more frequently. "It may appear ironic," declares the National Lawyers Guild, "that the first serious effort to revitalize Nuremberg into a binding legal and moral precedent has been undertaken by citizens of this country who assert that their own government has engaged in an illegal war in Vietnam in violation of international law and morality." And again, in the words of Eric Norden: "Our actions in Vietnam fall within the prohibited classifications of warfare set down at Nuremberg . . . the United States is clearly guilty of 'War Crimes,' 'Crimes against Peace' and 'Crimes against Humanity,' crimes for which the top German leaders were either imprisoned or executed."

So far as it concerns aggressive warfare, the case for these stark accusations is based on the conclusions that both South Vietnam and the United States violated the Geneva Declaration of 1954 by hostile acts against the North, unlawful rearmament, and refusal to carry out the 1956 national elections provided for in the Declaration, and that the United States likewise violated the United Nations Charter by bombing North Vietnam.

Eminently respectable and learned voices are raised on both sides of the debate. By what standards may it be judged? Critics of the Nuremberg condemnation of "aggressive war" often complain that neither the London Charter nor the tribunals' opinions embodied a definition of the concept. Is definition feasible, and would it help in identifying the aggressor in Vietnam? At the conferences during which the London Charter was formulated, the United States proffered two proposed definitions. But neither was accepted, and the Russian delegate, in words reminiscent of the man who doesn't know much about music but knows what he likes, declared: "When people speak about aggression, they know what that means, but, when they come to define it, they come up against difficulties which as yet it has not been possible to overcome." And in 1950, the Reporter to the International Law Commission of the United Nations concluded, even more bluntly, that any attempt to define aggression "would prove to be a pure waste of time."

That may be an overstatement, but certainly efforts at a definite formulation have not yet been successful. However, this is very commonly the case with general concepts, many of which are indispensable tools of law and philosophy. The Constitution of the United States contains numerous crucial phrases that equally defy definition: "Due process of law" and "unreasonable searches and seizures" come readily to mind. They are also to be found in common criminal and civil law—for example "negligence" or "reasonable doubt." The meaning of such words and phrases can be illuminated by descriptive comments, but invariably these also employ expressions of imprecise or imponderable content.

The lack of a satisfactory definition of "aggressive war" therefore, should not be taken as a sufficient argument against its use as a description of unlawful international conduct. In fact, as the discussion and application of the standard since it came into common parlance reveals, it is not significantly different from the tests for the lawful use of defensive force in our domestic criminal law. As we have already seen, the parallelism is of long standing. There is remarkable similarity between the criteria stated by Suarez and Grotius for distinguishing the just from the unjust war, and the provision of the New York Penal Law specifying the circumstances under which force may rightfully be used: to defend one's self, one's property or to assist other persons engaged in defending themselves or their property.

Over the course of time, the law has developed reasonable satisfactory statutory and judicial formulations of this right of self-defense. But there are no self-operating definitions. The policeman who comes upon a fracas may find it difficult or impossible to decide whether Cohen or Kelly struck the first blow, and the doubts may be equally impossible to dispel when the matter comes into court. And if run-of-the-mill criminal cases commonly present such difficulties, it is hardly surprising to encounter them in international conflicts. The question of initial responsibility, which is the essence of "aggression," may be vexingly complicated, as the Arab-Israeli hostilities abundantly demonstrate. And while there are many on both sides of the Vietnam dispute who declare that the original blameless or blameworthiness of the United States is readily demonstrable, the depth of disagreement among men of integrity and intelligence suggests that at least the issues are far from simple.

In practical terms, what difference does it make whether the American involvement in Vietnam is legal or illegal under the Nuremberg principles? Today there is no longer an international tribunal competent to render judgment. But the issue is being dramatically projected in a variety of domestic circumstances. May a soldier under orders to proceed to Vietnam refuse on the ground that he should not participate in an illegal war? May a draft registrant refuse induction on that basis? May taxpayers similarly persuaded of the war's illegality withhold a symbolic or proportionate part of their payments?

These and comparable questions, calling for a determination of the legality of our government's action in Vietnam, are being pressed before our domestic courts in a host of cases. Should the courts undertake to make such a determination? A strong affirmative opinion has been voiced by Richard A. Falk, Professor of International Law at Princeton:

> . . . the reassertion of an active judicial role in this area would appear to be a creative contribution to the doctrine of separation of powers in the war-peace context. . . . In addition, those who seek access to the courts in order to test the legality of the war—for instance, by refusing to pay all or part of their income taxes—are entitled to a substantive determination of the issue . . . it is important that judges become persuaded of their competence and responsibility to restrain the execution of government policy by either executive or legislative institutions if such policy is found to exceed the boundaries set by international law.

Thus far the Supreme Court has not heeded Professor Falk's call to battle, but the issue rings loudly in the lower court reports and law reviews. *Should* the Supreme Court engage itself with this issue? And if so, what would be the principles and problems attending such an adjudication?

We may best begin by taking a brief look at the merits of the aggression issue, not in order to answer it, but for an understanding of the range and complexity of its components. An answer would involve the interpretation of numerous treaties and other international documents, including the United Nations Charter, the Geneva Declaration of July 21, 1954, the reports of the International Control Commission established under the Geneva agreement, and the Southeast Asia Collective Defense Treaty (SEATO). It would involve the examination of hotly controverted evidentiary questions, such as when the infiltration of North Vietnamese guerrillas into South Vietnam began, and whether American destroyers were in fact attacked, or reasonably believed to have been attacked, by North Vietnamese torpedo boats in the Tonkin Gulf in the summer of 1964. It would involve scrutiny of the information available to, and the intentions of, the President of the United States and the military and civilian officials who helped him to shape and execute our policies and operations in Vietnam.

One example may serve to demonstrate the complexity of these issues. At Geneva in 1954 the dividing line between North and South Vietnam was drawn at the 17th Parallel. Indisputably, the ground fighting has all taken place in South Vietnam; it is the North Vietnamese who have joined the Vietcong "south of the border" and are seeking to subvert the Government of South Vietnam. On its face this would seem strong evidence that it is the North Vietnamese who are using war "as an instrument of national policy" (to echo the Kellogg-Briand Pact language) and are the aggressors. Indeed Professor John Norton Moore, one of the stoutest academic supporters of American policy, makes much of this very point: "As both Korea and Vietnam demonstrate, one of the greatest threats to world order today is external intervention seeking coercive change across a boundary separating the de facto halves of a cold-war divided country. This is a major reason why it is crucial that international legal scholars clearly condemn the strategy of Hanoi in seeking coercive change across such a cold-war dividing line."

But the matter is not at all that simple. The Geneva agreement of 1954 did not purport to establish two nations, but two "zones," and explicitly declared that "the military demarcation line is provisional and should not in any way be interpreted as constituting a political or territorial boundary." It was the basis for a cease-fire, and the purpose of the zones was specified as "regrouping." The agreement further provided for "free" nationwide elections, to be held in 1956, as the basis for a government based on "the principles of independence, unity and territorial integrity." But South Vietnam, with the support of the United States (which had not signed the Geneva agreement), declined to proceed with the elections on the ground that conditions in North Vietnam were not "free"; consequently the two zones took on the attributes of independent states, with South Vietnam in alliance with the United States. Many international lawyers support the North Vietnamese contention that the Geneva agreements were violated by the refusal to hold elections and unify the country, and that the demarcation line is not properly to be regarded as an international boundary. Consequently, it is said, the North Vietnamese were justified in aiding the Vietcong in South Vietnam, who are seeking to establish a government favorable to unification in line with the purpose of the Geneva agreement.

An American court undertaking to pass judgment on the legality of our Vietnam actions would have to review these and numerous other questions of comparable difficulty and complexity with little guidance from the Nuremberg and Tokyo judgments. Whatever might be said about the long-range causes of the Second World War, there was little question about who attacked whom, and the issue of aggression was comparatively easy to adjudicate.

There are also the vexed questions of intent and motive. At Nuremberg and Tokyo individuals were on trial, and it was possible to declare the wars to be aggressive because of their proven intentions and declarations. But if the issue arises not in a trial of persons accused of crimes against peace, but as a defense in a draft or tax case, it is the "government's" intentions that are called in question. The "government" is not an individual and cannot be said to have intentions of its own, and it might well transpire that the intentions and motives of government leaders were very diverse. Some might in good faith believe, in line with the arguments of Dean Rusk and Thurman Arnold, that the United Nations Charter and the SEATO treaty justified or even required intervention to protect South Vietnam from aggression. Others might talk this language only to conceal the intention to exploit South Vietnam as an American military base to "contain" Communism, or to dominate Southeast Asia and its enormous natural resources. In terms of individual guilt of crimes against peace, the question of intent might be decisive. But where only the "government" is the focus of inquiry, it might be quite impossible to determine the intent with which a particular decision was taken.

In this connection, it may be remarked that the policy-making machinery of the United States resembles much more that of the Japanese as it emerged at the Tokyo trial, than that of Nazi Germany. *"L'Etat, c'est moi,"* said Louis XIV, and Adolf Hitler could truthfully have echoed his words. Hitler's intention *was* the intention of the German Government. But there was no comparable figure in Tokyo, nor has there been in Washington. The President is a focus, but around him there are diverse and shifting groups and combinations of powerful military and civilian leaders, and the Congress likewise has its part to play. Declarations of intent in official documents are designed to be exculpatory, and are often less than candid, to say the least.

In summary, the nature of the issues that would have to be explored in assessing the legality, under the Nuremberg principles, of American participation in the Vietnamese war would present enormous difficulties to any court, and especially to a domestic court of one of the belligerents, convened during the course of hostilities. This is not a conclusive argument against making the attempt, but it is certainly a factor to be weighed in deciding whether or not this is a fit subject for judicial decision.

There is another question concerning the legality of our Vietnam involvement that is not a matter of Nuremberg or other international law principles, but is closely interlocked with them, both legally and politically. This other issue involves the respective powers of the Congress and the President in the fields of foreign relations and war-making. The tension between the two arises from the constitutional provisions that give Congress the power "to declare War," to "raise and support Armies" and "provide and maintain a Navy," and to "make Rules for the Government and Regulation of the land and naval Forces," while specifying also that the President "shall be Commander-in-Chief of the Army and Navy of the United States." Essentially, the contention is that the President has no authority to commit the armed forces to battle in Vietnam without Congressional authority, that no such authority has been given, and that the courts should, if properly called upon, declare the President's actions in Vietnam unconstitutional and subject to judicial restraint.

The constitutional provisions were originally intended to give Congress the principal power of decision as between war and peace. Chief Justice John Marshall, indeed, went so far as to say that "the whole powers of war" were "vested in Congress." The Founding Fathers, however, were well aware that the President must have authority to "repel sudden attacks," as Oliver Ellsworth put it, and the course of events soon led to a very broad interpretation of that phrase. During the Barbary Wars President Jefferson took a very cautious view of his powers, which was hotly disputed by Alexander Hamilton. The latter conceded that it was "the peculiar province of Congress, *when the nation is at peace,* to change that state into a state of war . . . in other words, it belongs to Congress only *to go to War.*" However, "when a foreign nation declares, or openly and avowedly makes war upon the United States, they are then by the very fact *already at war,* and any declaration on the part of Congress is nugatory; it is at least unnecessary."

Translated into modern terminology, Hamilton's distinction is drawn between "aggressive" and "defensive" wars. He wrote at a time when Grotian notions had gone out of fashion, and war was, in Lieber's phrase, "the means to obtain great ends of state." But the consequence of Hamilton's view under the United Nations Charter and the Nuremberg principles is indeed curious. If no Congressional authority is needed for defensive wars, and if aggressive wars are outlawed, then there is no room left for necessary and valid Congressional declarations of war, except perhaps in going to the aid of another country that has been wrongfully attacked.

If any event, Hamilton's expansionist approach to Presidential war powers prevailed, and today is conceived far more broadly than even he would have thought possible. In a military sense the world has diminished in size, and old distinctions between "direct attack" and "indirect threat" are blurred. Since the Second World War, all five Presidents—Truman in Korea, Eisenhower in Lebanon, Kennedy in Cuba, Johnson in Vietnam and the Dominican Republic, and Nixon in Cambodia—have taken military action in foreign parts on the basis of their authority as Commander-in-Chief, without Congressional sanction. A 1966 State Department public statement on "The Legality of United States Participation in the Defense of Viet-Nam" declares that the President, as Commander-in-Chief, has "the power to deploy American forces abroad and commit them to military operations when the President deems such action necessary to maintain the security and defense of the United States."

That, of course, is a 180-degree swing from John Marshall's view of the matter, and a virtual erasure of the Congressional role. The tortured course of the Vietnam war both at home and abroad, capped by President Nixon's Cambodian adventure, has aroused strong feeling in Congress that the executive power has been pushed much too far. During the Korean war President Truman, to avert a strike, seized the nation's steel mills and justified the act under his constitutional powers, without Congressional authority. The Supreme Court spanked him sharply, ruling that the President's powers as Commander-in-Chief did not support the seizure. There has never been a comparable judicial test of the President's power to commit troops to foreign wars, but if the courts should entertain such a case, it is doubtful that such sweeping claims of power as the State Department has made in connection with Vietnam would be upheld.

A much stronger case, however, can be made for the proposition that Congress *has* authorized our military operations in Vietnam, even though there has been no formal declaration of war. In the very same case in which he attributed "the whole powers of war" to Congress, Marshall recognized that by a series of statutes Congress had authorized "limited hostilities" against France, in the so-called "undeclared war" of 1798–1800.

There are a number of Congressional actions that might be cited to the same effect in connection with the Vietnam war. First and foremost is the Southeast Asia Resolution (better known as the Tonkin Resolution), taken in conjunction with the SEATO treaty. The latter provides that each party to it[1] "recognizes that aggression by means of armed attack . . . against any of the parties or against any state or territory which the parties by unanimous consent may hereafter designate, would endanger its own peace and safety, and agrees that it will in that event act to meet the common danger in accordance with its constitutional processes." A protocol to the treaty designated Vietnam (also Cambodia and Laos) as within the protection of the quoted clause. The Tonkin Resolution, enacted in August, 1964, approved the President's "determination . . . to take all necessary measures to repel any armed attack against the forces of the United States and to prevent further aggression," and declared that "the United States is . . . prepared, as the President determines, to take all necessary steps, including the use of armed force, to assist any

[1] The parties to the Southeast Asia Collective Defense Treaty, signed September 8, 1954 at Manila, are Australia, France, New Zealand, Pakistan, Philippines, Thailand, the United Kingdom and the United States.

member or protocol state of the Southeast Asia Collective Defense
Treaty requesting assistance in defense of its freedom."

Even those who most sharply dispute the constitutional validity of
the Vietnam war concede that this language pretty well covers subsequent military actions in Vietnam. But the actual intent and legitimate
effect of the Tonkin Resolution are hotly controversial questions today, and its original Congressional sponsors stoutly deny that it was
intended to authorize warfare limited only by the President's discretion. However, a few months later, and after the bombing of North
Vietnam had begun, Congress approved military appropriations that
the Administration explicitly labeled for support of the Vietnam operations. Again and again since, Congress has appropriated the
funds requested by the executive for this purpose, and there have
been other actions that seemingly conveyed approval of the Vietnam
venture, such as the 1965 penalties for the destruction of draft cards,
and the 1967 extension of the Selective Service Act.

But if all this makes a strong case it is still a debatable one, and
there remains the question whether the courts should undertake to
settle it. There is no doubt but that these issues of Presidential power
and legislative intent are much more familiar and congenial to
the judicial process than those involving the Nuremberg principles.
Furthermore, they are issues arising under the Constitution, the meaning and application of which are normally matters for the courts. But
there is serious question whether these particular constitutional issues—involving war, foreign affairs, and the respective powers of the
executive and legislative branches—do not fall within a category that
the courts have declined to adjudicate, under what lawyers call the
"political question doctrine."

An early and leading case illustrating this doctrine occurred in
1849, following a time of chaos in Rhode Island politics when there
were two rival state governments. The Constitution provides that
"The United States shall guarantee to every State in this Union a Republican form of Government," and it was asserted that one of the
two contenders did not meet this requirement and was therefore
illegitimate. But the Supreme Court declined to decide the point, on
the ground that the question was, as Chief Justice Taney put it,
"political in its nature," and thus committed entirely to Congress for
decision.

The political-question doctrine is itself controversial, and constitutional lawyers do not agree on its nature and purpose. For Herbert Wechsler it is itself a matter of constitutional Interpretation; it is finding in the words of the Constitution a direction that a particular provision, or area of governmental action, is removed from the judicial purview and committed exclusively to the legislative or executive branches. For Alexander Bickel, on the other hand, the doctrine is one of judicial discretion, to enable the Supreme Court "to maintain itself in the tension between principle and expediency." Adherents of the Bickel view lay stress on the inherent political weakness of the federal judiciary, dependent as it is on Congress for organization, jurisdiction and funding, and on the executive for appointments and enforcement of its orders. The courts' survival and ability to make their decisions "stick" depend heavily on public respect for and acceptance of their decisions, and there are occasions when political discretion suggests that the courts do well to stay clear of involvement in divisive and potentially explosive public controversies.

As a theory of constitutional interpretation the Wechsler view is much the more satisfactory, but it may well be that the Bickel approach more accurately reflects the workings of the judges' minds. Certainly there has been ebb and flow in the political-question doctrine's application, depending on the temper of the Supreme Court and its disposition to venture into new areas in a spirit of "activism." For many years the late Justice Felix Frankfurter was the leading spokesman of the school of judicial abstention or, as its opponents would call it, abdication. In 1962 his views suffered a sharp setback when the Court, after numerous refusals, finally decided to review the constitutional validity of the structuring of election districts. Many lawyers regard that case as signalling the decline of the political-question doctrine, and a greater willingness on the Court's part to step into the breach.

Foreign relations and war-making, however, have long been regarded by the Supreme Court as beyond the judicial ken. "The conduct of the foreign relations of our Government is committed by the Constitution to the Executive and Legislative—'the political'—Departments of Government," wrote Justice Clarke in 1918, "and the propriety of what may be done in the exercise of this political power is not subject to judicial inquiry or decision." More recently the late

Justice Jackson, in a case where Supreme Court review of an American war-crimes trial was sought, wrote: "Certainly it is not the function of the Judiciary to entertain private litigation—even by a citizen —which challenges the legality, the wisdom, or the propriety of the Commander-in-Chief in sending our armed forces abroad or to any particular region."

Today the indications are that these views still prevail with a majority of the Supreme Court. In 1966, three Army privates ordered to Vietnam sued to restrain the Army from shipping them out, on the ground that there had been no constitutionally sufficient authorization for American military activity in Vietnam. The lower federal courts dismissed the suit, and the Supreme Court declined to review that decision by the procedure known as "denial of certiorarl." This is a wholly discretionary process by which the Court indicates only that it does not wish to hear a case, without passing on any of the issues it presents. Justices Douglas and Stewart (an odd couple) dissented, saying that the Court should have heard argument, but did not indicate whether they thought the Court should decide the issue of the war's "validity" or, if so, how it should be settled.

This is inconclusive, but certainly suggests no eagerness on the part of the Court to grasp the nettle by telling Congress what it has or has not done, or the President whether he is acting within his constitutional powers. Of course, if a lower federal court should decide that our Vietnam involvement is unconstitutional, and that therefore the objecting registrant cannot be inducted or the soldier sent to war, the Court might well feel obliged to review the case, rather than let so portentous a ruling stand. But so far that has not happened; the lower courts have held the political doctrine applicable, on the basis of reasons such as those relied on by Judge Charles Wyzanski of the Federal District bench in Massachusetts:

> From the foregoing this Court concludes that the distinction between a declaration of war and a cooperative action by the legislative and executive with respect to military activities in foreign countries is the very essence of what is meant by a political question. It involves just the sort of evidence, policy considerations, and constitutional principles which elude the normal processes of the judiciary and which are far more suitable for determination by coordinate branches of the government. It is not an act of abdication when a court says that political questions of

this sort are not within its jurisdiction. It is a recognition that the tools with which a court can work, the data which it can fairly appraise, the conclusions which it can reach as a basis for entering judgments, have limits.

As matters stand today, it appears unlikely that the Supreme Court will confront the issue. Still these arguments continue to be pressed in a multitude of lower federal court cases. Whether or not this is a fruitful technique for resolution of the Vietnam crisis is a question to which I will shortly recur.

Issues such as those just discussed can be determined largely within the framework of United States domestic law, but of course that is not true of the so-called "Nuremberg defense," which rests on overriding principles of international law and treaties. In another recent case, wherein a draft registrant was convicted of failing to report for induction, the defendant unsuccessfully appealed on the ground that the war is illegal under the London Charter establishing the Nuremberg Tribunal. In this case, too, the Supreme Court declined to review the case, with Justice Douglas the lone dissenter. Supposing that the Court had taken the case, what "law" could it have looked to as the basis of decision?

On this point, the Supreme Court and all other American courts are governed by the so-called "supremacy clause" in Article VI of the Constitution, which provides:

> *This Constitution, and the Laws of the United States which shall be made in Pursuance thereof; and all Treaties made, or which shall be made, under the Authority of the United States, shall be the supreme Law of the Land; and the Judges in every State shall be bound thereby, any Thing in the Constitution or laws of any State to the Contrary notwithstanding.*

For present purposes, the most significant thing about this clause is that international law, except as embodied in treaties to which we are party, is not part of the "supreme law of the land." The second and almost equally important point is that treaties are not accorded any higher dignity than the "laws"—that is, the statutes enacted by Congress. Treaties and statutes stand on an equal footing, and it has long been settled that in the event of conflict or inconsistency between a treaty and a statute, whichever is of later date prevails.

The consequences of all this, as applied to a Supreme Court adjudication of a challenge to the Vietnam operations on "Nuremberg" grounds, is that the Court would have no authority, under the supremacy clause, to rely on doctrines of "just and unjust wars" or any other general international law principles. The Court could look only to treaties, and since the London Charter was never consented to by the Senate, it may not be a "treaty" within the meaning of the supremacy clause, though that is far from clear. Opponents of the war would have to place primary reliance on Article 2 of the United Nations Charter, under which the members agree to "refrain in their international relations from the threat or use of force against the territorial integrity or political independence of any state, or in any other manner inconsistent with the purposes of the United Nations." Supporters of our Vietnam policy would reply by reference to Article 51 of the Charter, which preserves "the inherent right of individual or collective self-defense if an armed attack occurs against a Member of the United Nations."

However, interpretation of the United Nations Charter would not end the matter, because of the parity of treaties and statutes. And here the issue would closely parallel the one just discussed concerning the constitutional basis of our Vietnam operations, for if Congress, by the Tonkin Resolution, appropriations, Selective Service legislation, or in any other statutory way has authorized those activities, these later statutory enactments would prevail in the event of any conflict with the United Nations or London Charters.

The Constitution, of course, is superior to both statutes and treaties. It is conceivable that, in some unlikely contexts, an argument could be made that the Fifth Amendment, in barring Congress from enacting any statute that deprives any "person" of "life, liberty, or property, without due process of law," might be held to embody basic elements of natural law. If in a fit of frenzy Congress should authorize the torture and execution of all prisoners of war, a constitutional barrier might thus be discovered. But it is quite beyond the bounds of possibility that the Court would use so blunt a tool to unravel the tangle of treaties, agreements and resolutions that are involved in determining the aggressive or defensive character of our Vietnam involvement.

In short, under the limitations of the supremacy clause, the Supreme Court *is not authorized* to render judgment on the validity of our participation in the Vietnam war under the Nuremberg principles or international law in general.

The direction in which the foregoing legal factors all point, I believe, is that the courts are not a suitable or sufficient forum for the settlement of our Vietnam problem. And apart from purely legal considerations, it seems to me that there are powerful political and practical considerations that lead to the same conclusion.

Contemplate, for example, the spectacle of the Supreme Court reviewing and pronouncing judgment on the question whether Congress has authorized our Vietnam operations, with Congress sitting at hardly a stone's throw and able to speak for itself. It is true that the Court made just such an adjudication in the steel seizure case, but there the arguments for finding Congressional approval were insubstantial compared to those that can be marshaled in connection with Vietnam. The steel seizure was a single Presidential act, important but paling into insignificance in comparison with the third costliest war in the nation's history, in the conduct of which the Congress has participated in many ways.

Of course, the fact that Congress has not said "no" is not *legally* significant, since the question is whether the war can be constitutionally waged if Congress has not said "yes." But politically, Congress' failure to act decisively to bring the war to an end is exceedingly significant in assessing the consequences of an adverse decision by the Court. As John Norton Moore remarks, "It is difficult for a President to pursue sustained military actions without the active support of a substantial segment of Congress and the American people." Through its power of the purse, its power to make rules for the regulation of the armed forces and if necessary its impeachment powers, a Congress determined to bring the Vietnam war to the quickest possible end can find ways and means to do so. After five years of bloody and costly war sustained by Congressional appropriations, if the President's course is to be checked by another branch of the government, it is the Congress and not the Court that can and should be the checking agent.

Quite apart from the limitations of the supremacy clause, the objections to a Court decision based on the antiaggression provisions of the Nuremberg or United Nations Charters are even more compelling. The political strain on the Court would be much greater, for while a decision on the constitutional basis of the war would appear as a sort of judicial arbitration between the two other branches' respective powers, a decision based on the Nuremberg principles would be regarded as putting international law over Constitution, Congress and President combined.

Furthermore, the evidentiary problems would be well-nigh insuperable. It is hardly to be thought that the United States and South Vietnamese governments would open up their secret diplomatic and military document files for inspection by the litigants. At Nuremberg and Tokyo alike, military conquest had accomplished just that, and especially at Nuremberg the volume and candor of the documents, as well as Hitler's focal role, greatly simplified the issue of intent.

But no such aids are available now. "An international lawyer writing about an ongoing war cannot hope to reach clear conclusions about all the legal issues involved," writes Richard Falk: "It is virtually impossible to unravel conflicting facts underlying conflicting legal claims." An American court, be it the Supreme Court or a lesser tribunal, would find the path to "clear conclusions" equally obstructed. Total military victories such as those that ended the Second World War are comparatively rare in modern history, and it is difficult to envisage other circumstances that would unlock the secret files. In the nuclear age, with the three greatest powers involved in the Vietnam war, total victory would probably leave few with any stomach for war crimes trials, or indeed any stomachs at all.

In some draft-resistance cases, the defendants have pressed the "Nuremberg defense" by contending that, if the Vietnam war is in fact aggressive, they will be liable to prosecution as war criminals if they engage in it. Professor Falk has given this argument a qualified blessing, writing that "the wider logic of Nuremberg extends to embrace all those who, knowingly at any rate, participate in a war they have reason to believe violates the restraints of international law."

Wherever the "wider logic" might lead, the Nuremberg judgments, as we have seen, have no such wide embrace. Those convicted at both Nuremberg and Tokyo of "crimes against peace" were all part of the inner circles of leadership, and the Nuremberg acquittals of generals and industrialists cut directly against Professor Falk's argument. Furthermore, there is much ambiguity in his phrase "reason to believe." No doubt there are today millions of Americans who, on the basis of generally available information, would claim a "reasonable belief" that we are "in the wrong" in Vietnam and, if educated in the terminology, would label it "aggressive." But there are more millions who think otherwise, and the issue between these disagreeing millions cannot rationally be projected in terms of criminal liability for rendering military service.

"There was no decision in Nuremberg," writes Benjamin Ferencz, one of the prosecutors there, "which would support a conclusion that the United States Armed Forces, like pirate ships, are criminal organizations." Nor was there any decision that international law confers immunity from military service on the basis of an individual's personal judgment that his country's foreign and military policies are wrong. Much less was it decided that domestic courts can be expected to sit in judgment on the foreign policies of the very government of which those courts are a part. The Nuremberg and Tokyo judgments were rendered by international tribunals on a *post mortem* basis (all too literally), surrounded by virtual libraries of the defeated governments' most secret papers. Professor Falk overlooks these factors, I believe, in suggesting that domestic courts sitting during the course of hostilities may be called upon to follow in the footsteps of Nuremberg, let alone embrace its "wider logic."

Lawyers called upon to represent young men who refuse to serve are abundantly justified in raising both the constitutional and the Nuremberg arguments in their defense. The force and sincerity of such contentions may serve their clients well even if they do not prevail as propositions of law. Judges and juries should be made aware of the tenuous basis on which they are asked to attribute criminal guilt to men whose driving motive may be that of obedience to a higher law. Furthermore, these arguments based on constitutional or international principle are of great public benefit in projecting profound moral and political issues in the legal dimension and expanding public understanding of our national predicament.

But the predicament itself is not, I believe, susceptible to solution by judicial decree. There is no such simple way to end the Vietnam tragedy, for the Supreme Court is not a *deus ex machina*. This war, and the agony and rancor that are its product, have been the work of the President and the Congress—the people's elected agents—and the war can be ended only by action of the national will, exerted through political, not judicial, channels.

VII WAR CRIMES: NUREMBERG AND VIETNAM

William L. Calley

LIEUTENANT CALLEY: HIS OWN STORY

Lieutenant Calley—at once the scourge of the American conscience and the hero of the toughminded "realists"—symbolized the dilemma of the United States fallen from grace. A nation which had prided itself on being the bearer of culture, democracy, and all that was good in the world suddenly found itself two decades after Nuremberg fighting a war that could not be won abroad and threatened with revolution at home. It came as a shock to many people when it was revealed during the course of the Calley court-martial that Americans were just as capable of committing mass murder as were the Fascists and Communists before them. As a result, the Calley memoirs are an extraordinary document; they reveal the thoughts of the "boy next door" who went to war for America in the 1960s.

We made a new assault on Mylai One in March. Remember the first one? How we were fired on from behind by "civilians" in Mylai Six? So now we landed outside of Mylai Six and were fired on from behind by "civilians" in Mylai Five. The soldiers said, "God, they're behind us," after which it was simply hell.

All this happened to Bravo company, the assault force that day. Our company was to the north again, and we were still milling there when it was called off. At noon, I got a radio call and Medina said, "So much for the second punch," and I took everyone to Uptight again. We had blown it again, and I went to walking around again. To getting guys up at seven. To listening to Medina tell me, "Calley, swing out and check out the village there." To listening to GIs ask me, "What in the hell for?" To never stopping, to hitting the ground when a VC fired, to hitting mines, to losing guys to dysentery, hepatitis, malaria: it had become routine now. I had come to Vietnam with forty-four men: I had twenty-four now.

At night, we would have to dig in. I'd have a beer, perhaps, and I would call in the defcons: the defensive concentrations, and I'd try to remember the damn registration numbers, the 711833 zulus and so on. I hated those, and I hated having to go waking guys up and

From *Lieutenant Calley: His Own Story* as told to John Sack, pp. 80–85, 95–121.

asking them, "Who is on guard here?" I'd go to sleep eventually, and god:

"Charlie One. This is Diamondhead Six," the Colonel.

"Diamondhead Six? This is Charlie One."

"Charlie One, I've got a situation here. I want you to get your troops up."

"What's up?"

"You're wasting time, Charlie One. I want you to get your troops moving out."

"At what time do—"

"Don't be smart with me, Charlie One! Right Now!"

It had become routine: the Colonel sending me shackle codes of coordinates, me then decoding them by a flashlight and just thinking, *Well, if I'm shot I'll save a hell of a walk*, the sergeants all asking me, "What in the hell's going on," the troops all screaming at me, "God-damn it! We walked all yesterday night, we walked all yesterday day, we got to walk tonight now? Don't they know, *We got to get some sleep*? Don't they have any respect for us—"

"Troop," I would say, "I don't give a damn if you go or go back to sleep: so shut up!"

Two o'clock in the pouring rain, and we would be moving out. Be starting another day by walking either in Indian style in that famous formation *hi diddle-diddle and file down the middle* and by being ambushed, or by keeping off trails and by falling into the holes, walking into the trees, falling into the paddies, stepping over the cliffs— We just were playing games here, and we were being laughed at. Cowboys, the Vietnamese called us. Boys with the pretty faces. Boy scouts.

Once, we came to a village where we really caught a VC, rifle and all. I don't exaggerate: I pulled him out of a secret room. He had gone through a crack, around a corner, and then behind a fireplace with an AK-41. We found him, though, and I sent him to military police with a manilla tag on: name, location, etcetera, and on the back something like "Found behind false wall." You won't believe it: I caught him again a few weeks later. In the same village again. And wearing the same manilla tag as though telling us, "I've been interrogated, and I'm okay. I've got a ticket to ride!" Of course, he had taken charcoal and he had crossed out the "Found behind false wall."

I told myself, *God. He has probably killed two or three of us. And the MPs didn't do a damn thing with him.* I went there angry: I said, "My god! I didn't call him a VCS," a VC suspect. "I said a VC!"

"Well, fine. So why didn't you go and shoot him? I can't," the MP said. "I'm at headquarters with the Geneva people on me."

"But you've got a POW camp—"

"A prisoner, I've got to give him a bed, a blanket, a pillow, and three square meals every day. And so many cubic meters space: I haven't space."

"But god! The guy's a VC—"

"All of these guys are VC. But they could tell me, 'I'm Egyptian,' and I'd have to believe them. We killed a man yesterday: the POW cannon zapped him. We aren't allowed to use coercion now."

"But if he's got an AK-41—"

"I'd love to be in the field with you. I'd take every prisoner and I'd kill every damn one. Do it, Lieutenant, or you're going to see these people back."

I didn't tell the GIs that: but I didn't have to. From then on, they would tell me, "My god, sir. Why don't we do something to these people?"

"What do you want to do? Send them to Task Force? They're going to send them back out."

"My god, sir. I want to do *something.*"

"Well, what do you want to do, troop? Talk to these people? Go in and pacify them?"

"Hell no! I want to go in and shoot them!"

I wouldn't let the GIs do it. I even hinted about the manilla tag guy, "He might be an Army intelligence agent." I just couldn't let the GIs kill without having orders to. Suppose an American politician told me, "That's horrible! If that woman was a VC, why didn't she have her uniform on? Her weapon?" I couldn't authorize that, and yet—I thought about it. I was troubled about it. My duty in our whole area was to find, to close with, and to destroy the VC. I had now found the VC. Everyone there was VC. The old men, the women, the children—the *babies* were all VC or would be VC in about three years. And inside of VC women, I guess there were a thousand little VC now. I thought, *Damn it, what do I do? Hack up all these damned people? Pull a machete out and kkk—? Chop up all of these people?*

Lt. William L. Calley, Jr. (right) walks with his military defense counsel, Maj. Kenneth A. Raby, at Fort Benning, Georgia. (*Wide World Photos*)

Standing at attention, Lt. William L. Calley, Jr. hears Col. Clifford Ford, left, read the court-martial verdict finding him guilty. He later was sentenced to life imprisonment. Beside Calley are his attorneys, George Latimer, left, and Major Kenneth Raby, right. The drawing is by CBS artist Howard Brodie for the Walter Cronkite' News Show. (*Wide World Photos*)

That's what the VC themselves will do. Kill the rear echelon people: ones in the quartermaster corps, the transportation corps, the ordnance corps—

Everyone said eliminate them. I never met someone who didn't say it. A captain told me, "Goddamn it. I sit with my starlight scope, and I see VC at this village every night. I could go home if I could eliminate it." A colonel: he told me about a general's briefing where the general said, "By god, if you're chasing dead VC and you're chasing them to that village, do it! I'll answer for it! I'll answer for it!" The general was in a rage saying, "Damn, and I'll lose my stars tomorrow if I tell those politicians who haven't been out of their bathtubs that." Americans would say, *It's wrong*, if American women fought in Vietnam, but the VC women will do it. And the VC kids: and everyone in our task force knew, *We have to drop the bomb sometime.*

And still people ask me, "What do you have against women?" Damn, I have nothing. I love them. I think they're the greatest things since camels. And children: I've nothing against them. "Why did you kill them?" Well damn it! Why did I go to Vietnam? I didn't buy a ticket for it. A man in Hawaii gave it to me. "Why did you go? Why didn't you go to jail instead?" Oh, you dumb ass: if I knew it would turn out this way, I would have. . . .

The briefing broke up. The troops went to supper: I didn't, I had too much to do. I got another map, I cut out the Mylai part, and I memorized it: the coordinates of the centers of Mylai Four, Five, Six, and One. I got the coordinates for Alpha and Bravo companies and the radio frequencies that day. I went to Medina's hooch for an order-of-battle briefing and to the military police: where the VC prisoners were. I said, "Any intell on Mylai?"

"Not much. If you want to talk to the prisoners—"

"All right."

I went to the tiger cage: a cage of ASP runway stuff that was sandbagged over. A dungeon: the POWs had to squat there. And get stiff, and if they escaped from it they could be caught: a tiger cage.

I squatted too, and asked a VC prisoner. *"VC Quangngai?"* It meant—oh, I didn't know. A million things, "Are you a VC from Quangngai?" "Are there any VC in Quangngai?" "Are you going to answer me?" If so, I would get an interpreter and I would ask—I still didn't know. I would ask for the moon, perhaps. For his telling me, "The battalion isn't in Mylai One. It's in Mylai Four." Or Five. Or Six, and I would call the Phantoms in. A battalion there in a five hundred meter by three hundred meter area, the Phantoms could easily burn it. With napalm: I say anything but to send soldiers in and lose lives. And so I asked that man, *"VC Quangngai?"*

"No bitt."

"VC number one?"

"VC number ten."

I shrugged. There was a POW cannon there: I might get us some intelligence that way. It had just killed a POW, though, and now the MPs were petrified: *It's illegal.* What if some autopsy shows that he was electrocuted? And someone investigates? "Well, we were interrogating him. And shining lights in his eyes. And using him as a filament—" No, they didn't want to go to Leavenworth for that damned war. And the POW cannon was half destroyed then. I knew, *No intell.*

I still hadn't eaten. I went where the MPs lived, and I saw a bottle of A-1 sauce. I asked them, "How did you get it?"

"PX."

"Mind if I use it?"

"No. Ah, Lieutenant? About POWs," the MP went on. "Our tiger cage is filled up. Brigade and Division are filled too. And the Vietnamese tell us, '*We* didn't capture them.'"

"So—?"

"So don't send us POWs tomorrow."

I didn't answer: hell, the MPs had always said it. I took the A-1 sauce, and I made pizza pies out of C-ration bread, C-ration cheese, and C-ration beef. I thought, *Anyone with an AK rifle, I will send to Dotti tomorrow. For intelligence:* a Vietnamese would really be safer tomorrow with an AK-41. I gave the MPs some pizza pies, we had beer and we turned on the armed forces television channel: I think the Miss America. No, that wouldn't be in March then. The Academy Awards? Or the Grammies: I didn't really watch, and I left telling the MPs, "See you." I should have but I didn't say, "I hope."

I went along the platoon perimeter. I knew, *We must be ready tomorrow. We must be sharp or*—Well, if we're ready we needn't worry. I asked the men, "Is everything ready?"

"Yes sir."

I woke up Sergeant Mitchell and Sergeant Bacon, "The men. Are their weapons clean?"

"Yes sir."

I woke up Platoon Sergeant Cowen: I had a thousand questions for him. "How are the C's? How are the RTO's batteries? The helicopters: who's on the first one? The second one? The—"

"Everything's ready, sir. You give the Top the promotion list?"

"The promotion list? I will tomorrow."

"And tell him I want a cot here, please."

"I will, Sergeant Cowen."

"And also. I got to get to Division soon, I got this shoulder—"

He talked of everything else but Mylai. I went to the second platoon leader's hooch: to Lieutenant Brooks's. And they had a poker game on! His playing cards and his MPC, or his military payment certificates, were on the ammunition boxes, and his RTO was asleep with a radio on him playing the Cream, perhaps. A card player told me, "Come in. Got any money?"

"No—"

"Three sixes. Get you a Bud?"

"No—" I told him. "I think I'll rack out."

I went outside again. It was dead silent there. It was dark out, and I got snagged on the concertina wire as I went through it. I knew, *I'm as ready as anyone can be*: I felt empty anyhow. I wanted to keep asking questions so I wouldn't think, *I feel empty*. Or maybe to get some honest answers. "Are you ready, troop?"

"No sir."

"I am not ready either. I will never be."

I admit it: I was afraid. I can see now, *Everyone was*. And everyone hid it: Calley, Cowen, Brooks. And everyone hid it a different way. I kept walking, but I looked up and said softly, "Help us to be good soldiers tomorrow. Help us to make the right decisions: amen."

And slept. The next day, I got up roughly at six o'clock. I put some water in a steel pot: a helmet, and I shaved with it. And washed my armpits and groin area to keep fungus off. I dressed, and I had chow: scrambled eggs, a creamed hamburger, coffee, and I drew water for six canteens. I put those and the C-rations into a rucksack, and I saddled up: a cartridge belt, the rucksack, a flak jacket perhaps

(I can't really remember that), and a brassiere sort of bandolier of ammunition clips. A rifle, and I just really swabbed it: I had done everything there was to do. It's weird, I even combed my hair thinking, *Why in the hell am I doing this?* And put on a helmet over it.

The troops. For once, I didn't try to speed them up. Or chew their ass: I just didn't want the platoon pissed off. Medina yelled, "Get your goddam people down to that helicopter pad!"

"I don't think they'll start the firefight without us."

"Get your people down, or I'll get someone who can!"

On the choppers: there the adrenalin started. We felt as automobile racers do: *A split second, and I might hit the very edge of disaster. Or pass it.* We had about twenty thousand rounds for our M-16s with us: four hundred every man. And fifteen thousand for our machine guns, and four hundred grenades for our M-79 launchers, and a dozen shells for our 81-millimeter mortar. The choppers around us had fire behind them: the M-5 grenade launchers, the rocket launchers, and the miniguns were on Mylai already. A minigun: a super machine gun, in a minute it can have holes in every square foot of a football field. It was just devastating fire! We saw the artillery hit: a battery of four 105-millimeter cannons at Uptight and a heavy battery of 155-millimeters and 175-millimeters at Dotti. We saw them hit on the tree tops of Mylai. And the Navy had swift-boats for us with thirty-caliber and fifty-caliber machine guns. And mortars. If need be destroyers and, I think, the *New Jersey,* and the Air Force its Phantom jets. And that, I think, was really piss-poor: the Phantoms if *need* be. I wanted the Phantoms ready to go! On the runway itself! I had said to Captain Medina, "I don't care if I get them after I'm dead!"

For remember. I didn't know if a VC squad, or platoon, or company —*what* was in Mylai Four. Or the goddamn battalion even. I only knew, *It is shooting at us*: I got that from the chopper pilot. He brought her in and shouted at me, "A hot one!" It meant, "We are under fire!" It meant a lot more, though, "I hope you'll make it. I hope *I'll* make it. I am not staying here! Get out!" I thought, *Well, here we go,* I got up, I jumped—I didn't move. I tried, I just forced myself, I jumped a few meters into the paddies under me. The troops jumped out of the chopper behind me. Ahead of us: Mylai Four.

I'm going to die sometime: I had always known it. Ignored it: and knocked on the door of death today, and I couldn't ignore it. The fear now: I was saturated with it. I *felt* it, I kept running but it took extra effort to. A bullet: a pretty good way to go, I knew. No fuss. No muss, I wouldn't even know it was hitting me. A mine: that's worse, to wake up and think, *Now, what did I lose? My legs: I still have my arms, though*, I would try to think positively. Of the great guys who run around, jump out of planes, hop up a mountainside with an artificial leg. I would think, *I'm out, I don't have to worry anymore.* I had that mechanism: and I kept running to Mylai Four. It whirled, it was like seeing a bomb burst or a person blow up.

The fear: nearly everyone had it. And everyone had to destroy it: Mylai, the source of it. And everyone moved into Mylai firing automatic. And went rapidly, and the GIs shot people rapidly. Or grenaded them. Or just bayoneted them: to stab, to throw someone aside, to go on. Supposedly, the GIs said, "Chalk one up," "Hey, I got another one," "Did you see the fucker die?" I didn't hear it: I just heard Medina telling me, "Keep going," and I said, *"Keep going! Keep going! Keep—"*

"God," people say. "But these were old men, and women, and children." I tell you: I didn't see it. I had this mission, and I was intent upon it: I only saw, *They're enemy.* Of course, I still was in South Vietnam. I knew, *There are old men, women, and children in South Vietnam.* It was common sense: sure, but in combat there is damn little common sense.

To start with, we had come in the wrong way: I had been where the second platoon was to be. We had switched sides, and I had been called by Captain Medina, "Any body count?" I had seen bodies out in a tapioca patch: the artillery's doing. Or the grenades, rockets, or miniguns. Or ourselves: I didn't know, but I had said to Medina, "Six to nine bodies." He said to Task Force, "Sixty-nine bodies." In Mylai, the GIs had slowed up for hedges, bushes, trees, for fences, for houses: and then fired at GIs ahead, and I had thought, *God, we are just going to kill each other.* It's true: I hadn't heard any VC rifle fire. Or mortar fire, but I didn't say, *Gee, I can breathe easy now.* A cross-country runner doesn't say, *Gee whiz, I'm out ahead. I can slow up—* He keeps saying, *Keep going.*

Medina says now, "You have to use common sense." Well, I wasn't taught at OCS to use common sense: I was taught, "Do this!

Do this like this!" In combat, if Medina had really told me, "Use common sense," I'd have said, "Sure, I'm going back to Hawaii." In December! To use saturation fire: to use rifles, rockets, cannons, mortars, miniguns, and machine guns on a little guerilla—hell, to go to Vietnam to fight him, is that common sense? It is America's strategy though. To keep putting the "stuff" out: to kill everyone in Mylai before someone gets an AK rifle out. And still people tell me, "But these are old men, and women, and children." Now, *they* ought to have common sense. And give us a bullet which won't hurt the old men and women and children.

And babies. On babies everyone's really hung up. "But babies! The little innocent babies!" Of course, we've been in Vietnam for ten years now. If we're in Vietnam another ten, if your son is killed by those babies you'll cry at me, "Why didn't you kill those babies that day?" In fact, I didn't say, "Kill babies," but I simply knew, *It will happen.* I knew if I was in Mylai with twenty thousand rounds, if I didn't shoot at paper targets there would be men, women, children, and babies hurt. It's chaos in combat, and I couldn't tell the GIs that day, "Be careful now." We aren't there to coddle them now. Or be cowboys, or be laughed at. Or listen to people say, *"No bitt."* Not any of us! And we didn't deny it at Fort Benning, Georgia. A squad sergeant from the second platoon testified, "We complied with the orders, sir."

"Did you kill men, women, and children in Mylai Four on March 16, 1968?"

"Yes." A squad sergeant from the third platoon said, "We could see people running from the first and second platoon. We stopped the peoples, and one of the GIs asked, 'What are we to do with them?' I said, 'Well, everything *is* to be killed—' And one of the individuals opened up on these individuals."

"Did your entire squad fire?"

"I can't really say."

"Did you fire?"

"Yes. I figured, *They're already wounded, I might as well go and kill them. This is our mission.*"

"Well now. Men, women, and children?"

"And your estimate of the number?"

"Ten."

All the platoons did it. And the Vietnamese knew, *I'm obstructing them. I had better fight or get out of their way.* And fled: and the pilots outside of Mylai just devastated them. I've heard of as many as five hundred killed that day. It's possible.

As for me, a leader who is shooting them is doing someone else's job. Not his own: and I had just taken seven clips or 125 rounds with me. Mostly tracers, so I could fire one and say, "Follow my tracer." I had just had to fire twice in Mylai Four. I had been alone at a big brick house, and I had looked inside. In the fireplace there was a Vietnamese man. At the window another one—and I shot them, I killed them. And strange: it just didn't bother me. I had once had a BB gun, and I shot a sparrow with it. I cried then, but now? I thought, *Sonofabitch's dead, and I got a body count now.* The worst thing about it had been the noise. My rifle made noise. It went bang: and that was the worst thing about it. I can't answer those who say, "Man, how can you kill someone?"

"I don't know," I say. "Use a rifle, I guess. Or stab him. Or burn him. Or some other way. And you?"

"I couldn't kill anyone."

"Even if they would kill *you?*"

"I couldn't kill anyone."

"Well, you'll be a poor soldier then."

"I couldn't live with it."

A silly statement, I think. Most of America's males were in Korea or World War II or I. They killed, and they aren't all going batshit. They simply escaped it. The human mind: I think it has more defense mechanisms than it has smarts. As for me, killing those men in Mylai didn't haunt me. I didn't—I couldn't kill for the pleasure of it. We weren't in Mylai to kill human beings, really. We were there to kill *ideology* that is carried by—I don't know. Pawns. Blobs. Pieces of flesh, and I wasn't in Mylai to destroy intelligent men. I was there to destroy an intangible idea.

To destroy communism. Now, I hate to say it, but most people know a lot more about communism than I do. In school, I never thought about it. I just dismissed it: I looked at communism as a Southerner looks at a Negro, supposedly, *It's evil. It's bad.* I went to school in the 1950s, remember, and it was drilled into us from grammar school on, *Ain't is bad, aren't is good, communism's bad, democ-*

racy's good. One and one's two, etcetera: until when we were at Edison high, we just didn't think about it. Well: Mary did. Mary was a timid girl at Edison who still would evaluate things. Who if someone said, "Sex isn't good," she would try it and answer, "No, its great," and if someone said, "Communism's bad," she would ask, "Why?" A friend of mine called her a communist once, but Mary simply told him, "I'm not," and sent him a Christmas subscription to—What is it? *Pravda?*

I wasn't like her. I was a run-of-the-mill average guy: I still am. I always said, *The people in Washington are smarter than me.* If intelligent people told me, "Communism's bad. It's going to engulf us. To take us in," I believed them. I had to. I was sure it could happen: the Russians could come in a parachute drop. Or a HALO drop or some submarines or space capsules even. It could happen today in Los Angeles, I guess, or in San Francisco. A surprise attack: the Russians on a direct trajectory to City Hall. To the head honcho and say, "Surrender. Or watch us kill every man, woman, and child here." And if the mayor hesitates for a moment, they do it! They line up a thousand people and kill every single one. And get the mayor on his knees thinking, *God. These people are horrible. These people are monsters. God, to kill little children!* The mayor would say, "I surrender."

They did it in Vietnam, the communists. I had once known the Vietnamese village chief at Dotti. A hard rugged man: a John Wayne, but I had seen how the communists beat him. He had come to me sobbing, screaming, carrying with him a large earthen water jar. In it I saw what looked like a lot of stewed tomatoes. Blood. And a jagged bone. And hair. And some floating lumps of flesh. The interpreter said, "It was on his doorstep today."

"What is it?"

"His son."

"Who did it?"

"VC."

They had won. They had done him in. Those people are monsters, and they have no qualms, no hang-ups, no holding-backs to the extremes they'll go to. I mean butcherings: this is what communism does, and we were there in Mylai to destroy it. Personally, I didn't kill any Vietnamese that day: I mean personally. I represented the United States of America. My country.

I came out of Mylai on the other side: the eastern side, and I saw some people ahead of me. Vietnamese, and Americans watching them: I understood why. One squad at Mylai wasn't supposed to kill everyone there. We had those mines to go through, and the Vietnamese people would know the way. Would know if a zigzag wire, a bamboo stick that is slanted west, or is slanted east—if any of these meant mines, and Medina had told me, "Save some of the people." I'd said to Sergeant Mitchell, "Save some," and clearly those were the Vietnamese ahead of me. In fact, I'm not even sure if I saw them: I knew I had ordered it, *They're there*. It was just incidental to me. I was indifferent about it, I *wasn't* indifferent about the VC bunkers there on the eastern side. We could be fired at from those bunkers, and I said to Sergeant Bacon, "Check them out."

Bacon said, "Roger." And went to the northern bunkers.

"Sir—" Sergeant Mitchell. "Do you want the others checked out?"

"Roger," and Mitchell went to the southern ones.

A call came from Captain Medina. "Where are you?"

"I'm on the eastern edge, and I'm checking the bunkers out."

"Well, damn it! I didn't tell you to check them out. Get your men in position."

"I have a lot of Vietnamese here," I said, or "I have a lot of VC—"

"Get rid of 'em. Get your men in position now." Medina knew, *We still have a VC battalion ahead. Any damn minute—*

"Roger," I said, and I started to where those people were. In the paddy ahead of me. At this irrigation ditch: a ditch that the Vietnamese get the water from. And were squatting there with a GI guarding them: PFC Meadlo. He was very afraid, I know. He thought, *Any minute, they'll have a counterattack. And pull on a piece of string somewhere. Or a chain somewhere or*—I know because he would testify so. I went up to Meadlo and asked him, "Do you know what you're to do with those people?" A damn illogical question. How in the hell could a PFC know what to do?" *I* didn't know what to do. I may have thought, *Well, if Meadlo knows what to do, I won't have to worry about it.* A damn illogical question in this illogical place: in Vietnam. "Do you know what to do with those people?"

"Yes—"

And right then, I saw a GI with one of those individuals: a Vietnamese girl. He had hold of her hair to keep holding her to her knees.

He had a hand grenade (I was later told) to threaten her little baby with. He wanted a blow job.

I ran right over. "Get on your goddamn pants," I said. "Get over where you're supposed to be!"

I don't know why I was so damn saintly about it. Rape: in Vietnam it's a very common thing. And Mylai, I've even heard that's a twelve-year-old in the photograph in *Life*. A soldier from the platoon that did it would testify about it. "There were girls in that group, weren't there?"

"I imagine there were."

"Didn't one of you molest one?"

"I couldn't say. He tore her blouse off, if that's what you call molest."

"One of you fired then, is that correct?"

"That's right."

"Why?"

"I figure, *He thought this was his orders. Kill everything.*"

"Was it his orders to tear the girl's blouse off?"

"I object—"

In the other platoon, a GI raped a girl, another was in her mouth, another was in her hand, soldiers say. And even say, "She waved goodbye." Well, I guess lots of girls would rather be raped than be killed anytime. So why was I being saintly about it?

Because: if a GI is getting a blow job, he isn't doing his job. He isn't destroying communism. Of course, if I had been ordered to Mylai to rape it, pillage, and plunder—well, I still don't know. I may be old-fashioned, but I can't really see it. Our mission in Mylai wasn't perverted, though. It was simply "Go and destroy it." Remember the Bible: the Amalekites? God said to Saul,

> Now go . . . and utterly destroy all that they have, and spare them not; but slay both man and woman, infant and suckling, ox and sheep, camel and ass.
> But the people took of the spoil—

and God punished them. No difference now: if a GI is getting gain, he isn't doing what we are paying him for. He isn't combat-effective.

"Get on your goddamn pants," I said.

He didn't argue. He complied, and I went north to Sergeant Bacon.

He may have had a few rapists too: I couldn't tell, he was still at those bunkers, anyhow. I told him to hurry up, and showed him a cemetery a hundred meters east.

"For your machine gun. And spread your men to the right of it."

"Roger."

And again. A call from Captain Medina, "What are you doing now?"

"I'm getting ready to go."

"Now damn it! I told you: Get your men in position *now*! Why did you disobey my damn order?"

"I have these bunkers here—"

"To hell with the bunkers!"

"And these people, and they aren't moving too swiftly."

"I don't want that crap! Now damn it, *waste* all those goddamn people! And get in the damn position!"

"Roger!"

I really moved. I said to Sergeant Bacon, "Get your people together right now! *Move out,*" and I went south to Sergeant Mitchell. Telling the RTO, "Now shut the damn radio off," or anyhow thinking it. The screaming: I was sick of it, Medina was right behind me and pulling my string. And the Colonel his?

I passed by PFC Meadlo. He still had the Vietnamese there. I didn't even stop, I said, "Damn it! You said, *I know what to do with these goddamn people.* Get rid of 'em!" I meant—hell, I didn't think this out. I meant, "Get rid of 'em." I meant, "Go wave a magic wand. And say, 'Disappear.'" I meant, "Waste them," but I didn't think of what *that* meant. If it meant to Meadlo, "Kill them," I must admit it: I had that meaning. I had those orders: "Get in the damn position." A hundred meters ahead, and the Vietnamese were all in the goddamn way. I wasn't playing games here! I said to Meadlo, "Get them on the other side of the ditch. Or get rid of 'em!"

"Roger." Or some affirmative word.

I didn't stop, I went on to Sergeant Mitchell. He had some stuff from the bunkers there, such as cartridge cases. And nothing much, and I told him, "Forget it! Do you see the three trees there? Set up your machine gun—" And then, I heard shooting near us: north of us. I said to Sergeant Mitchell, "And spread your men to the left: to Sergeant Bacon."

"Roger."

And went to where the shooting was. I went around a few bushes, and I saw people down in the irrigation ditch. And dead: and a few more still stepping in. I saw Meadlo there. And Dursi, *"I like kids, and I can't tell them, Go away."* And the prosecutor says Conti. And Grzesik, *"It's futile. I don't want to question them."* And some others, and I fired into the ditch myself. A few rounds: I had those tracer rounds, and they're bad for the M-16. They're painted red: it peels off in the chamber, generally. You can jam, and I fired at the most a half-dozen rounds, at the most sixty seconds. At the whole mass, and at a Vietnamese just rolling away. Or crawling away, and I told the GIs, "Now damn it! Get over on the other side! In position!"

I was mad! To begin with, I had those mines ahead, and I had wanted the Vietnamese ahead of me. Not dead, and especially not in the goddamn ditch. What if I had gotten hit? And needed this to fight out of? I knew the GIs wouldn't *jump* in with corpses around, and I knew damn well *I* wouldn't. It's sort of a messy trench, and I was damn irritated about it. But mostly about the GIs themselves. I didn't want Medina bitching at me: I wanted them in position. *Now,* and I said to Dursi, "Hurry up. Get on the other side of the ditch before you're sick." He had an *Ohhh* look, as though he were hunting deer and he had looked in a dead deer's eyes. It had been dirty work: a GI's a human being, and I said to Dursi, "Move out." He testified later, "It was in a sympathetic tone." I suppose so.

Meadlo was someone else. A kick in the ass wouldn't humiliate him: it wouldn't even get him mad. And the GI just needed one. He was still shooting down at the dead people down in the ditch. On automatic (there is some madness in war, believe me). He was afraid, remember, and he may have thought, *If there's someone alive, he'll be after me.* He would testify later that he had kept switching clips and ("I imagine") crying. I can believe it: Meadlo was simply losing grip. I kicked him, I told him, "Get on the other side of the god-damn ditch."

"All right—"

"Now go!"

He stopped shooting. He got reoriented: a day later, though, he would become hysterical. He would step on a booby trap, it would take his right foot off, he would be just bananas. "My little girl. My little girl. Oh, what have they done? She's innocent—" As for me, I would get a powder burn and a rock in my throat: nothing much, but Meadlo would cry, "They'll get you, Lieutenant Calley. They'll get you, Lieutenant Calley. You've got to get out of Vietnam." I'd have a few tears myself: *I'm alive,* but mostly for Meadlo. A perfect soldier. He always obeyed me. He didn't say, "Why? Why? Why," as I didn't say to Medina, "Why?"

At the ditch again. It had a log across it: a bridge, and the GIs walked over it. Into position, and I went north to Sergeant Bacon. I told him to tell everyone, "No more shooting."

"We weren't shooting—"

"And this raping, too. The next time I catch—" I named the GI who wanted the blow job, "I will court-martial him and you too! So you better watch out."

"I wasn't—"

"Now get in position!"

"Yes sir, but I wasn't shooting."

I'm not really sure of the sequence now. I saw a man in a white shirt and shorts, and I questioned him, *"VC adai?"*

"No bitt."

"VC adoe?"

"No bitt."

I thought, *You people. I only want to communicate with you. Now what in the hell must I do?* I asked him, *"VC adai!"*

"No bitt."

"VC adoe!"

"No bitt."

You sonofabitch. And bam: I butted him in his mouth with my M-16. Straight on: sideways could break the M-16. He had frustrated me! He bled, but I didn't kill him: I wanted him to interrogate later. He was about the same age I was, twenty-four.

He was drop-kicked into the ditch by—I don't know who. On the other side, a "Skeeter" or a small helicopter landed, the helicopter pilot left and a sergeant told me, "He wants whoever's in charge." I went where the helicopter was.

Where the pilot was. He told me, "There's lots of wounded here." He didn't say, "Vietnamese wounded," or "American wounded here."

But either way, it would be the third platoon's job: I was supposed to keep going on. "There's wounded here."

"Yes."

"So what will you do about it?"

"Nothing. Relay it to higher."

"I already did. Can you call for a Dustoff?"

"Can *you*?"

"I already did. But they don't respond."

"If they don't respond to you, they won't respond to me." The pilot left, and I may have said to my RTO, "He doesn't like the way I'm running the show. But I'm the boss," and I called Medina. "He doesn't like the way things are being done."

"Roger. Where are you now?"

"I'm just about in position."

"Get in the goddamn position. And don't worry about the casualties."

"Roger," and I went south again to Sergeant Mitchell. To check out the—Suddenly, I saw a man crawling near me. I shot and I killed him, I had my RTO check him, and the RTO said, "He was just a small boy." He had been crawling away: or pulling pins out of VC mines, I wouldn't know. I went on to Sergeant Mitchell, I checked out the GI positions, and I went to Sergeant Bacon. And checked out the GI positions: I was in position now. I was secure now. I didn't have to go on: I could come up with sense now.

I could evacuate people. Ahead, I saw ten old men, women, and children, and the Skeeter again. And that pilot again: I went over.

He said, "The civilians. Are you going to evacuate them?"

"The only way I have to evacuate them is a hand grenade." It was true: the Army had just given us the grenades and the M-16, that was all. I said, "*You* have the helicopters here."

He looked sort of surprised. As though thinking, *Gee, I guess that I do.* He had three: his small helicopter or Skeeter had two big Scorpions with it. And the Skeeter would look for the VC, and the Scorpions would hit the VC with rockets, grenades, and minigun fire. All morning long, and now the Skeeter pilot had the Scorpions come in. And take the old men, the women, and children. I helped him to carry them on: and then never saw the Skeeter pilot until it was fifteen months later. At the inspector General's Office, in Washington. He was wearing a sports shirt then: a red plaid one. He said, "The second one," and I stepped out of an Army lineup.

I asked them, "Who's that?"

"It's someone. He thinks he knows you."

"Fine."

Now in Mylai. It was lunchtime now: I sat with the mortar platoon leader and the forward observer for the artillery that day. I had some fruit, and I made small talk. "How is everything going?"

"Fine."

"Getting beer in?"

"Yeah. I guess I'll request it."

"We can get together tonight. Where did you get the two little girls?"

"Back there."

"Where?"

"In the hooches."

I opened a C-ration cracker can. I dipped them in C-ration cheese for the two Vietnamese with us. One was about four. And silent, the other was four, perhaps, and as cute as could be. A doll, a red little dress and all. I fed them the C-ration crakers, but I didn't play: I knew, *They're cute and all*. But they'd be alone in a little while. And starve. And stay there and rot, I knew. And the rats—well, it wouldn't be too nice being involved.

I felt the temperature now. I took my helmet off, and I used my rucksack to lie back on. To relax on: I knew I couldn't be fired on. For thirty years, the Japanese, the French, the Vietnamese, the GIs had never been in Mylai and not been fired on. I felt no jubilation, though: I was dead tired. To be in all that hysteria, the Captain's talk, the choppers in, the terror out in the paddies outside of Mylai, the hours inside it: everything, and to stop is to come right down. To crash: I was never on drugs, but I think that to "trip" and "to crash" is a similar thing to a morning at Mylai or anywhere else. To be at D-day or Iwo Jima, to do that shooting and TV shit, and to stop is a similar thing, I'm sure. All your adrenalin's gone, and you ask, *Now, what have I done? I've killed lots of German or Japanese or Vietnamese people. Big deal.* I felt I could really cry now. I lay in that paddy, I felt extremely tired, and I looked at the village ahead of me: Mylai

Five. A few minutes more, and we would assault it. And destroy it. So this is what war is. Big fucking deal.

Medina said. "What is the body count?" We sat on a log together a few minutes later.

It always aggravated me, the body count. I would say to Medina, "Three," Medina would tell the Colonel, "Six." He would double it. But anything went in a body count: the buffalos, cows, the Vietnamese, and I always wondered, *Who gives a flying*—? All right: the American people did. The reporters did. And the Army would tell us, "Everyone else has a body count. Why haven't you?"

"What is the body count?"

I said to Medina, "I don't know."

"What is your estimate then?"

"I don't know. Go to the village yourself. Or go over there to the ditch. And count 'em."

"Anything off the top of your head—"

"Oh hell. Thirty. Forty."

"Lieutenant Brooks?" Medina had all the platoon leaders there, and asked every one. He then called the Colonel, and he reported fifty for the first platoon, fifty for Brooks's platoon, fifty for the third platoon, fifty for the mortar platoon, fifty for the helicopter units, and fifty for the artillery. And maybe some for the headquarters troops: it appeared as one hundred and twenty-eight in *The New York Times*. Front page.

I didn't argue with him. I couldn't care less, and I sat and I talked to Lieutenant Brooks. "It'll be a hot damn day."

"Yeah. A hot one."

"We ought to shoot an azimuth on Mylai Five."

"Yeah—"

I heard Medina say, "Wait out." He was still on the radio to higher: to the task force, and it had some question, apparently. "The bodies," Medina asked us. "What per cent were civilians?"

Brooks said, "How do you tell?"

I said, "They're all VC. Or they're all civilians."

Medina said, "They want a per cent."

"Everyone's dead," I said. "So what per cent were civilians this morning?"

"I don't know."

"Or what per cent were VC this morning?"

"I don't know."

I thought, *You dumb ass. You already told us, "Everyone is."* "So classify them as civilians now. As far as I care."

"Well—" Medina went on. "What per cent did the artillery do?"

"*You* tell them. You told them twenty per cent a minute ago." Or less, really: fifty out of three hundred bodies.

At last, Medina called in twenty per cent civilians. I *think,* I just didn't listen. And gave us another briefing on Mylai One: on Pinkville. It was deserted now. The battalion had already left it. We wouldn't attack it, Medina said. We would just do the usual: go through the villages here and ask, *"VC adai?" "VC adoe?"* He said, "I don't want any shooting."

"Roger," I said.

My rifle. I drew back the bolt, and I cleared it: I knew, *The operation's over.* And that day, we hardly saw anyone in Mylai Five and Mylai Six. An old man. An old woman. A very attractive girl in a Saigon gown: I thought, *She's out of place around here.* About twenty people, and we simply asked them, *"VC adai?"* We didn't shoot them: the Vietnamese police came and did. One man, the Vietnamese shot in the skull, and it flattened out: it looked like a Halloween mask now. "You better guard him," a GI kidded me. "He might crawl away."

"I don't think so," I said. "He has a terrible headache."

Death: we were getting used to it. Sometime that day, a GI shot the Vietnamese in white shorts, apparently: I heard from my RTO, "He isn't in any shape to interrogate now." The next day, we saw a Vietnamese woman down on the ground moaning, groaning, and carrying on: just dying, and I gave her a cinnamon roll. But someone shot her: a day later we saw another one, a Vietnamese nurse, and I thought, *She's dead.* But no: simply knocked out. By the man I had said to, "Put on your goddamn pants."

"Well," someone asked him. "Is she a good piece of ass?"

"Hell, no. She is too damn dirty to screw."

The next day, we went north again, and we were on operations all of March, April, May, and June. The months of Operation Golden Fleece, of Operation Norfolk Victory, of Operation Dragon Valley—. . . .

WAR CRIMES AND
THE AMERICAN CONSCIENCE

In 1970 a group of concerned congressmen sponsored the Congressional Conference on War and National Responsibility, which featured a remarkably frank discussion of American atrocities and war crimes in Vietnam. The participants included Robert J. Lifton, professor of psychiatry at Yale, Hans Morgenthau of Chicago, Jonathan Schell, a writer for the New Yorker, *Daniel Ellsberg, who leaked the Pentagon Papers, and Gabriel Kolko, New Left historian at the University of Buffalo. In the following excerpts from the conference transcript, it becomes clear that mass murder on the scale of My Lai is the inevitable result of a guerrilla war.*

Robert Jay Lifton: The massacre at My Lai is a product of our self-deception. By no means an outgrowth of the ordinary stresses of war, My Lai is the result of a psychological state created by specific features of the war in Vietnam. Americans fighting that war are intruders in an Asian revolution, and become profoundly confused by their inability to distinguish the enemy from the people. Their anger at allies who do not fight, and who seem to be part of an environment of general deterioration, becomes readily converted into racist perceptions of the Vietnamese as nonpeople. Such perceptions are furthered by our military policy of compensating for our "blindness" by saturating the environment with our technology of destruction, thereby conveying to the GI the sense that Vietnamese are expendable. Seeing their buddies killed, but finding themselves unable to take revenge upon or even locate the adversary, GIs experience a desperate need to find an enemy who can be made to stand still. Their diffuse rage against all Vietnamese can lead to something close to an illusion that, by gunning down little babies and women and old men, they have finally "engaged" the enemy—can lead, in other words, to My Lai. . . .

Hans Morgenthau: I do not agree with the proposition that the massacre at My Lai is the result of self-deception. It is the logical consequence of the enterprise in which we are engaged. For if you are engaged in a war directed not against a distinguishable army, not

against a particular group within a population, but against the population as a whole, it becomes perfectly logical—perfectly rational, I
would even say—to regard every man, woman, and child as an actual
or potential enemy who has to be eliminated. So I am firmly convinced
that what happened in My Lai and elsewhere were not accidents, or
deviations created by self-deception, but the inevitable outgrowth of
the kind of war we are waging.

Robert Jay Lifton: My point was simply that the political illusions lead directly to psychological illusions on the part of our
troops in Vietnam or, putting the matter more strongly, that political
madness leads to behavioral madness. It is a very direct relationship.

Consider what Sergeant Michael Bernhardt, the man who did not
fire at My Lai, has said about this: "You know, when I think of somebody who would shoot up women and children, I think of a real nut,
a real maniac, a real psycho, somebody who's just completely lost
control and doesn't have any idea of what he's doing. That's what I
figured. That's what I thought a nut was. Then I found out that an
act like, you know, murder for no reason could be done by just about
anybody." What that reveals is that in a certain kind of extreme environment moral standards are totally reversed, and, as Professor
Morgenthau said, what has been sane becomes psychotic and what
has been psychotic becomes sane.

Jonathan Schell: The war in Vietnam has a dream-like quality—
not simply because it is happening on television, but because like a
dreamer we face a reality that is of our own creation. Although a
dreamer may be surprised or shocked by what he encounters in the
dream, those surprises have been authored by himself. In the same
way, we have imposed definitions on Vietnam that have created the
reality we face. . . .

Robert Jay Lifton: I have talked to many returning GIs about their
experience—their psychological experience—in Vietnam. No soldier
I have talked to—and none of the two hundred or so that a friend
and colleague and historian has talked to in his investigations—has
ever been surprised by the news of My Lai. That is an interesting
fact. They have not been surprised because they have either been
party to, or witness to, or have heard fairly close-hand about hundreds
or thousands of similar, if smaller, incidents. My Lai is outstanding,
it would seem, only for its size.

One cannot separate policy from My Lai. A psychological state formed in Americans in pursuing the war in Vietnam leads directly to My Lai, and that psychological state is directly influenced by their witnessing larger military policies, such as the free-fire zones, where the Vietnamese become expendable. . . .

Daniel Ellsberg: . . . The question remains, how did this particular face-to-face massacre come about? Is it the nature of this war? Is it inevitable in this sort of war? These questions have all been raised. I would suggest that it is in the nature of this war and to be expected. This is the major reason I have concluded that the war in which I participated is one we should not have been fighting. But the cause, I would suggest, is not so much strategic or tactical in any objective sense, but psychological, in terms of the pressures that this war puts on those who participate in it. These pressures lead daily to smaller, unrecorded atrocities, but sooner or later they were likely to produce a My Lai.

The first thing to be mentioned is the frustration to both planners and soldiers of fighting in a war where nothing seems to work, where the rules either don't exist or obviously don't apply, and where they are confronted by impotence and failure day after day. My Lai had to be destroyed not because its occupants posed any threat, but because there was a felt need to destroy some village like it. . . .

But if My Lai was still exceptional, it was separated only by a very fine distinction from incidents that occur regularly and that are regarded as permissible. A few shots from the village, a few uniforms found in a hut, a measure of resistance, would have removed any question about what happened at My Lai. We operate on the principle that any action is permissible against a foe—even if he is a thirteen-year-old boy who is carrying a rifle—or even, when we come to strategic bombing, against anyone whose death might inconvenience a foe. . . .

Rep. John Conyers, Jr.: When I questioned American officials in Vietnam about the violence and oppression perpetrated against the Vietnamese by their own government, I received this kind of response: "Well, you know, we are dealing with Orientals now. They are not used to the same level of legality of conduct that we are. You cannot expect the prisons, the interrogation camps, the detention centers, the inquisitional methods and techniques that might be employed, to be comparable to ours. These are Orientals. You can't expect them to hold to what a white western society would regard as normal standards under these circumstances."

The attitude reflected in that comment raises the question of racism. Is not the racism inherent in this country relevant to some of our conduct toward the enemy in Vietnam? If the enemy were white, would we not treat him a bit differently?

Jonathan Schell: I think the question of racism does arise, although it is hard to judge because we have no way of telling whether we would behave in a similar fashion toward a white enemy. But just the words used to describe the enemy in Vietnam—such as "gooks," and "slopes," meaning sloping eyes—certainly do indicate a strong element of racism in our soldiers' attitude toward the Vietnamese.

You see more of the Confederate flag in Vietnam than you see of the Stars and Stripes. You hear the kind of comment cited by Congressman Conyers that they have an "Oriental mentality." This is brought up again and again.

One man said to me, "You see, we have to torture them because they are two thousand years behind us, and the only thing they understand is force." The notion that the Vietnamese belong to a different, strange race, that they don't have the same kind of values we have, is certainly a very strong element in the way we have chosen to treat them.

Gabriel Kolko: The application of American power overseas is the one area in which the United States believes in equal rights.

The firebomb raids against Germany, which were carried on with the same kind of brutality in World War II, did not discriminate in favor of the white people of Germany. After the war, the first United States intervention overseas was against Greece, and it was carried on in a very bloody way, in an area that was exclusively white.

The United States planned its initial interventions after World War II essentially in Europe. It did, indeed, contemplate intervention in France, and drew up plans for that eventuality. I don't think the United States is fighting any differently in Vietnam than it would in France or in Spain, if that should prove necessary. . . .

Gordon Livingston: Responsibility for American actions in Vietnam cannot reasonably be ascribed to any small number of our representatives there, nor can it be attributed to some fundamental defect in human nature or the nature of war itself.

Our search for culprits leads us to the mirror of reality, there to confront ourselves with Walt Kelly's triumphant cry, "We have met the enemy and they is us."

America's presence in Vietnam, indeed its place in the world, is predicated on a self-image of moral rectitude. The belief in the essential humaneness and good will of Americans, even in time of war, is ingrained in our national mythology. The events in our history which contradict the myth are neither widely known nor celebrated, but they are there. For example, in the "incident" at My Lai some observers heard echoes of another day in 1890 when at Wounded Knee Creek, South Dakota, soldiers of the U.S. 7th Calvary massacred about three hundred Sioux, most of them women and children, in what was the last significant event in the ignoble conquest of the American Indian.

The ethic of the legitimate use of violence is deeply rooted in our culture. Our folk heroes, real and imaginary, have almost all been violent men. The level of violence in our entertainment parallels that in our streets, and we have learned to accept, if not enjoy, both. The reporting of the war itself, with the incessant repetition of violent images, seems to produce, if I may borrow a term, psychic numbing on a national scale.

Dr. Maccoby made a profound and important observation when he described the war as the triumph of the principles and values of the industrial bureaucracy. In trying to describe the feeling I had toward the military organization of which I was a part in Vietnam, I have called it the "General Motors of Death." The magnitude of the effort, the paperwork, and the middle-management attitude of many of the participants, as well as the predilection for charts and statistics —including that most dehumanizing and absurd figure of all, the body count—all these represent the triumph of technocracy over reason. One has the distinct impression that a majority of Americans object to this war not because it is wrong, but because it is so demonstrably inefficient.

Nevertheless, we think of ourselves as a peace-loving people, slow to anger, quick to forgive. The ideals for which we have fought our wars have been clearly stated and almost universally supported. More than this, the manner in which we prosecuted the fighting has been accepted as reflecting a moral superiority over our enemies which has found expression in the sanctimonious and chauvinistic assumption of "God on our side." Implicit in this view of our country reluctantly at war was a picture of the American soldier as a character out of a Mauldin cartoon—a flower in his helmet, a candy bar in his hand for the children of the war, determinedly but decently fighting to roll back the well-identified forces which were the current threat to human freedom.

What, then, happened at My Lai? What does it say about us as a people and about the war we have chosen to wage in Vietnam? To answer this, we might try to consider the total impact of our presence there, with special emphasis on relations between Americans and the people of Vietnam, for herein lies the key to the tragedy that is war.

In addition to the bombs and the napalm, we have exported to Vietnam some of the most degrading aspects of American culture. For example, drug use among the U.S. troops is so widespread as to have reached epidemic proportions. The magnitude of the problem is impossible to document accurately, but estimates of drug experimentation run as high as 80 per cent of the troops, with many of them becoming habituated. The boredom, loneliness, and anxiety engendered by their situation make many soldiers welcome this form of escape. Vietnam, unlike some other Oriental nations, does not have a tradition of widespread narcotic usage, but there have been some changes since we arrived. The American market has been exploited by Vietnamese entrepreneurs whose own society did not generate sufficient demand to support them before we came.

Among the basic services which the Vietnamese economy provides our forces is prostitution. Venereal disease is, in fact, consistently the health problem of highest incidence among U.S. troops. Even in relatively remote rural areas our units are magnets for the aptly named "short-time girls." Often they are brought from a distance and are received by the local Vietnamese with the same lack of enthusiasm one would find in a small town in this country in an equivalent situation.

A related and particularly tragic aspect of our presence in Vietnam —and perhaps the one with the most lasting consequences—is in the large number of children of mixed parentage who have been produced and abandoned there. Pearl Buck has coined the term "Amerasian children," but by whatever name their abandonment represents the ultimate in our contemptuous treatment of that people. At some of the orphanages fully half the infants are of American fathers. They lie there, bottles propped against their bassinets, facing a future of rejection in an ethnically proud society. Perhaps someone could include them in a separate body count. . . .

Frank Kowalski: Each of us has brought to this discussion views and ideas conditioned by his background and experiences. Though I have served in Congress and have tasted both the sweet and bitter of politics, I spent most of my adult life in the Army. Accordingly, I would like to comment essentially from that background.

To begin with, soldiers don't make wars—they die in them. We are not in the senseless war in Vietnam because any mad-dog general or militarists decided to wage war there. We backed into that bottomless pit through a series of mistakes and misguided policies of a succession of presidents—with the acquiescence of Congress.

Nor can we put the blame for the way the war is fought in Vietnam on the military. The Army, Navy, and Air Force have a fantastic assortment of horrendous weapons available not only to destroy North Vietnam but to wipe civilization from this planet. The weapons and strategies the military employ in Vietnam, however, are determined by the legally constituted heads of our civilian government. We have not used nuclear and biological weapons there because the President of the United States has not authorized their use. On the other hand, we have carpet-bombed North Vietnam, blasted forests, jungles, rice paddies, towns, and villages in South Vietnam, spewed flaming napalm on both friend and foe, defoliated hundreds of square miles of Asia, herded millions of people about the country like cattle, and crushed and made governments at will, because the presidents of the United States, past and present, either initiated or approved the use of these strategies of war in that unhappy land. Specifically, there is no evidence that the military of the United States violated any instructions of the Administration in power regarding limitations on the use of weapons or the strategies to be employed.

There is evidence, however—distressing evidence—that a deplorable slippage in behavior has been developing in the military structure. In Vietnam this slippage is the natural consequence of fighting a war we cannot win. The resulting frustration unhinges men at all levels from traditional American concern for humanity. In a war where the enemy is everywhere and nowhere at the same time, military men no longer plan or hope for victory—they seek only to survive themselves and to punish the "gooks." And so, if designated targets cannot be bombed, bomb loads are dumped on anything that moves or on any area that looks like enemy ground. When one cannot come to grips with the enemy on the battlefield, assassination of suspected "gooks" becomes acceptable to men who otherwise abhor murder. Prisoners and civilians are shot on orders or on a whim, dragged behind trucks, dumped into the sea, or thrown out of aircraft. When the elusive guerrillas fade into the jungle, frustrated troops get some consolation in venting their artillery, mortars, or rockets on a village through which the enemy escaped. The massacre at My Lai, accordingly, where not even babies were spared, was the inevitable consequence of a gradual erosion of human restraints and military controls. I want to believe that this monstrous slippage in conscience has infected individuals rather than the body of our military.

In light of my long service in the Army, I am convinced that there are sincere military men who deplore, as much as I do, the wholesale dishonor My Lai has heaped upon American men and units fighting in Vietnam. Moreover, I am sure these men are doing everything in their power to cleanse the Army from within.

Specifically, I applaud the Army for bringing to trial the officers and men who participated in the My Lai and other killings of civilians and prisoners in Vietnam. Whatever may be the outcome of these courts-martial—and certainly those charged must be assumed innocent until found guilty by proper authorities—the Army command, by initiating these trials, has served notice on its young officers and men, those engaged in close combat, that the military will not tolerate wanton killings. In this action the Army is responding to the spirit of Nuremberg and the conscience of humanity. . . .

Russell International War Crimes Tribunal
PROCEEDINGS

Lord Bertrand Russell (1872–1970), whose life spanned nearly a century, was a seminal mind of extraordinary brilliance. Principia Mathematica, *which he published with Alfred North Whitehead before World War I, was a pathbreaking work in the field of mathematical logic. Russell's later years were devoted in great part to the burning issues of the day. He was courageous and outspoken, although his enemies accused him of posturing and a senile predilection for histrionics. He was the force behind the Russell International War Crimes Tribunal which met in Stockholm and Copenhagen in 1967 to condemn the United States in a mock Nuremberg Trial. The following selections include the "verdict of the Tribunal" as well as a statement by Lord Russell.*

VERDICT OF THE STOCKHOLM SESSION

The International War Crimes Tribunal, during the session held at Stockholm from the 2nd to the 10th May 1967, studied the two following questions included in its program, adopted in London on the 15th November 1966:

"Has the United States Government (and the governments of Australia, New Zealand and South Korea) committed acts of aggression according to international law?"

"Has there been bombardment of targets of a purely civilian character, for example hospitals, schools, sanatoria, dams, etc., and on what scale has this occurred? . . ."

The Tribunal has heard the qualified representatives of the Democratic Republic of Vietnam and of the National Front of Liberation of South Vietnam as well as those of the Neo Lao Haksat of Laos and of Cambodia, and has heard the grievances that they have presented. It has heard numerous witnesses from the most varied countries, and in particular Vietnamese citizens from the North and the South who are war victims, and citizens of the USA having belonged to the American Army in Vietnam.

From John Duffett, ed., *Against the Crime of Silence* [Proceedings of the Russell International War Crimes Tribunal] (Stockholm, Copenhagen, 1968), pp. 302–312, 643–649. Copyright © 1968 by Studies in the Third World. Reprinted by permission of Clarion Books, a division of Simon & Schuster, Inc.

It has heard the reports drawn up by the investigative commissions which it had sent itself to Vietnam, both in the DRV and in the areas controlled by the NLF, and the USA, as well as the reports of the investigative committees of Japan and of the Democratic People's Republic of Korea. It has studied numerous reports furnished by scientific and legal experts and by historians. Abundant documentation in photographs and motion pictures has been presented, as well as samples of weapons and products, accompanied by the results of experiments made in connection with these.

On the First Question. Resort to force in international relations has been prohibited by numerous international agreements, the chief of which is the 1928 Pact of Paris, known as the Kellogg-Briand Pact.

In its Article 2, the United Nations Charter solemnly recalled the said principle immediately after the Second World War.

Article 6 of the Statute of Nuremberg qualified as crimes against peace "the conduct of, preparation for, starting or pursuit of a war of aggression or a war in violation of international treaties, pledges or agreements, or participation in a concerted plan, or plot for the accomplishment of any of the foregoing acts."

Finally, it must be recalled, as in the United Nations resolution of December 1960, that all peoples have fundamental rights to national independence, to sovereignty, to respect of the integrity of their territory, and that breaches of these fundamental rights may be regarded as crimes against the national existence of a people.

The accession to independence and to national existence of the people of Vietnam dates back to 2nd September 1945. This independence was called in question by the old colonial power. The war of national liberation then embarked upon ended with the victory of the Vietnam Army.

The Geneva Agreements of the 20th and 21st July 1954 intended to put an end to the previous conflict, created in Vietnam a state of law, the respect of which was incumbent on all, and particularly on the United States. These Agreements recognized the guarantees, independence, unity and territorial integrity of Vietnam (Articles 6 and 7 of the final Declaration). Although a line of demarcation divided the country into two parts on a level with the 17th Parallel, it was expressly stipulated that as the essential aim of this division was to settle military questions, it was of a provisional nature "and could in no way be interpreted as constituting a political or territorial boundary" (Article 6 of the final Declaration).

The Geneva Agreements stipulated that general elections should take place over the whole of the country in July 1956 under the supervision of an international commission, and that consultations on this subject were to take place between the competent representatives of the two zones as from July 1955.

The Agreements specifically excluded all reprisals or discrimination against persons and organizations by reason of their activities during the previous hostilities (Article 14 of the Armistice Agreement). They formally prohibited the introduction of fresh troops, of military personnel, fresh arms and munitions, as well as the installation of military bases (Article 16 of the Armistice Agreement) and the inclusion of Vietnam in military alliances, this applying to the two zones (Article 9 of the final Declaration).

This state of law, intended to create a peaceful situation in Vietnam, was replaced by a state of war in consequence of successive violations and the responsibility for the passage to a state of war lies with the government of the United States of America.

It transpires from the information of a historical and diplomatic nature that has been brought to the knowledge of the Tribunal:

—that numerous proofs exist of the American intention prior to 1954 to dominate Vietnam;
—that the Diem government was set up in Saigon by American agents several weeks before the conclusion of the Geneva Agreements;
—that the Saigon authorities, subservient to the United States, systematically violated the provisions of the Geneva Agreements which prohibited reprisals, as has been established on several occasions by the International Control Commission;
—that in defiance of the Geneva Agreements the United States has, since 1954, introduced into Vietnam increasing quantities of military equipment and personnel and has set up bases there.

The elections that were fixed for July 1956 and which were to be the subject of consultations in July 1955 did not take place in spite of numerous diplomatic notes from the government of the Democratic Republic of Vietnam calling for the said consultations. Information from United States sources make it possible to ascribe to the USA the refusal by Saigon of the most essential provisions of the Geneva Agreements.

In this manner there was created in South Vietnam a situation of foreign intrusion by force against which the people of Vietnam had to launch a struggle of national liberation in a political form until 1959 and in the form of an armed struggle since that date, a struggle led by the National Liberation Front of South Vietnam since 1960, which has succeeded in controlling vastly greater territories than those controlled by the United States.

This attack against the South was followed by an attack against the North, begun in 1964, and intensified since 1965 in the form of aerial bombardments and naval and land shellings in circumstances which form the subject of the second question studied by the Tribunal. The United States has not ceased to increase the power of these attacks by practicing what it has itself called a policy of escalation.

The Tribunal has made a point of examining scrupulously the arguments put forward in American official documents to justify the legality of their intervention in Vietnam. Special attention has been paid to the document entitled: "Juridical Memorandum on the Legality of the Participation of the United States in the Defense of Vietnam," which document was submitted to the Senate Foreign Affairs Committee on the 4th March 1966. The main argument formulated by this text consists in claiming that the American intervention in Vietnam merely constitutes aid to the Saigon government against aggression from the North. Such argument is untenable both in law and in fact.

In law, it is hardly necessary to recall that Vietnam constitutes a single nation which cannot be seen as an aggressor against itself.

The fact is that no proof of this alleged aggression has ever been produced. The figures stated of infiltration of personnel from the North into the South, often contradictory, mixing up armed men and unarmed men, are thoroughly disputable and could in no case justify the plea of legitimate defense provided for in Article 51 of the United Nations Charter, an article, moreover, none of the other conditions of which are complied with.

From the foregoing it follows that the United States bears the responsibility for the use of force in Vietnam and that it has in consequence committed a crime of aggression against that country, a crime against peace. . . .

On the Second Question. The Tribunal has gained the conviction that the aerial, naval and land bombardments of civil targets is of a massive, systematic and deliberate nature.

The massive nature of these bombardments is attested by innumerable reports from American sources on the tonnage of bombs dropped and the great number of American aerial sorties. . . .

All of the witnesses heard, in particular the members of the investigating teams, have confirmed that the greater part of the civilian targets (hospitals, sanitoria, schools, churches, pagodas) are very obvious and very clearly distinguishable from the rest of the Vietnam countryside. . . .

The Tribunal ascertained the vital importance to the people of Vietnam of the dams and other hydraulic works, and the grave danger of famine to which the civilian populations were exposed by the attempted destruction by the American forces.

The Tribunal has received all necessary information in the diversity and power of the engines of war employed against the Democratic Republic of Vietnam and the circumstances of their utilization (high explosive bombs, napalm, phosphorous and fragmentation bombs, etc.). Seriously injured victims of napalm bombs have appeared before it and medical reports on these mutilated people have been provided to it. Its attention in particular has been drawn to the massive use of various kinds of antipersonnel bombs of the fragmentation type, also called in American parlance, CBU, and in Vietnamese parlance, pellet bombs. These devices obviously intended to strike defenseless populations, have the following characteristics:

> containers, called by the Vietnamese the "mother bombs," release hundreds of small, oblong or spherical bombs ("pineapple" or "guava" bombs) which in turn release hundreds of small pellets. A single "mother bomb" can therefore cause the dispersion of nearly 100,000 pellets; these pellets can cause no serious damage to buildings or plants or to protected military personnel (for example, civil defense workers behind their sandbags). They are therefore intended solely to reach the greatest number of persons in the civilian population.

The Tribunal has had medical experts study the consequences of attacks with these pellets. The path of the particles through the body is long and irregular and produces, apart from cases of death, multiple and various internal injuries.

The Hague Convention No. 4 of the 18th October 1907 laid down the principle that belligerents may not have unlimited choice so far as the means of injuring an enemy are concerned (Article 22); the said Convention specially prohibits the use of arms, projectiles and material deliberately destined to cause pointless suffering (Article 23); attacks on or bombardments by any means whatsoever of town, villages, dwellings or undefended buildings are prohibited (Article 25). During bombardments all necessary steps must be taken to spare, so far as possible, buildings devoted to religion, art, science or charitable purposes, historical monuments, hospitals or places where sick and injured persons are assembled, provided that these places are not used for military purposes (Article 27).

Article 6 of the Statutes of the Tribunal of Nuremberg has qualified as war crimes the destruction without reason of towns and villages or devastation not justified by military requirements.

The Geneva Convention of the 2nd August 1949 also laid down the principle of absolute prohibition of attack on civilian hospitals (Article 18) and private and collective property not rendered absolutely necessary by the conduct of the operations (Article 53).

The government of the United States cannot override such treaties, to which it has subscribed, whilst its own Constitution (Article 6, para. 2) gives them preeminence over domestic law. Furthermore, the official manual (Department of the Army Field Manual) entitled "The Law of Land Warfare" published by the U.S. Defense Department in 1956, under reference F.M. 27-10, refers to all of the foregoing provisions as being obligatory on all members of the American Army.

In consequence, the Tribunal considers that in subjecting the civilian population and civilian targets of the Democratic Republic of Vietnam to intensive and systematic bombardment, the United States of America has committed a war crime.

Apart from condemnation of this war crime, the Tribunal makes a point of declaring that fragmentation bombs of the CBU type, which have no other purpose than to injure to the maximum the civilian population, must be regarded as arms prohibited by the laws and customs of war.

Meeting with the resistance of a people who intended to "exercise peacefully and freely its right to full independence and to the integrity of Its territory" (United Nations resolution of the 14th December 1960), the government of the United States of America has given these war crimes, through their extent and frequency, the character of crimes against humanity (Article 6 of the Statute of Nuremberg).

These crimes cannot be regarded merely as a consequence of a war of aggression, whose prosecution is determined by them.

Because of their systematic employment with the object of destroying the fundamental rights of the people of Vietnam, their unity and their wish for peace, the crimes against humanity of which the government of the United States of America has rendered itself guilty, become a fundamental constituent part of the crime of aggression, a supreme crime which embraces all the others according to the Nuremberg verdict.

Findings of the Tribunal

1. Has the government of the United States committed acts of aggression against Vietnam under the terms of international law? YES (Unanimously).
2. Has there been, and if so, on what scale, bombardment of purely civilian targets, for example, hospitals, schools, medical establishments, dams, etc? YES (Unanimously). . . .

Endorsed "ne variatur"
The President of the Tribunal
Stockholm, 10th May, 1967   *Jean-Paul Sartre.*

CLOSING ADDRESS TO THE STOCKHOLM SESSION, BY BERTRAND RUSSELL

The International War Crimes Tribunal has been subject to abuse from people who have much to hide. It has been said that the conclusions of this Tribunal were known in advance. The conclusions of our Tribunal are built out of the evidence. The evidence is abundant. It is precisely because the knowledge of crime is a cause for inquiry that we are holding this session. When the evidence on aggression and the systematic bombardment of the entire population of Vietnam becomes known this evidence will be compelled to reach the same conclusions. . . .

We have heard evidence for many days on the sustained aggression by a great power against a small, heroic people. A large power has occupied an impoverished nation to subdue a popular movement seeking land, independence and social advance. It is not the evil which is new; nor is it the crisis which has changed. We have celebrated in history the struggles waged by oppressed people against large, cruel and powerful invaders. The sense of identity with the small victim of a cruel and large tormentor touches our deepest impulses and is part of our mythology, religion and literature. The concern for the weak, struggling after long suffering against the strong for their simplest rights is the source of our ethics and the great moments in our common history. David and Goliath, the Greeks at Salamis, the Vietnamese and Genghis Khan—the partisans of Vietnam and the United States Air Force and mechanized army—are part of a continuous tradition.

The International War Crimes Tribunal defies the powerful rulers who bully and butcher with abandon. Who would compare the 100,000 tons of napalm with a peasant holding a rifle? Who can fail to distinguish the power which destroys hospitals and schools of an entire people from the defenders who attack the airplanes carrying napalm and steel fragmentation bombs? The difference between the victims and the criminals who oppress them is part of the evidence before us compelling honest men to speak loudly and to risk much.

The United States is using fascist states to facilitate its plans for new levels of crime. Each day bombers leave Thailand to saturate Vietnam in steel pellets and liquid fire. Has one American city been attacked? Are Canada and Mexico bases for the destruction of America by a power on the other side of the world? If one American city suffered two hours of bombing such as has been inflicted for two years on Vietnam the world press would inform us rather fully. This imbalance is a clear indication of the great injustice we are investigating. The difference in power is matched by the indifference of the powerful and those who serve them or depend on their favor.

During the 1930s when millions of people could see the nature of Adolf Hitler and Nazism, there was too little understanding and insufficient will to act in time. In Germany there were no great strikes or mass demonstrations. The large political parties opposed only in words but did not mobilize their large support. Even now the great political parties fail to act and the nominal opponents of the aggressive violence of the United States satisfy themselves with pious complaint in institutions dominated by the aggressor.

Nazism emerged from a nation unable to stabilize itself and degenerated to unforeseen limits of depravity. The policy of aggression in Washington has brought a comparable degree of scientific extermination and moral degeneracy. The International War Crimes Tribunal must do for the peoples of Vietnam, Asia, Africa and Latin America what no Tribunal did while Nazi crimes were committed and plotted. The napalm and pellet bombs, the systematic destruction of a heroic people are a barbarous rehearsal. The starving and the suffering will no longer die in silence. We must discredit the arrogant demand that they protect our comfort with their quiet agony. Our social institutions, impregnated with racism, must be reconstructed. The Tribunal must begin a new morality in the West, in which cold mechanical slaughter will be automatically condemned. The Tribunal must inspire a new understanding that the heroic are the oppressed and the hateful are the arrogant rulers who would bleed them for generations or bomb them into the stone age. The Tribunal must warn of the impending horror in many lands, the new atrocities prepared now in Vietnam and of the global struggle between the poor and the powerful rich. These are themes as old as humanity. The long arduous struggle for decency and for liberation is unending. A Tribunal such as ours will be necessary until the last starving man is fed and a way of life is created which ends exploitation of the many by the few. Vietnam struggles so others may survive. The truths we must declare are simple truths. Great violence menaces our cultural achievements. Starvation and disease cannot be tolerated. Resistance at risk of life is noble. But we know this. Western Europe and North America are drenched in the blood of struggle for social change. Feudalism, the reduction of men to starving hulks, the purchase of their minds, the eradication of their spirit —these are blights on human culture. These are vicious forms of aggression at once more fundamental and more pervasive than the crossing of frontiers by foot soldiers. Wherever men struggle against suffering we must be their voice. Whenever they are cruelly attacked for their self-sacrifice we must find our voices. It is easy to pay lip-service to these ideals. We will be judged not by our reputations or our pretenses but by our will to act. Against this standard we too will be judged by better men.

May 10, 1967   *Bertrand Russell*

SUMMARY AND VERDICT OF THE SECOND SESSION ...

Agenda of Second Session

In the course of its Roskilde session, the Tribunal was to study the following questions:

- First, the complicity of Japan, Thailand and the Philippines in the acts of aggression committed by the government of the United States of America.
- Second, the use of weapons and products prohibited by the laws of war.
- Third, the treatment of war prisoners.
- Fourth, the treatment of the civilian populations by the forces of the USA and those which are subordinate to them.
- Fifth, the extension of the war to Laos.
- Sixth, and finally, the Tribunal was to pronounce whether the combination of the crimes imputed to the government of the USA could not receive the general qualification of genocide. ...

It is in a position to give the following replies to the questions which it has studied.

*   *   *

Second, on prohibited weapons and products: The Tribunal wishes to recall the uncontested principles of the law of nations, as well as those which were set down in The Hague in 1907, and with respect to which the legality of a weapon must be appraised: the principle of the immunity of the civilian population, the prohibition on the use of toxic products, the prohibition of weapons that may cause superfluous harm. It has attached a special importance to the Martens clause, which appears in the preamble of The Hague Conventions of 1907, and according to which the law of war depends on the principles of the law of nations resulting from the usages established between the civilized nations, the laws of humanity and the requirements of the human conscience. It is in the application of these principles that the official manual of the American Army (Department of the Army Field Manual) entitled "The Law of Land Warfare," published in July 1956, under the reference F.M. 27-10, by the Department of the Army, makes it an obligation for campaigning armies not to use any kind and degree of violence not really necessary for military objectives and aims. . . .

The Tribunal wants today to condemn:

* The wholesale and indiscriminate use of napalm, which has been abundantly demonstrated before the Tribunal.
* The use of phosphorous, the burns of which are even more painful and prolonged and have, in addition, the effects of a poison on the organism.

As for the use of gases, the Tribunal considers that the failure of the United States to ratify the Geneva Protocol on June 17, 1925, concerning the prohibition of the use in war of toxic or similar asphyxiating gases is without effect, as a result of the voting by the General Assembly of the United Nations (a vote joined in by the United States) of the resolution of the 5th of December 1966, inviting all states to conform to the principles and objectives of the said Protocol, and condemning all acts contrary to these objectives.

The scientific reports of the most qualified experts, which have been submitted to the Tribunal, demonstrate that the gases used in Vietnam, in particular CS, CN and DM, are used under conditions which make them always toxic and often deadly, especially when they are blown into the hideouts, shelters and underground tunnels where a large part of the Vietnamese population is forced to live. It is impossible to classify them as simple incapacitating gases; they must be classified as combat gases.

The Tribunal has studied the current practice of the American Army consisting of spraying defoliating or herbicidal products over entire regions in Vietnam. It has noted that the American manual on the law of war already cited forbids destroying, in particular by chemical agents—even those theoretically nonharmful to man—any crops that are not intended to be used exclusively for the food of the armed forces.

It has found that the reports of the investigative commissions confirmed the information, from both Vietnamese and American sources, according to which considerable areas of cultivated land are sprayed by these defoliating and herbicidal products. At least 700,000 hectares [about 1,750,000 acres] of ground were affected in 1966.

Third, on the treatment of prisoners of war: The Tribunal recalls that prisoners of war must receive humane treatment, under conditions which are defined by the Geneva Conventions of 1949, which the United States has signed, and the terms of which it has incorporated in its own manual of the law of war. Tortures, mutilations and serious physical and mental coercion are not only prohibited but must be punished. The prisoner is entitled to life and to the medical aid that his state requires.

Numerous testimonies, both Vietnamese and American, were heard (among the American witnesses was a former soldier whose function for ten months had been to question prisoners from the time of their capture), and it was established that these principles are a dead letter for the Americans in Vietnam. The finishing off of the wounded on the battlefield and summary executions are frequent. Prisoners are thrown into the air from helicopters. Torture in all forms, by electricity, water, burns and blows, is practiced daily. All the witnesses have confirmed that these practices always occur in the presence and under the direction of American soldiers, even when they do not themselves participate. These tortures are aimed at obtaining information or confessions. Medical care is systematically refused to the wounded and ill who refuse to speak.

Finally, in contempt of the provisions of the Geneva Convention, the prisoners held by the United Sates, which is the detaining power within the meaning of this Convention, are handed over to the authorities of the so-called Saigon government, which engages in a dreadful repression accompanied by acts of torture, numerous examples of which have been furnished, including those in which women are frightfully tortured.

Fourth, treatment of civilian populations: The Convention of The Hague of 1907, the Nuremberg and Tokyo judgments, the Universal Declaration of Human Rights, the 4th Geneva Convention of August 12th 1949, lay down the undeniable principle of the protection of civilian persons in time of war. The manual of the law of war of the American Army includes as one of its parts the entire 4th

Convention of Geneva, the binding character of which is undeniable.

The Tribunal heard: the testimony of three American veterans, and the report of the interrogations undertaken by its investigative mission in the United States, some Vietnamese victims, the report to the investigative mission of the Tribunal in the areas controlled by the NLF (which has collected 317 depositions, the minutes of which have been put into its files) and an important witness, a citizen of the German Federal Republic who has lived several years in South Vietnam. It considers that the following facts are established:

- First, in the course of raiding operations which take place both systematically and permanently, thousands of inhabitants are massacred. According to serious information from American sources, 250,000 children have been killed since the beginning of this war, and 750,000 wounded and mutilated for life. Senator [Edward] Kennedy's report, of October 31, 1967, points out that 150,000 wounded can be found every month. Villages are entirely leveled, fields are devastated, livestock destroyed; in particular the testimony of the American journalist Jonathan Schell describes in a startling way the extermination by the American forces of the population of the Vietnamese village of Ben Suc, and its complete destruction. Precise testimony and documents that have been put before the Tribunal have reported the existence of free-fire zones, where everything that moves is considered hostile, which amounts to saying that the entire population is taken as a target.
- Second, one-third of the population of Vietnam has been displaced according to the very terms of the address of Senator Kennedy at the International Rescue Committee, and shut up in the strategic hamlets which are now baptized New Life Hamlets. The living conditions, according to published reports that have been brought to the Tribunal's attention, are close to those of a concentration-camp life. The interned—women and children in most cases—are packed like cattle behind barbed-wire fences. Food and hygiene are almost entirely lacking, which often makes survival impossible. The social structures and traditional structures of the Vietnamese families are thus destroyed. One must also take account of the fact of the impressive number of prisoners held in the jails of South Vietnam—400,000 according to estimates that are worthy of attention. Arbitrary arrests, parodies of justice, interrogations accompanied by

abominable tortures, are current practice. All the testimony agrees in establishing that inhuman and illegal methods are daily being used by the American armed forces and their satellites against the civilian populations, who are thus threatened with extermination. . . .

*   *   *

Therefore, the International War Crimes Tribunal, does as a result of deliberations render its verdict as follows:

Is the Government of Thailand guilty of complicity in the aggression committed by the United States Government against Vietnam?
Yes, by Unanimous Vote.

Is the Government of the Philippines guilty of complicity in the aggression committed by the United States Government against Vietnam?
Yes, by Unanimous Vote.

Is the Government of Japan guilty of complicity in the aggression committed by the United States Government against Vietnam?
Yes, by 8 Votes to 3

(The three Tribunal members who voted against agree that the Japanese Government gives considerable aid to the government of the United States, but do not agree on its complicity in the crime of aggression.)

Has the United States Government committed aggression against the people of Laos, according to the definition provided by international law?
Yes, by Unanimous Vote.

Have the armed forces of the United States used or experimented with weapons prohibited by the laws of war?
Yes, by Unanimous Vote.

Have prisoners of war captured by the armed forces of the United States been subjected to treatment prohibited by the laws of war?
Yes, by Unanimous Vote.

Have the armed forces of the United States subjected the civilian population to inhuman treatment prohibited by international law?
Yes, by Unanimous Vote.

Is the United States Government guilty of genocide against the people of Vietnam?

Yes, by Unanimous Vote.

Telford Taylor

WAR CRIMES: SON MY

General Taylor has made an important contribution to the literature on My Lai by focusing on the anomalous nature of international law on guerrilla warfare. Guerrilla wars provide the international lawyer with an extraordinary set of circumstances. They do not feature a common battlefront, nor are friend and foe easily distinguishable; indeed an entire population in some cases can become the potential enemy. Such is the case in Vietnam, and Mr. Taylor claims that the refusal of the Vietcong to wear uniforms in order that they might be differentiated from the civilian population is a violation of the Geneva Conventions. The thrust of this argument is that the Vietcong themselves are responsible for the massacre at My Lai.

What actually happened at Son My (better but inaccurately known as My Lai) in March of 1968 is and may well remain obscured by the fog of war, the passage of time, and the self-interest of surviving participants and observers. Especially in view of the criminal charges pending against a number of those involved, it is no part of the purpose of this book to point the finger of guilt at any individual. Whether the killings constituted a war crime is the question first to be examined and, for this purpose, it can be taken as undisputed that on March 16, 1968, American troops at Son My killed a large number of the village residents of both sexes and all ages. According to President Nixon, who presumably was well briefed: "What appears was certainly a massacre, under no circumstances was it justified. . . . We cannot ever condone or use atrocities against civilians. . . ."

Son My is a village in Quang Ngai Province, situated close to the

Reprinted by permission of Quadrangle Books, Inc. from *From Nuremberg to My Lai: The Search for Justice and World Order* by Telford Taylor. Copyright © 1970 by The New York Times Company. (Footnotes abridged.)

seacoast in the narrow northern neck of South Vietnam, about 100 miles south of the 17th Parallel demarcation line. In 1954, at the time of the partition, thousands of Quang Ngai's inhabitants preferred the Hanoi regime and moved north. In later years many returned as Vietcong organizers; the entire province became a stronghold of the National Liberation Front (NLF), and Son My village came under Vietcong control in 1964. From time to time there were skirmishes between the Vietcong and the South Vietnamese (ARVN) units, and in 1967, after the great American buildup, American Army patrols appeared from time to time, but without untoward incident. In January 1968, the Tet offensive brought severe fighting in the nearby provincial capital of Quang Ngai, but Son My itself did not suffer. By this time, however, a large number of other villages in the province had been destroyed, as a result of American search and destroy operations coupled with extremely heavy air strikes.

The Son My killings took place in the course of a standard type of American military operation in Quang Ngai, the nature of which was a sudden lift of troops by helicopter, in and on all sides of a reported enemy unit, in an attempt to close a trap on it and destroy it. In this instance the operation, under the code name "Muscatine," was carried out by an ad hoc unit of three infantry companies, called "Task Force Barker" after its commander, the late Lieut. Col. Frank A. Barker, Jr. The parent unit of the task force was the 11th Brigade, which in turn was part of the newly formed Americal Division, commanded by Maj. Gen. Samuel W. Koster.

About mid-March 1968, the American command received information that a strong Vietcong unit, the 48th Local Force Battalion, was regrouping after the Tet offensive at Son My, in the hamlet of My Lai. Task Force Barker thereupon planned a helicopter operation for March 16, under which one of its three companies would go into My Lai and engage the enemy, while the other two companies would be set down to the north and east of the target, to prevent the Vietcong from escaping the trap.

It appears that there was in fact a Vietcong unit in My Lai, centered in the subhamlet of My Khe, shown on American military maps as My Lai (1). Whether because of linguistic and map confusion or for some other reason, however, the central target of the attack on the morning of March 16 was the subhamlet Xom Lang in the hamlet Tu

Cung, labelled My Lai (4) on the American maps, about two miles distant from My Khe where the Vietcong were based.

Consequently, when C Company of Task Force Barker went into Xom Lang that morning, expecting heavy opposition, it encountered none. The company had had little combat experience, and had recently suffered casualties from mines and booby-traps that had enraged and frightened the men; apparently there had been brutal and inexcusable killings of Vietnamese before the assault on Xom Lang.

What happened when the soldiers reached the dwellings is too well-known from newspaper and magazine photographs, and the accounts of numerous participants to warrant repetition. It appears certain that the troops had been told to destroy all the structures and render the place uninhabitable; what they had been told to do with the residents is not so clear. However that may be, the accounts indicate that C Company killed virtually every inhabitant on whom they could lay hands, regardless of age or sex, and despite the fact that no opposition or hostile behavior was encountered. There were few survivors, and based on the prior population of the area, the deaths attributable to C Company in Xom Lang and Binh Dong, together with other killings said to have been perpetrated a few hours later by a platoon of B Company a few miles to the east in the subhamlet My Hoi, amounted to about 500.

There was certainly nothing clandestine about the killings. About 80 officers and men went into the Xom Lang area on the ground. Above them, at various altitudes, were gunship, observation and command helicopters. There was constant radio communication between the various units and their superiors, and these were monitored at brigade headquarters. A reporter and a photographer from an Army Public Information Detachment went in with the troops and witnessed and recorded the course of events virtually from start to finish. The pilot of an observation helicopter, shocked by what he saw, reported the killings to brigade headquarters and repeatedly put his helicopter down to rescue wounded women and children. Command helicopters for the divisional, brigade and task force commanders were assigned air space over the field of action, and were there at least part of the time.

Such were the tragic fruits of Operation Muscatine in the village of Son My. Beyond doubt there were crimes, but were they "war crimes"? The answer to this question is not altogether simple, and neither is it unimportant, as it may bear closely on issues of personal liability, and the authority under which alleged perpetrators may be tried.

The complications arise from the multilateral nature of the Vietnam war and its guerrilla character, marked by the absence of any military "front" dividing the two sides. Directly involved in the fighting are on the one side the North Vietnamese Army and the Vietcong, and on the other the South Vietnamese units and the greatly stronger allied forces of the United States, as well as contingents from South Korea, the Philippines, Thailand, Australia and New Zealand. Until the Cambodian excursion, all of the ground fighting took place on the territory of South Vietnam, but large parts of the country are controlled by the Vietcong, and Son My might well have been regarded as "enemy" territory in that sense at the time of the assault.

With the exception of the NLF, all participants in the conflict are parties to the four Geneva Conventions of 1949, of which the two most important for present purposes are the "Prisoners of War" and "Protection of Civilian Persons in Time of War" conventions. But in June 1965, when the International Committee of the Red Cross addressed a letter to the four principal belligerents declaring that they were all bound by the 1949 conventions and asking for information concerning the steps being taken to comply with the prisoner-of-war provisions, North Vietnam as well as the NLF declined to acknowledge that they were obligated under the conventions, while declaring that prisoners were being "well treated" (North Vietnam) or "humanely treated" (NLF). And in fact neither of the two has complied with the conventions. North Vietnam in particular has consistently refused to carry out the reporting, correspondence and neutral inspection provisions relating to prisoners of war, and the Vietcong units have commonly disregarded the requirements that combatants shall carry arms openly and "have a fixed distinctive sign recognizable at a distance."

The legal situation is further complicated by the fact that the Geneva Conventions as a whole apply only to "armed conflict . . . between two or more" signatory nations, while Article 3, containing certain "minimum" prohibitions of inhumane treatment of prisoners or civilians, applies also to "armed conflict not of an international character in the territory of" a signatory power. Whether the Vietnamese war is a "civil" or "international" war is one of the points in dispute, and the phrase "international civil war" is nothing but a handy verbal compromise that solves nothing. However that may be, there is no room whatsoever for a North Vietnamese contention that they are not bound at least by Article 3 and, since their regular troops are engaged with those of South Vietnam and its allies in South Vietnamese territory, there appears to be little force in their effort to escape responsibility under the conventions in their entirety. The NLF, as a nonsignatory, is in a much stronger position with respect to the particular provisions of the conventions but, of course, is bound, as is every organized military force claiming or aspiring to sovereignty, by the customary laws of war.

International lawyers have discussed at length whether and to what extent North Vietnam and the NLF are bound by the conventions and, if negative answers are supportable, the question then arises whether South Vietnam and the United States are bound if their opponents are not. The conventions themselves do not say that a signatory's obligation to comply is dependent on reciprocity, and in any event customary law binds the United States as it does the NLF.

But so far as concerns the obligations of the United States, we need not pursue these vexing questions further. Claiming as it does to be intervenor only to protect South Vietnam against aggression, and to be fighting under the banner of justice and humanity, the United States cannot possibly take the position that her forces are not bound by the laws of war, whether customary or embodied in treaties to which she is signatory. To the credit of our government, it has made no such claim, and acknowledges that its conduct of military operations, whether against North Vietnamese or Vietcong, is subject to those laws and treaties.

The crucial difficulty is that neither at Son My, nor in most of the other actions charged against our forces, has it been clear that the victims were either North Vietnamese or Vietcong. Indeed, the basis of the charge is that often they are *not,* and that we are indiscriminately killing civilians who may be and often are South Vietnamese innocent of any hostile action against our troops. What laws of war, if any, govern the relations between those troops and the civilian population of South Vietnam?

Before 1949, this question would have been governed by Section III of The Hague Convention of 1907, entitled "Military Authority over the Territory of the Hostile State," and reflecting in the title its basis in the customary laws of war, which apply only between belligerents. The issue would generally be whether the place where the challenged action took place should be regarded as "friendly" territory controlled by our allies, or "enemy" territory controlled by the NLF and to which the laws of war would apply.

The Geneva "Civilian Persons" Convention, however, applies to "all cases of partial or total occupation of the territory of" a signatory, and the persons protected by the convention include "those who, at a given moment . . . find themselves, in the case of a conflict or occupation, in the hands of a Party to the conflict or Occupying Power of which they are not nationals." On their face, these provisions would appear to cover the situation of South Vietnamese nationals who, like the inhabitants of Son My, find themselves "in the hands" of the United States forces, but this is rendered dubious by still another provision, which excludes from the convention's coverage "nationals of a co-belligerent State" which "has normal diplomatic representation in the State in whose hands they are." The theory of this clause is that the inhabitants can rely on normal diplomatic processes for protection against abuse, but it is certainly doubtful whether the South Vietnamese Government is either able or disposed to furnish such protection for its nationals "in the hands of" the United States. On this basis it could be argued that *all* South Vietnamese nationals enjoy the protection of the Geneva Convention vis-à-vis the American forces, but this conclusion is by no means clear.

If the more conservative view that the laws of war do not apply to American-South Vietnamese relations generally is taken, then one must fall back on the orthodox distinction between "friendly" and "enemy" territory. If an American soldier rapes and murders a South Vietnamese girl in Saigon, it is a crime punishable by court-martial under the articles of war,[1] but not a war crime. The terrible episode

---

[1] The crime would also be punishable under Vietnamese law, but Americans in

poignantly described by Daniel Lang in "Casualties of War," involving the American patrol that kidnapped a South Vietnamese girl to serve as luggage-carrier and lust-gratifier, and then murdered her, was apparently not a war crime, for the same reasons.

But Son My was in an area regarded as a Vietcong stronghold, and the hamlets assaulted were thought to be Vietcong military bases. The troops went in expecting to encounter resistance, and under orders to destroy the habitations and deal ruthlessly with any resistance. It would be highly artificial to say that this was not "hostile" territory within the meaning of The Hague Convention, or to question the applicability of the laws of war to the events of March 16, 1968, at Son My. What, then, were the applicable laws?

The presence of infants and the aged, as well as many women, among those killed at Son My underlined the horror of the episode, but is not directly relevant to the legality of what was done. It is sad but true that the weak and helpless are not exempt from the scourge of war. Indeed, they are likely to be the first to succumb to the starvation and other deprivations that are the consequence and, indeed, the purpose of an economic blockade. In this day and age they are at least as often the victims of aerial bombardment as are regular troops. The death of an infant in consequence of military operations, therefore, does not establish that a war crime has been committed.

All this is as true in Vietnam as in any other war. Furthermore, in Vietnam the weaker inhabitants are not only victims, but often also participants. It is not necessary to be a male, or particularly strong, to make a booby-trap, plant a mine, or toss a hand grenade a few yards. American soldiers are often the losers in these lethal little games played by those who appear helpless and inoffensive. Furthermore, these actions are not occasional aberrations; on the contrary, they are basic features of Vietcong strategy. As the leading military figure of North Vietnam, General Vo Nguyen Giap, has put it:

> *The protracted popular war in Vietnam demanded . . . appropriate forms of combat: appropriate for the revolutionary nature of the war in relation to the balance of forces then showing a clear enemy superiority. . . . The form of combat adopted was guerrilla warfare . . . each inhabitant a*

South Vietnam, under the applicable assistance treaties, are immune from Vietnamese criminal process.

soldier; each village a fortress. . . . The entire population participates in the armed struggle, fighting, according to the principles of guerrilla warfare, in small units. . . . This is the fundamental content of the war of people.

Now, guerrilla warfare is not intrinsically unlawful, but as waged by the Vietcong it is undeniably in violation of the traditional laws of war and the Geneva Conventions, based as they are on the distinction between combatants and noncombatants. Combatants need not wear uniforms (which the North Vietnamese generally do) but must observe the conventional four requirements: to be commanded "by a person responsible for his subordinates"; to wear "a fixed distinctive emblem recognizable at a distance"; to "carry arms openly"; and to "conduct their operations in accordance with the laws and customs of war." The Vietcong commonly disregard at least the second and third provisions, and in response to the Red Cross inquiry, declared that they were *not* bound by the Geneva Conventions, on the grounds that they were not signatories and that the conventions contained provisions unsuited to their "action" and their "organization . . . of armed forces."

Like a spy, a guerrilla may be a hero, but if he engages in combat without observing the requirements, he violates the laws of war and is subject to punishment, which may be the death penalty. Nor is there any special court for juveniles; the small boy who throws a grenade is as "guilty" as the ablebodied male of military age. This may seem a harsh rule, but it is certainly the law, and its continuing validity was reaffirmed in several of the Nuremberg trials. As one of the tribunals put the matter:

> *We think the rule is established that a civilian who aids, abets, or participates in the fighting is liable to punishment as a war criminal under the rules of war. Fighting is legitimate only for the combatant personnel. . . . It is only this group that is entitled to treatment as prisoners of war and incurs no liability beyond detention after capture or surrender.*

However, Richard Falk and other international lawyers have strongly pressed the argument that an insurgent revolutionary movement cannot possibly comply with the rules for the identification of combatants, or other laws of war, especially when confronting a foe so vastly superior in mobility and firepower as the United States. "I would suggest," Falk writes, "that the insurgent faction in an undeveloped country has, at the beginning of its struggle for power, no alternative other than terror to mobilize an effective operation."

This is, of course, the familiar argument of "military necessity" which we have already examined. If emblems and the other indicia of combatant status are to be discarded and the whole population engaged in combat, as Giap describes, then the same argument of necessity may justify the power against whom this type of war is directed in resorting to hitherto unlawful means to counter the guerrilla forces. As will shortly appear, this point may have some relevance to the lawfulness of the population transfers and "free-fire zones" that have become a common feature of our military policy in Vietnam.

But however far the "necessity" argument be stretched, it cannot justify what was done at Son My. Given the history and location of the village, the Americans might have had reason to suspect that many of the inhabitants were sympathetic to the Vietcong. There has been no suggestion, however, that there was reason to believe that any particular individual had engaged in hostile conduct. Even had there been such grounds, the slaughter of all the inhabitants would have been an unlawful and atrocious reaction; the Geneva Conventions are explicit that persons suspected of violating the laws of war shall "be treated with humanity" and not punished without trial and opportunity to contest the charge. And while small boys can toss grenades, infants in arms cannot, and were nonetheless killed along with the rest.

I have dealt with the Son My killings at length because of the scale of the disaster, the extensive though belated publicity it has received, and the fact that it is the only mass killing of the Vietnam war that our government has acknowledged as a crime. It has been said that "the massacre at Son My was not unique," but I am unaware of any evidence of other incidents of comparable magnitude, and the reported reaction of some of the soldiers at Son My strongly indicates that they regarded it as out of the ordinary. There have, however, been numerous indications that our troops have killed many other civilians under parallel circumstances, and equally in violation of the laws of war. Obviously, this state of affairs poses questions far more searching than the criminal liability of the soldiers who did the shooting at Son My.

Richard A. Falk
NUREMBERG: PAST, PRESENT, AND FUTURE

In this concluding selection, Richard Falk engages General Taylor once more, offering a penetrating, unrelenting attack on nearly every point of law the latter has raised. He argues that although the United States made a major contribution to the normative, communitarian approach to international affairs at Nuremberg, our behavior in the Vietnam War has been motivated almost exclusively by traditional national power considerations. As a result, the Nuremberg precedent and the international approach to world order have suffered a nearly irreparable blow. Professor Falk concludes with an admonition directed not only to Americans but to all the peoples of the world to let a universal love for humanity guide their affairs.

"What happens in Nuremberg, no matter how many objections it may invite, is a feeble, ambiguous harbinger of a world order, the need of which mankind is beginning to feel." These words addressed by Karl Jaspers to the German people shortly after the end of World War II have peculiarly vivid relevance to the situation Americans now must deal with in relation to the momentous issues of war crimes and individual responsibility presented by the continuing American involvement in the Indochina War.

Whatever else, Telford Taylor's book, *Nuremberg and Vietnam. An American Tragedy,* helped greatly to move the issues of war crimes and individual responsibility toward the center of public consciousness in this country. Professor Taylor's credentials of career and craft, his balanced and lucid style of analysis, and his lawyer-like restraint made his contention that America's involvement

Reprinted by permission of the author, The Yale Law Journal Company and Fred B. Rothman & Company from *The Yale Law Journal,* Vol. 80 (1971), pp. 1501–1528. (Footnotes omitted.)

in Vietnam was, in many respects, criminal in the Nuremberg sense much more difficult to shrug off than some of the prominent earlier efforts, directed at mobilizing antiwar sentiment, to demonstrate the same conclusion. Also, Professor Taylor's timing was superb. His book rode the crest of indignation, confusion, and concern that was created by the sensationalism of the disclosures of the My Lai massacre and the prosecution of some of the leading participants. In addition, antiwar veterans were beginning to speak out on their experiences in the combat theater that routinely involved intentional killing and cruelty toward innocent Vietnamese civilians. And, finally, Taylor's book came out at a time when prowar sentiment had virtually vanished from the scene and the political debate was confined to disagreement about exit strategies. The recital of these factors is not, of course, meant to draw attention from Professor Taylor's central achievement in writing on this difficult and controversial subject an illuminating book that conveys a great deal of knowledge and wisdom in relatively few pages.

The war goes on, however, and the debate evolves. Professor Taylor has been a vigorous participant in this debate and has since developed his position in response to criticism and the pressure of events. In the late spring of 1971 a portion of the so-called Pentagon Papers was placed in the public domain and managed to dissolve many carefully cherished ambiguities about the motives, intentions, and objectives of Washington's leading policy-makers with respect to America's involvement in Indochina. When the full corpus of McNamara's task-force study of the history of United States involvement becomes available later this year, these materials will establish two propositions having a direct and important bearing on Taylor's book:

1. There is clear proof that American civilian and military leaders did not take into account the moral dimension of their decisions to bring high-technology weaponry to bear in massive fashion on a low-technology society.
2. The case against the United States on the aggressive war issue is much stronger than when Taylor was writing his book.

Even before the release of the Pentagon Papers it was clear that the issue of war crimes had developed on its own. The public outcry

after Lt. Calley's conviction (inducing presidential gestures of conciliation) and the mere persistence of the war have driven the issue
deeper into "the hearts and minds" back here. Furthermore, the
irony of putative "war criminals" being rewarded with such jobs as
the presidency of the World Bank, the presidency of The Ford
Foundation, the editorship of *Foreign Affairs,* and high-salaried pro-
fessorships at leading American institutions of learning has not been
entirely lost on the widening antiwar community in this country—
nor, I might add, has the further irony of treating those who have
struggled to bring this war to an end as "enemies of the people,"
as criminals, exiles, or traitors. The situation, then, is one of inflamed
awareness, a sense that war crimes have been committed on a large
scale by American officialdom, a consciousness that "the system"
remains under the control of those who participated or conspired
with these "war criminals." As a result, a tension is developing
between the *clarity* of the facts and the law on the war crimes issue
and the *inability* to bring this clarity to bear on policy, even to the
extent of hastening the end of the war.

Under these circumstances the occasion calls for a reconsidera-
tion of the approach taken after World War II toward individual
criminal responsibility for the war leaders of Germany and Japan. In
essence, we need to determine whether those war crimes trials
should be viewed as precedents in an evolving legal tradition of
individual responsibility or as special events associated with the
conditions of victory in World War II which have been by now, *as a
result of ensuing patterns of statecraft,* denied any status as legal
precedents. Naturally, this issue cannot be resolved in a decisive
way, but the question raised underlies the discussion of individual
responsibility for American leaders in connection with the Vietnam
War and is of vital importance in appraising Professor Taylor's book.
In the remainder of this article, then, I will consider the Nuremberg
idea as it emerged, as it relates to the present controversy, and as
it might evolve in the future.

I. The Nuremberg Idea Reconsidered

It is not surprising that in the present situation people are skeptical
about the moral stature of international law in the Nuremberg area.

There is, indeed, a rebirth of cynical realism, often proclaimed under the peculiar contention that it is excessive moralism—not immorality or even amorality—that has been responsible for the most serious excesses of American battlefield practices in Vietnam.

The underpinning of this dismissal of a kind of ethnocentric moralism and of its relacement by the revival of national-interest thinking has been well expressed in a recent article by Arthur Schlesinger, Jr.: "Until nations come to adopt the same international morality, there can be no world law to regulate the behavior of states. Nor can international institutions—the League of Nations or the United Nations—produce by sleight of hand a moral consensus where none exists. World law must express world community; it cannot create it." On this basis Schlesinger condemns the American war as "immoral" because the *scale* of the commitment

> *burst the limitations of national interest. Our original presence in South Vietnam hardly seems immoral since we were there at the request of the South Vietnam government. Nor does it seem necessarily contrary to our national interest; conceivably it might have been worth it to commit, say, 20,000 military advisers if this could preserve an independent South Vietnam. But at some point the number of troops, and the things they were instructed to do, began to go beyond the requirements of national interest. This point was almost certainly the decision taken in early 1965 to send our bombers to North Vietnam and our combat units to South Vietnam and thus Americanize the war.*

According to Schlesinger it was the moralism of the architects of escalation that "intensified senseless terror till we stand today as a nation disgraced before the world and before our own posterity." In essence, this approach associates the immorality of the war mainly with the *disproportion* of the means adopted, given a reasonable construction of the geopolitical ends in view, and argues that had the policy-makers engaged in these sorts of calculations rather than in crusading or missionary claims relating to "freedom," "commitment," and "communism," then the threshold of immorality would never have been crossed. There is an apparent paradox here—immorality arises because moral issues are emphasized as the roots of policy. For Schlesinger this paradox is overcome by realizing that statist imperatives of rival national governments prevent the formation of any moral consensus in world society, and by finding that the invocation of moral considerations as a justification for national policy is a self-serving *moralism* that prevents the operation of the only kind of *morality* possible on an international level—namely, the prudential calculation of means and ends. Within such a framework, law follows morality, and the role of law is confined to reinforcing the logic of the moral order. As such, it would be appropriate to limit the role of law to questions of *means,* not *ends.*

But what, then, of Nuremberg as a basic orienting tradition? Clearly, the logic of Nuremberg rests on a moral order in which the *ends* of policy are crucial and in which the assessment of means is based on their *intrinsic* character as well as by links of *proportionality* to ends. That is, the prime effort at Nuremberg was to regard "aggressive war" both as illegal and as entailing individual criminal responsibility for its principal planners. In the language of the Judgment: "To initiate a war of aggression, therefore, is not only an international crime; it is the supreme international crime differing only from other war crimes in that it contains within itself the accumulated evil of the whole." Such a position rests on the view that it is the nature of the war policies, not their proportional relationship to the national interests at stake, that is the basis of moral and legal appraisal. In Schlesinger's terms the whole effort by Japan to wage war to expand its zone of economic and security control would appear to have been a reasonable, if ultimately disastrous, calculation of means/ends in the context of national interest. The Tokyo Tribunal found that aggression was committed by Japan because of its initiation of the war by military attacks. And certainly it is this view of the central teaching of Nuremberg that underlies Taylor's view of the relevance of legal criteria to war policies. But oddly enough even Schlesinger argues that "the Charter, Judgment, and Principles of the Nuremberg Tribunal constitute, along with other treaties, rudiments of an international consensus" that warrant enforcement:

> Such documents outlaw actions that the world has placed beyond the limits of permissible behavior. Within this restricted area a code emerges that makes moral judgment in international affairs possible up to a point. And within its scope this rudimentary code deserves, and must have, the most unflinching and rigorous enforcement.

Schlesinger seems confused about the content of Nuremberg, as well as about the extent to which his endorsement of substantive rules does not comport with his insistence on means/ends judgments rather than intrinsic appraisals of foreign policy. He writes that these "international rules deal with the limits rather than with the substance of policy," and, as such, "do not offer grounds for moral judgment and sanction on normal international transactions (including, it must be sorrowfully said, war itself, so long as war does not constitute aggression and so long as the rules of warfare are faithfully observed)." But, of course, this is as much as the most morally and legally inclined analyst would contend. Why, then, does Schlesinger write with such indignation about "moral absolutism" as a "malady" that "may strike at any point along the political spectrum"? Why does he state that "[f]rom the standpoint of those who mistrust self-serving ethical stances, the heirs of John Foster Dulles and the disciples of Noam Chomsky are equal victims of the same malady. Both regard foreign policy as a branch of ethics." This strikes me as sheer nonsense in light of Schlesinger's earlier comments on Nuremberg and wars of aggression. Clearly, in the context of Indochina, Noam Chomsky (and his disciples) have done nothing more than to document his conclusions about the aggressive character of the war and the barbarous tactics by which it has been waged. How can Schlesinger possibly explain his Vietnam position as merely one of the *degree* of violence used to crush the National Liberation Front? One can, to be sure, contend that carrying the war beyond a certain point was stupid ("counter-productive" as the authors of the Pentagon Papers tend to put it), but surely it did not become "aggression" at some point because of an increase in its magnitude.

Something very fundamental is exhibited by Schlesinger's confusion. Oddly enough, given Taylor's background and intellectual rigor, the same confusion lies latent in his book. Richard Wasserstrom has mounted a strong attack on Taylor, properly calling attention to the opening of the final paragraph of the book which Taylor begins as follows: "One may well echo the acrid French epigram and say that all this 'is worse than a crime, it is a blunder'— the most costly and tragic national blunder in American history." Wasserstrom goes on (in my opinion unfairly) to say that "Taylor's point of view is defective, inadequate, and dangerous because unlike him (and the French, apparently) I happen to believe that crimes are much worse than blunders." What Wasserstrom is on to is Taylor's effort to appear realistic and tough-minded. The risk with so doing is to appear both hopelessly confused and basely insensitive; it is one thing to reject the Nuremberg tradition out of hand as dangerous humbug, but quite another to affirm its relevance, as does Taylor, in such a way that Pentagon and State Department hardhats in the Acheson-Kissinger tradition won't slam the door in your face. Liberals in the Kennedy-Johnson mold of Schlesinger (and probably Taylor) want it both ways—to be in on the talk because they know what international conflict is all about and to remain somehow in touch with such minimal traditions of human decency as are embodied in the Nuremberg tradition.

This kind of normative (moral/legal) ambivalence is, I think, a characteristic of a period of transition within international life itself. I have tried to depict both the normative tension and the transition process in relation to the interplay between the *statist* imperatives of the Westphalia tradition and the *communitarian* drift of the Charter tradition. The Westphalia tradition is a shorthand description of the system of world order that has prevailed in international life since 1648 when the Peace of Westphalia was concluded at the end of the Thirty Years' War. The main characteristic of this system is the acknowledgment of the sovereignty of national governments in domestic and international affairs. The Charter tradition, which is as yet far weaker and of much more recent origin, can be understood as seeking to qualify the discretion of sovereign governments in the area of war and peace through the establishment of rules of restraint and the creation of international institutions of review. One consequence of the coexistence of these two approaches to the organization of international life is the exposure of a number of contradictions between sovereign discretion at the national level and community judgment at the global or regional level. The present structure of power and authority in the world order system is weighted down on the Westphalia side of the seesaw. Principal governments control military capabilities and exercise effective discretion over their employment. The political organs of the United Nations function mainly as instruments of statist diplomacy rather than as world community actors of the sort envisaged by much of the language of the United

Nations Charter. These considerations make it appear, on one level, naive and misguided to invoke the Nuremberg tradition as a basis for judging the dominant actors in world affairs. What is the point of fulminations put forward in moral and legal language against the powerful and mighty? The only realistic hope, given this outlook, is to persuade them that it is contrary to their own welfare to wage wars that do not promote the national interest. Hence the practical appeal of Schlesinger's plea for amorality and a sober national-interest calculus; hence, also, Taylor's tendency to allow his critique of the Vietnam War to confuse its military failure as an exercise in intervention with its normative status as an aggressive war involving criminal tactics. It is revealing that Taylor acknowledges that he was "one who until 1965 supported American intervention in Vietnam as an aggression-checking undertaking in the spirit of the United Nations Charter," and then, like Schlesinger, goes on to emphasize the drastic changes in that year in "the nature, scale, and effect of intervention" as the decisive elements in altering his attitude.

Some of this ambivalence is embedded in the Nuremberg experience itself. Only the victorious nations participated in setting up the Tribunal and passing upon the charges. More important, ghastly Allied actions in the war such as the destruction of Dresden, the fire-bombing of Tokyo, and the atomic bombing of Hiroshima and Nagasaki were kept outside the orbit of war crimes inquiry. Standards of negative reciprocity were relied upon, namely, that the leaders of the defeated states brought before the bar of international justice were not charged with any actions—such as submarine attacks without prior warning or the bombardment by air of enemy cities—that were also the common practice of the victorious side. Such forbearance at Nuremberg can be interpreted to mean that *anything* the victor does is beyond condemnation as *criminal* and that the defendant might succeed with a *tu quoque* argument. So interpreted, Nuremberg is deeply flawed if understood as moral education. However, there is more to Nuremberg than its Judgment. Certainly part of the experience was the creation of a precedent contributing to an international learning experience on world order that would, with the passage of time, broaden its significance beyond the original circumstances of its application. Part of the ideology of Nuremberg itself was contributed by Mr. Justice Robert Jackson, the Chief Prosecutor for the United States at the Nuremberg Trials, in his celebrated assertion that "[i]f certain acts in violation of treaties are crimes, they are crimes whether the United States does them or whether Germany does them, and we are not prepared to lay down a rule of criminal conduct against others which we would not be willing to have invoked against us." Certainly Professor Taylor's book is a testimonial to the accuracy of Jackson's prediction. The United States has not been defeated in Indochina in anything like the way that Germany was defeated in World War II. The military mission has failed and has been widely discredited, but the military and economic prowess of the country remains preeminent in world affairs. Nuremberg has reached beyond itself when applied to Vietnam, and this moral growth, so to speak, was implicit within its initial historical dimensions.

Those who are working for a new world order system based upon some form of effective central guidance in matters of war and peace reject as obsolescent and regressive the "realism" of national interest approaches to foreign policy. There is a new realism emerging out of the need to adapt the state system to the multiple challenges of war, population pressure, global pollution, resource depletion, and human alienation. It is this new political consciousness that insists upon regarding America's involvement in the Indochina War as illegal and immoral *from the beginning* in the late 40s and early 50s. Such an assessment can be made more authoritatively since the publication of the Pentagon Papers. But the main point is that we are in a situation of transition from one world order system to another, from a statist logic which is *no longer adequate* to a normative logic associated with the United Nations Charter and the Nuremberg Principles that *does not yet pertain.* In the midst of such a process rigid distinctions between what the law "is" and what it "ought to be" obscure the central reality of movement from one position to another. Those who identify with a progressive vision of world order are primarily agents of value change. In this sense, to pass judgment on one's own government, to discredit those who planned and waged aggressive warfare in Vietnam for so many years, and to seek an application of the Nuremberg concept is to embody the future in the present to some small extent. We become—in a normative way—what we do.

II. Problems of Application: Wars without Victors

The facts available make it increasingly evident that the United States has violated the Nuremberg Principles, and that its chief policy-makers could be prosecuted before a Nuremberg-type court for crimes in all three categories. In this section I address the question of what action is appropriate given the unavailability of a proper adjudicating tribunal. Since the evidence is now increasingly available to support allegations of criminality, the nonavailability of an adjudicating forum is at present the most crucial policy issue.

The Nuremberg concept presupposed an Allied victory in World War II. In the context of the Vietnam War there is no prospect that the United States will be defeated in the sense of surrendering to North Vietnam or the National Liberation Front. The other side would not, as a consequence, be in a position to convene a tribunal that would hear charges against United States military and civilian leaders. Moreover, the organized international community has neither the will nor the capability to proceed against the most powerful country in the world. There is no prospect, in other words, of bringing United States leaders before the bar of international justice, even as it was so imperfectly enacted at Nuremberg.

There is some sentiment among legalistic observers who argue that the inability to convene an international war crimes tribunal should put to rest, once and for all, allegations about war crimes. Taylor is somewhat ambiguous about his own position. On the one hand, he says that at the end of the war crimes trials after World War II

> the United States Government stood legally, politically and morally committed to the principles enunciated in the charters and judgments of the tribunals. The President of the United States, on the recommendation of the Departments of State, War and Justice, approved of the war crimes programs . . . . The United States delegation to the United Nations presented the resolution by which the General Assembly endorsed the Nuremberg principles. Thus the integrity of the nation is staked on those principles [of Nuremberg] . . . .

In short, we created a precedent intended to bind ourselves in the future. On the other hand, Taylor does not deal at all directly with these difficult issues of application in the altered setting of the American involvement in Vietnam. Indeed, Taylor comes down hard against entrusting domestic courts in the United States with any role in assessing the legal status of the American involvement or the battlefield tactics relied upon. Thus, despite a reasonably clear set of judgments in the book that a Nuremberg problem has been created by our role in Vietnam, there is absolutely no guidance given as to what can (or should) be done about it. Taylor has said in response to this criticism of his book that he regards the question of application as "a political one" outside the scope of his technical competence. I suppose it is "political" in the sense of involving the current mood of public opinion. Obviously, if 90 per cent of the American public (rather than a tiny number—say 1 per cent) was clamoring for war crimes trials against Westmoreland, Abrams, Rusk, Rostow, and others, then there would be a powerful movement in this country to constitute some sort of tribunal.

There are also, however, serious legal questions presented. The growth of international law has always depended on the vigor of its domestic enforcement. The absence of an international tribunal is not indispensable to serious judicial treatment of war crimes issues. After all, the *Eichmann* case was heard before a domestic court in Israel, and there is a Security Council Resolution calling upon nations to use their domestic legal system to punish World War II war criminals. In a variety of areas, ranging from the apprehension of international pirates (and more recently hijackers) to the enforcement of antitrust and expropriation norms, domestic courts have performed valuable functions when international tribunals were nonexistent or unable to act. Furthermore, a particularly strong case for the development of a more active judicial role could be made in light of certain tendencies to downgrade Congress' constitutional role. The expansion of executive prerogatives has eroded the constitutional scheme envisioned by the framers and led to other undesirable effects as well. In particular, the presidential power to maintain secrecy and to manage the release of news has virtually nullified the development of legal restraints on war-making at the global level.

Taylor advances a number of grounds for concluding that a domestic court should not undertake inquiry into the legality of the American involvement in the Vietnam War, either on constitutional grounds of executive usurpation of congressional privilege, or on international law grounds of incompatibility with treaty obligations to refrain from nondefensive (or aggressive) uses of force.

1. To resolve the issue would require "the examination of hotly controverted evidentiary questions" for which much relevant material is unavailable; these questions involve the quantum and timing of infiltration from North to South Vietnam, the status of the 1954 Geneva Accords, the relevance of the SEATO Treaty;
2. Unlike the situation after the Second World War, the perception of who is "the aggressor" in the setting of Vietnam is very difficult to adjudicate because even the issue of "who attacked whom" is factually and legally murky; Taylor also stresses here the inability of governments through the years to evolve an agreed definition of aggression;
3. In Nuremberg and Tokyo it was possible for the prosecution to establish intent and motivation by relying on the "proven intentions and declarations" of the defendants;
4. Congress has endorsed the war by means of the Tonkin Resolution in 1964 and by voting appropriations since that time;
5. The judicial capacity to act in the area of foreign affairs is severely restricted, even if it is not entirely clear whether this is a matter of constitutional requirement or judicial self-restraint.

On these bases Taylor concludes that "the Supreme Court *is not authorized* to render judgment on the validity of our participation in the Vietnam War under the Nuremberg Principles or international law in general." It is Taylor's view that "[a]fter five years of bloody and costly war sustained by Congressional appropriations, if the President's course is to be checked by another branch of the Government, it is the Congress and not the Court that can and should be the checking agent." This line of argument is very statist in character, for it overlooks the degree to which the denial of standing and judicial relief to individual citizens raising these legal issues undermines the legitimacy of government. It should be understood that efforts to gain judicial relief in relation to the war have grown out of refusals to enter the armed forces or pay taxes—out of refusals, in other words, to contribute to the war. I have argued elsewhere that in this situation "the wider logic of Nuremberg" supports such assertions, whereas Taylor writes that "Nuremberg acquittals of generals and industrialists cut directly against Professor Falk's argument." Not at all. My argument is not based on Nuremberg as a precedent in a strict sense of what was decided there, but rather by conceiving of Nuremberg as a set of directives about individual responsibility in relation to aggressive war-making. In this regard "the wider logic" includes such actions in the Nuremberg setting as President Roosevelt's appeal of 1944 to the German citizenry on the ssue of war crimes:

> *Hitler is committing these crimes against humanity in the name of the German people. I ask every German and every man everywhere under Nazi domination to show the world by his action that in his heart he does not share these insane criminal desires. Let him hide these pursued victims, help them to get over their borders, and do what he can to save them from the Nazi hangman. I ask him to keep watch, and to record the evidence that will one day be used to convict the guilty.*

There is an implicit civic responsibility to resist and oppose any war that it *seems reasonable* to believe is aggressive, and, hence, whose furtherance involves the commission of crimes against peace.

Part of the "wider logic" also involves the generalized responsibility of all actors at every level of social organization to implement the basic Nuremberg directives. The United Nations Security Council has urged governments to facilitate the prosecution of World War II war criminals. By preparing the Nuremberg Principles—merely a codification of what was decided at Nuremberg—the United Nations has set forth general standards of responsibility that pertain to all who hold high public office.

And, finally, the wider logic has to do with giving effect to the Nuremberg concept in other contexts than the prosecution of those leaders responsible for the policy. The effort of war resisters to turn the legal system against illegal and criminal warfare involves a symbolic effort to use these ideas of personal responsibility to inhibit unrestricted sovereign discretion in the area of war and peace. America is *not* Nazi Germany, and, precisely for this reason, the vulnerability of the war-making apparatus may be in the responsiveness of its institutions to the values embedded in Nuremberg thinking rather than in the vulnerability of the power apparatus to decisive battlefield defeat. "The wider logic" explores the possibilities of enforcing Nuremberg in a situation where "victor's justice" is unavailable, and where the war machine and its underlying criminality persist.

In responding to Taylor I would like to deal in sequence with each of his five points.

1. *Evidence of criminal behavior.* Since the publication of the Pentagon Papers there is ample documentary material on which to assess the central issue of whether the United States Government has been waging a war of aggression in Indochina. Some difficult issues of interpretation remain, but these issues are not inherently more difficult than those confronting courts in many other areas of the law, nor do they seem to hamper greatly the prospect of reaching a clear conclusion. On the issue of war crimes and crimes against humanity there is less documentary evidence, but there is also less need for it as alternative sources of reliable evidence exist. For instance, there are now available numerous Vietnam veterans who are willing and eager to testify about the tactics, methods, and weapons of warfare used, and who, in many instances, themselves participated in specific massacres. There is no longer, if indeed there ever was, any reasonable doubt about the main patterns of warfare relied upon by the United States in Vietnam that have been challenged as illegal. The evidence is there.

2. *Identity of the aggressor.* It is correct, as Taylor suggests, that the setting of the Vietnam War is different from that of World War II, but I do not find it significantly different. The extension of the combat zone to North Vietnam in 1965 and the character of the interventions by both sides in South Vietnam seem susceptible to legal analysis and inference. Indeed, pro-Administration and anti-Administration legal scholars have long shared the conviction that the law and the facts are clear enough to support an inference of aggression— though they do not agree on who the aggressor is. Why under such circumstances is it impossible for a court to make a comparable assessment? Indeed, the government as a whole seems estopped from even contending that it is impossible to identify the aggressor in the Vietnam context since it has itself so frequently argued that it was acting in defense against aggression.

The failure of governments to reach an agreement on the international definition of aggression is surely not a plausible obstacle to a domestic court reaching a determination in relation to specifically challenged conduct. This assertion takes on more weight when it is realized that the growth of American law has proceeded on the assumption that the content of general concepts has generally depended on a case-by-case development rather than by applying some sort of definition agreed to in advance. Indeed, the United States has been a leading opponent of international attempts to define aggression, and has consistently opposed the definitional initiatives of the Soviet Union and others on these general grounds of legal policy. Finally, there was enough clarity about the character of aggression at Nuremberg and Tokyo to permit authoritative inferences of aggression in the absence of a definition. It is not at all clear that striking first is a decisive indicator of the identity of the aggressor (consider, for example, the legal debate about the outbreak of the 1967 Middle Eastern War, or the American threat to use force, if necessary, to prevent the deployment of Soviet missiles in Cuba in 1962) or that there was an undisputed chain of aggressive actions by Germany and Japan and of defensive responses by the Allied Powers. Taylor's argument that the identity of the aggressors in World War II was clear by comparison with Vietnam is merely self-serving in relation to his conclusion.

3. *Evidence of intentions.* Taylor's argument here, too, has been undercut by the publication of the Pentagon Papers. Even if these documents are incomplete or onesided, as claimed by most of the principal officials depicted therein, a prima facie case has still been made and a burden to come forward imposed on those who would repudiate the available evidence of intentions. Furthermore, the issue before domestic courts would not be the criminality of specific government officials, as to which intent is relevant, but the legality of state action, as to which it is not relevant. If the concerns under 1 and 2 are dissipated, then 3 seems immaterial in many contexts where judicial redress has been sought. This issue of intent seems relevant only to the formation of some Nuremberg-type operation against specifically identified defendants.

4. *Congressional endorsement.* By now, there is ample indication that the passage of the Tonkin Resolution should not be viewed as an endorsement of the legality of the war as a whole any more than its later repeal should be viewed as a repudiation of the war. Several

prominent Senators who voted for the Tonkin Resolution have been outspoken opponents of the war for several years and have denied their intention to give the President blanket authority to expand the combat theater. The argument on appropriations seems even weaker since it has been made abundantly clear by many Congressmen and Senators that votes for appropriations have reflected an overriding concern for the physical welfare of Americans in the battlefield. However misconceived and implausible such a rationale may be (i.e., the welfare of American soldiers could be best safeguarded by earmarking appropriations "for withdrawal purposes only"), nevertheless it suffices to establish the view that a vote for appropriations cannot properly be construed as a vote for the war. In any event, congressional approval of the war is not strictly relevant to its legal status. Congress might (and often has) given its formal approval to executive policy that courts deem unconstitutional. The doctrines of judicial review and of constitutional supremacy as developed in American legal history presuppose that courts have the last word on issues of this kind. Obviously, the need for a court to reach a decision that challenges fundamental policy of both coordinate branches poses political problems of great delicacy for a society that prides itself on popular sovereignty and representative government, but these difficulties are not properly viewed as obstacles to adjudication. Especially where individual issues of life and death and collective issues of war and peace are concerned, the right of judicial redress seems to take clear precedence over the prospect of potentially harmful clashes among coordinate branches of government.

5. *Judicial incapacity in the area of foreign affairs.* Taylor's argument that courts are severely restricted in the area of foreign affairs also seems unconvincing. There have been very few tests of the scope of judicial power in the area of foreign affairs, and these have been in relation to special circumstances favoring judicial prerogatives. The "political question doctrine" as a basis for deference seems to be the most persuasive ground on which to urge courts to side-step the legal issues raised by the Vietnam War, but even this argument is not very strong. As *Baker* v. *Carr* made clear there is no fixed context for a "political question." In the present context, there seems to be a powerful basis in law and policy to reverse past dispositions of courts to treat all issues of foreign policy as falling

within the domain of executive discretion and outside the domain of judicial scrutiny. Until the Kellogg-Briand Pact of 1928, no effort was ever made to outlaw aggressive war, but since that time numerous events have confirmed the growth of this prohibitive rule of law. As I have argued under 1, 2, and 3, there are no technical difficulties in the Vietnam context to prevent applying this rule in a substantive setting. In more general terms, the importance of this rule of international law, which is central to the United Nations Charter, makes it desirable for domestic courts to enforce it. The incapacity of the political organs of the United Nations to proceed effectively against a principal state, and the general unavailability of an adjudicating tribunal on the global level, make it especially important to establish the responsibility of domestic courts in this area. It has been generally true that *domestic* courts have been far more important than international courts in developing and upholding international law. The particular situation, in which the United States is the most powerful actor on the world scene and is deeply involved in foreign military operations, makes it evident that if legal limits are going to be made relevant at all, these limits must be generated on a domestic level. Since the executive part of the government is already engaged in evolving the policy, normally with the acquiescence of Congress, the courts are the only conceivable arena in which a serious legal challenge can be mounted. Admittedly, such a position requires "a new patriotism" in which the national interest in law-abidingness in international undertakings is given an unprecedented priority.

I close this section with some general observations that go beyond the response to Taylor's specific arguments. Professor Taylor underestimated the strength of the Nuremberg imperative within our political culture when he wrote that "it is difficult to envisage other circumstances [than "total military victories"] that would unlock the secret files." Without "the wider logic," Daniel Ellsberg would probably not have been motivated to act as he did. It is significant to note that Ellsberg spoke of hmself as a war criminal warranting prosecution before he apparently decided that he had a duty to unlock "the secret files."

The issues of separation of powers and "political question" seem an insufficient basis for judicial passivity. Legal criteria now exist by which to appraise a challenge directed at war policies. The flow of power from Congress to the Executive in the war/peace area has badly distorted the constitutional notion of checks and balances. Where Congress fails to act and a clear issue of urgent national welfare is at stake, courts have an obligation to act.

Obviously, it is tempting for an American court to dispose of such issues as belonging to the province of the Executive or as having been resolved by subsequent congressional action that governs judicial action, but to yield to such temptation is to consign our institutions to a state of impotence during times of emergency. The differences between Nazi Germany and ourselves need to be stressed in considering the benefits and burdens that would result from allowing this conflict within our public consciousness to be dealt with by domestic courts. To shut off judicial redress leaves conflict to the streets; to control the streets is to initiate a program of "pacification" at home that seriously endangers the fragile institutions of our kind of democratic polity.

III. Nuremberg and the Present

In writing recently about the waning impact of the Pentagon Papers, Walter Pincus suggested that "[a] year from now, Dr. Daniel Ellsberg may look back and wonder why he did it." As with the invasion of Cambodia in May 1970, the My Lai disclosures, and the Calley trial, the revelations of the Pentagon Papers have generated some temporary furor in the country, but have not exerted any decisive influence on either public opinion or government policies. In each instance, the war persists, bureaucratic momentum is maintained, public apathy is restored, and the bipartisan elite that conceived and executed the Vietnam intervention remains in or close to power. There has been neither a turn against the war, nor against the warmakers, nor even against the military-industrial complex. To be sure, there are ripples of discontent, but the dominant mood of the country appears to stress the *continuity* between the recent past and the hoped-for future.

If we consider this evidence of continuity from the perspective of the Nuremberg tradition, the implications are extremely discouraging. Interpreting Nuremberg for the benefit of German society in 1947,

Karl Jaspers wrote that "[t]he essential point is whether the Nuremberg trial comes to be a link in a chain of meaningful, constructive political acts (however often these may be frustrated by error, unreason, heartlessness and hate) or whether, by the yardstick there applied to mankind, the very powers now erecting it will in the end be found wanting." As of 1971, the United States has clearly not carried forward the Nuremberg tradition either with respect to the use of its military power against a foreign society or with regard to attitudes toward individual responsibility. Despite the evidence of war crimes, crimes against peace, and crimes against humanity, one detects neither public indignation of any magnitude nor any effort to hold the main policy-makers accountable to any degree for the moral consequences to Vietnam and to America of the involvement. What public indignation there is has to do with *costs* and *failure,* that the war plans were too expensive given the interests at stake and that these plans did not accomplish the mission of securing South Vietnam for an anticommunist Saigon regime. To discredit policy-makers for their failure to achieve stated goals is a normal accompaniment of any democratic system of political accountability. But it represents only a pragmatic, and not a normative basis of judgment, for such criticism happens also when the means and goals of policy were admirable.

This American repudiation of the Nuremberg tradition is part of a more general pattern of international behavior. The Soviet interventions in Eastern Europe, the French colonial wars in Indochina and Algeria, and the Anglo-French cooperation in the Suez campaign are examples of international conduct that appear to be criminal if measured by Nuremberg standards. These examples of criminality are taken only to show that none of the powers that sat in judgment at Nuremberg has kept the implicit promise of establishing a precedent for the future. Indeed it is a tribute to the public consciousness of America that the Nuremberg issue has been raised at all, although this consciousness also reflects the length, the frustrations, and the overall failure of the American effort in Vietnam. The basic international reality, tragic from the perspective of Nuremberg, is that world public opinion, at least as it has crystallized in the setting of the United Nations, neither expects nor insists upon carrying forward the Nuremberg tradition. This is partly because the pattern of repudiation seems so pervasive, and partly because there is no international capability to pass judgment upon the actions of a state that has not been utterly defeated in a war.

The failure of Nuremberg is a matter both of behavior and of public consciousness. On both levels the Nuremberg tradition has been virtually repudiated by the *governments* that dominate international life. The only open question is whether some popular movement could revive and sustain this tradition in defiance of the statist logic that prevails in international life. And it is for this reason that unorganized efforts by "peace criminals," peace groups, and journalists seem so important. They are important because the future of world society ultimately depends on keeping the promises of Nuremberg. For, again quoting Jaspers, "Ever since European nations have tried and beheaded their monarchs, the task of the people has been to keep their leaders in check. The acts of states are also the acts of persons. Men are individually responsible and liable for them." Jaspers' book is especially relevant to the present discussion because he is so keenly aware of the small degree to which Nuremberg as an *external judgment* really disposed of the genuine issues for German society of coping with the Nazi experience. These issues have their proper locus within the national consciousness of the state that has acted in such criminal fashion. The external judgment by its externality tends to divert attention from the need to emphasize internal processes of renewal.

IV. Keeping the Nuremberg Idea Alive

My purpose here is to set forth very briefly some lines of constructive initiative. This discussion is based upon the assumption that it may well be impractical and undesirable to press for formal trials of those American political and military leaders principally responsible for the overall drift of the Vietnam involvement and for the main battlefield tactics. The formation of an American commission of inquiry into the issue of war crimes that would assemble evidence and draw conclusions on these questions could have a constructive impact. It also seems essential for the moral status of law in American society that steps be taken to exonerate draft resisters, tax evaders, and others who committed nonviolent "crimes" to manifest their opposition to the Vietnam War. There seems to be ample basis for the

United States to pay reparations to Vietnam (and to Laos and Cambodia) to help overcome the war damage that has been done; these reparations should be gathered on as public a basis as possible, perhaps being collected from a 1 per cent income tax surcharge for a number of years and from cuts in the counter-insurgency portion of the Defense Department budget. In any event, the idea that America has some ongoing responsibility toward those war-ravaged societies seems essential for our civil health. This assertion of an American responsibility does not imply direct participation in postwar Indochina. Funds should be channeled through an international trust arrangement and given to the Indochina governments to spend according to their own priorities.

There are some other steps that can be taken even given the low state of public consciousness in these matters. Governments could press for a new world conference, on the order of The Hague Conference in 1899, to establish new laws of war incorporating, to the extent possible, both the normative (for instance, the Nuremberg experience and the United Nations Charter) and technological developments of the last several decades. At a minimum, the process of preparing for such a conference would bring many of the issues into the field of awareness in a vivid way. Participation by governmental delegations would reaffirm the restraints of law and morality upon the discretion of governmental officials, and the pressure to produce something tangible might lead to a renewal of the law of war on a realistic and effective basis. The international climate seems somewhat receptive to an initiative of this type, given such bloody struggles as those in Indochina, Nigeria, Pakistan, and the Middle East.

Another area of change involves structuring our own governmental system to make it more responsive to normative restraints in relation to warfare. Congress could clarify its own relation to the Presidency and establish definite procedures to authorize limited objectives within fixed times and periods; in other words, except for an emergency response to a sudden attack, recourse to war should be based on specific congressional declaration, although it need not be technically treated as a Declaration of War. If the President acted without such authorization or beyond its express terms, then he could be made subject to a series of congressional remedies ranging from censure to impeachment, and any member of Congress should be given judicial access to seek declaratory, and possibly injunctive, relief. Congress could also grant the courts an express mandate to hear arguments about the legal status of any war and confer standing upon individuals to seek judicial redress for alleged infringement of personal and property rights.

Of great potential importance would be the creation of some post within the government which would have responsibility for conforming the action of the country to the requirements of international law. This post could be conceived of as an Attorney General for International Affairs or as an Under-Secretary in a yet-to-be-created Department of Peace. The function of this job would be to report privately to the President on the legal status of any contemplated undertaking by the United States and to report publicly any doubts about the legal status of ongoing policies. Such a public official would serve notice on the President that legal consequences of foreign policy activity would receive explicit attention. Of course, there are many difficulties with such a proposal:

—How does one prevent the government official entrusted with the task of being an international law watchdog from becoming a presidential lap dog?
—How does one take account of reasonable differences of opinion as to the requirements of international law, requirements that are often controversial in the extreme, especially in determining "aggression," "armed attack," and "self-defense"?
—How can such a public official gain access to the facts upon which a persuasive legal appraisal depends?
—How can an international law argument prevail in relation to a determined President, a militant Congress, a mobilized electorate?
—How would such legal judgment be enforced?
—How should account be taken of the failure of "the other side" to show comparable respect for the restraints of international law?

These difficulties are generally characteristic of efforts to bring law to bear on human behavior. Pitfalls, weaknesses and ambiguities are unavoidable at all levels of social and political organization. Nevertheless, the legal approach seems a valid method of inhibiting aggressive war-making and discouraging criminal methods of warfare. The national and human peril of allowing the discretion of governmental centers of power and authority to determine the occasions and character of warfare seems clear enough. We need to build barriers against war-making carried on in the name of national populations who are often victimized by the process without ever participating in it. In general, the next great movement of mankind needs to involve decisive action by the public "to keep their leaders in check" in the area of war and peace.

The sorts of steps that I have outlined are intended only to indicate a sense of direction on the most immediate level of response. In more fundamental terms, I am persuaded by the view so eloquently and persuasively held by J. Glenn Gray that "to resolve the problem of warfare, civil or international," requires that "a transformation of a deepgoing inner sort will have to come over men." I also share Gray's view that "a changed attitude toward our habitat must precede—or at least accompany—a changed attitude toward our fellow man."

Law is largely a dependent variable in both accomplishing and sustaining change, although it may symbolize emerging human aspirations and precede a wider social adjustment to new challenges. The Nuremberg idea needs to be understood as a statement both of aspiration and of necessity. Our indebtedness to Telford Taylor, Daniel Ellsberg, and the Berrigans is essentially the same: they remind us of our ideals in a period of national and international danger. And Taylor has further demonstrated that in earlier days of triumph we even acted to translate these ideals into norms of judgment and conduct. The question before all of us, at this time, is whether we who originally lit the Nuremberg torch can keep it aflicker in these times of barbarism. The question will not be answered affirmatively by governments, but only by popular forces who are committed to building a new world order in which tenderness toward nature and fellow man is the basis of organization and action. It is this greater struggle that is being prefigured by the debate surrounding Nuremberg and Vietnam.

Suggestions for Additional Reading

Students desiring to undertake studies related to the trials of individuals at Nuremberg should consult the following official government publications: International Military Tribunal, *Trial of the Major War Criminals before the International Military Tribunal,* November 14, 1945–October 1, 1946, 42 vols. [Blue Series] (Nuremberg, 1949); Office of United States Chief of Counsel for Prosecution of Axis Criminality, *Nazi Conspiracy and Aggression: Opinion and Judgment,* 8 vols. [Red Series] (Washington, 1947); *Trials of War Criminals before the Nuremberg Military Tribunal under Control Council Law No. 10,* October 1946–April 1949, 15 vols. [Green Series] (Washington, 1949–1954). The legal background for the Nuremberg trials is found in two works by Sheldon Glueck: *War Criminals: Their Prosecution and Punishment* (New York, 1944), and *The Nuremberg Trial and Aggressive War* (New York, 1946). There are also several works by American participants at Nuremberg, including Robert H. Jackson, ed., *The Nürnberg Case* (New York, 1947), and "Final Report to the President from Supreme Court Justice Jackson," *Dept. of State Bulletin* 13, October 27, 1946, pp. 771–776; Telford Taylor, *Final Report to the Secretary of the Army on the Nürnberg War Crimes Trials under Control Council Law No. 10* (Washington, 1949), and "Nuremberg Trials, War Crimes and International Law," *International Conciliation* 450 (April 1949): 241–371. Inge S. Neumann's *European War Crimes Trials: A Bibliography* (New York, 1951) is a useful source book.

There are numerous books and articles dealing with the complex legal issues of the Nuremberg trials. A selected list of some of the most provocative and informative titles would include the following: Nathan April, "An Inquiry into the Judicial Basis for the Nuremberg War Crime Trial," *Minnesota Law Review* 30 (April 1946): 313–331; Peter Calvocoressi, *Nuremberg: The Facts, the Law, and the Consequences* (New York, 1948); Eugene Davidson, *The Trial of the Germans* (New York, 1966); Felix Hirsch, "Lessons of Nuremberg," *Current History* 11 (October 1946): 312–318; E. Janeczek, *Nuremberg Judgment in the Light of International Law* (Geneva, 1949); August von Knieriem, *The Nuremberg Trials* (Chicago, 1959); Hans Leonhardt, "The Nuremberg Trial: A Legal Analysis," *Review of Politics* 11 (October 1949): 449–460; Harold Leventhal, Sam Harris, John Woolsey, and Warren Farr, "The Nuremberg Verdict," *Harvard Law Review* 60 (July 1947): 857–907; Franz Neumann, "The War Crimes Trials," *World Politics* 2 (October 1949): 135–147; Max Radin, "Justice at Nuremberg," *Foreign Affairs* 24 (April 1946): 369–384; F.B. Schick, "The Nuremberg Trial and the International Law of the Future," *American Journal of International Law* (hereinafter cited as *AJIL*) 41 (1947): 770–794; Robert K. Woetzel, *The Nuremberg Trials in International Law* (London, 1960); Quincy Wright, "Legal Positivism and the Nuremberg Judgment," *AJIL* 42 (1948): 405–414.

The legal issues of the trial may be viewed from the German perspective by reading Wilbourn Benton and Georg Grimm, eds., *Nuremberg: German Views of the War Trials* (Dallas, 1955), and Hans Ehard, former Minister President of Bavaria, "The Nuremberg Trials against the Major War Criminals and International Law," *AJIL* 43 (1949): 223–245. Oliver Schroeder, Jr. raises many issues which have relevance to Vietnam in *International Crime and the U.S. Constitution* (Cleveland, 1950), while Otto Kirchheimer poses many troubling issues in *Political Justice: The Use of Legal Procedure for Political Ends* (Princeton, 1961). Those wishing to pursue the subject of mass murder and the Nuremberg precedent should consult George Finch, "The Genocide Convention," *AJIL* 43 (1949): 732–737 and Josef Kunz, "The United Nations Convention on Genocide," *AJIL* 43 (1949): 738–745. William Bosch analyzes American attitudes toward the trials in *Judgment on Nuremberg* (Chapel Hill, 1970).

The problem of aggression, still undefined in international law, is treated by Philip C. Jessup, "The Crime of Aggression and the Future of International Law," *Political Science Quarterly* 62 (March 1947): 1–10; and Walter Millis and James Real, *The Abolition of War* (New York, 1963). T.J. Farer takes a reckoning of the Nuremberg precedent after the lapse of a quarter century in "The Laws of War 25 Years after Nuremberg," *International Conciliation* (May 1971).

The Japanese war-crimes trials have become the subject of renewed interest. Besides A. Frank Reel's *The Case of General Yamashita* (Chicago, 1949), interested students should read Willard Cowles, "Trials of War Criminals (Non-Nuremberg)," *AJIL* 42 (1948): 299–319; Horwitz, *The Tokyo Trial* (New York, 1950); and R. Minear, *Victor's Justice: The Tokyo War Crimes Trial* (Princeton, 1971). The torrent of criticism against Hannah Arendt's *Eichmann in Jerusalem*

(New York, 1963) included Jacob Robinson, *And the Crooked Shall be Made Straight* (New York, 1965); and Gideon Hausner, *Justice in Jerusalem* (New York, 1966). Jacob Robinson has appended an excellent bibliography to his work. Also recommended are Peter Papadatos, *The Eichmann Trial* (New York, 1964); Yosal Rogat, *The Eichmann Trial and the Rule of Law* (Santa Barbara, 1961); and L.C. Green, "Legal Issues of the Eichmann Trial," *Tulane Law Review* 37 (1962–1963): 641–684.

The charge that the United States is guilty of aggression in Vietnam according to Nuremberg law has occasioned the growth of a considerable literature on the subject. Among the books analyzing the constitutional issues involved are A. Austin, *The President's War* (New York, 1971); and J. Goulden, *Truth is the First Casualty: The Gulf of Tonkin Affair—Illusion and Reality* (New York, 1969). Articles dealing with the legality of United States involvement include John N. Moore, "The Lawfulness of Military Assistance to the Republic of Viet-Nam," *AJIL* 61 (1967): 1–34; Quincy Wright, "Legal Aspects of the Viet-Nam Situation," *AJIL* 60 (1966): 750–769; Wolfgang Friedmann, "Law and Politics in the Vietnamese War," *AJIL* 61 (1967): 776–784; John N. Moore, "Law and Politics in the Vietnamese War: A Response to Professor Friedmann," *AJIL* 61 (1967): 1039–1053; Neil Alford, Jr., "The Legality of American Military Involvement in Viet-Nam: A Broader Perspective," *Yale Law Journal* 75 (1966): 1109–1121; Ralph White, "Misperception of Aggression in Vietnam," *Journal of International Affairs* 21 (1967): 123–140; and E.B. Firmage, "International Law and the Response of the United States to 'Internal War'," *Utah Law Review* 1 (1967): 517–546. Roger H. Hull and John C. Novogrod, *Law and Vietnam* (Dobbs Ferry, 1968) is a commendable analysis of the legal problems involved. Richard A. Falk has collected the most outstanding literature on both aggression and atrocity law in *The Vietnam War and International Law,* 2 vols. (Princeton, 1968–1969).

Any serious study of atrocities committed by either the Vietcong or American troops should begin with the normative law for the troops in the field: The United States Army Field Manual 27-10, "The Law of Land Warfare" (Washington, 1956). For one reason or another, American atrocities have concerned writers to a greater degree than those perpetrated by the enemy, and are detailed in Edward S. Her-

man, *Atrocities in Vietnam* (Philadelphia, 1970). Among the outstanding works dealing with alleged and proved American atrocities are:
Noam Chomsky, *At War with Asia* (New York, 1969); Seymour Hersh,
Chemical and Biological Warfare (New York, 1969); Richard A. Falk,
Gabriel Kolko and Robert J. Lifton, eds., *Crimes of War* (New York,
1971); Seymour Melman, ed., *In the Name of America* (New York,
1968); and Jonathan Schell, *The Villiage of Ben Suc* (New York, 1969).

Among the most outstanding publications on My Lai are Seymour
M. Hersh, *My Lai 4* (New York, 1970); and Richard Hammer, *One
Morning in the War* (New York, 1970). The defense of "superior
orders," denied the Nazis at Nuremberg, has relevance in the context
of Vietnam, and literature on this subject includes David G. Paxton,
Superior Orders as Affecting Responsibility for War Crimes (New
York, 1946); Martin Redish, "Military Law: Nuremberg Rule of Supe-
rior Orders," *Harvard International Law Journal* 9 (Winter 1968): 169–
181; and Richard Wasserstrom, "Criminal Behavior," *New York
Review of Books,* June 3, 1971, pp. 8–13.

4 5 6 7 8 9 10